THE ROBERTSONS, THE SUTHERLANDS, AND THE MAKING OF TEXAS

THE ROBERTSONS, THE SUTHERLANDS,

and the

MAKING *of* TEXAS

by Anne H. Sutherland

TEXAS A&M UNIVERSITY PRESS
College Station

The paper used in this book meets the minimum requirements of the
American National Standard for Permanence of Paper
for Printed Library Materials, z39.48-1984.
Binding materials have been chosen for durability.

The publisher gratefully acknowledges support from the
Milam Country Historical Commission and other individuals and
organizations who helped make this book possible.
Illustrations from *Texas History Movies* © Texas State Historical Association.
Used by permission.

Library of Congress Cataloging-in-Publication Data

Sutherland, Anne.
The Robertsons, the Sutherlands, and the making of Texas /
by Anne H. Sutherland.—1st ed.
p.   cm. — (Elma Dill Russell Spencer series in the West and Southwest ; no. 25)
Includes bibliographical references and index.
ISBN-13: 978-1-58544-520-2 (cloth : alk. paper)
ISBN-10: 1-58544-520-7 (cloth : alk. paper)
1. Scots-Irish—Texas—History. 2. Scots-Irish—Texas—Biography.
3. Texas—History. 4. Texas—Biography. 5. Sutherland, Anne—Family.
6. Robertson family. 7. Sutherland family. I. Title. II. Series.
F395.S4S87   2006
976.4—dc22
2006005037

To the Memory of

Thomas Shelton Sutherland (1911–1991)
and
Lois Hartley Sutherland (1911–2005)

Contents

Illustrations

A Family Tale

his book is at once a particular ethnographic history of Texas, a family memoir, and an essay on how identity and culture are made and remade over many generations. I have written it to answer these questions: Why do Texans have such a strong sense of themselves? Why are they so cussedly proud of being Texans? How did that identity develop?

The families in this book do not represent all Texans, but their stories are representative of the American colonization of Mexican Texas, which in itself is only part of the whole story of the Lone Star State. The research is based on hundreds of people related to each other by blood or marriage — for example, the Sutherland, Menefee, Rogers, Heard, Dever, Wells, White, and Robertson families, who came to Texas in the early 1830s. Some of them are my ancestors. Their experiences up to the twentieth century are valuable in themselves. These were real people who lived real lives. Thus, in the first instance, my story is a witness to their existence, a way to bring them back to life in the present.

At the same time, their story is worth preserving for reasons beyond its intrinsic value. First, in the process of settling Texas, these people developed a strong, unique family culture of very close kinship ties based on complex marriages among groups of sisters and brothers over several generations. These intermarriages created a powerful family relationship that became an intriguing piece of the larger Texas story. Their association of the 1830s grew out of affiliation, in contrast to the later popularized idea of West Texas "cowboy" culture, which was an identity of isolation. I have documented the development of that familial connection. Since these people are my forebears, I have privileged access to their original, unpublished documents, letters, poems, diaries, and oral histories. My membership in these families is advantageous in another way as well. The story is richer because I know from my own experiences the myriad versions of things that happened to them and how their lives evolved. I am also familiar with the contradictions built into their existence and the many views of what "becoming Texan" meant to them. All of this is deeply embedded in my own psyche.

In addition, the family culture I have described is interesting not only because it is unusually interconnected but also because these families played an important role in the construction of Texas history. They made a significant contribution to the larger texture of Texas history and ultimately the history of the United States. Texas became a nation through a series of highly contested struggles that are now viewed as canonical events in nineteenth-century U.S. history—the movement westward, the battles at the Alamo and San Jacinto, and the displacement of Indians and Mexicans by American settlers. This local record is an integral part of the history of this vast nation. It is also the bedrock of the Texas mystique, which is reinforced, often somewhat tastelessly, by the exotic stereotypes of Texas created in newspapers, books, and films. The family narrative I have written is one window onto the strong feelings of identity and pride that Texans have today. It also contributed to the stereotypes about Texas, and I draw on these because they too are an essential part of a Texas identity.

To show how Texas identity has been constructed and reproduced up to the present, I first introduce my family's current culture and describe the acquisition of my own identity. Then I show the way in which Texas history was taught in schools and books and portrayed in movies to those of us who grew up in the Lone Star State during the 1950s, before the civil rights movement of the 1960s. The most influential text during that time was a comical pamphlet called *Texas History Movies,* which was distributed free to all Texas schoolchildren.[1]

Next I chronicle the history of my early Texas ancestors, who include two groups of people: the Robertson colony and the Alabama Settlement of the Austin colony. Both of these are well known in Texas history, but they have never been thoroughly mined and written up as part of it. Instead, historians have viewed them as peripheral to the main account of the Lone Star State.

I begin with the high-level political shenanigans of Sterling Clack Robertson, a nephew of Gen. James Robertson in Tennessee and a man from a privileged and wealthy Nashville family. He established Robertson's colony, a huge settlement that covered a two-hundred-mile area between Austin and Fort Worth. Because of various setbacks and a longtime tenuous legal status, Robertson's colony was founded in fits and starts. More a buffer outpost for the stable and surer settlement of Stephen F. Austin to the south, Robertson's colony never really flourished. Nevertheless, as a part of Texas history, the colony is fascinating, fraught as it was with subterfuge, alleged planned assassinations, and vicious legal battles that make the shenanigans on a soap opera like *Dallas* seem warm and fuzzy in comparison.

I also describe the Alabama Settlement, which landed in Austin's colony in 1830. Led by George Sutherland and his wife, Frances Menefee Sutherland, this huge migration involved hundreds of kinfolk, including the families of Frances's brothers, William and Thomas Menefee, as well as those of Jesse White, Stephen Heard, and James Dever, each one married to a sister of George Sutherland. Closely bound together by these sibling marriages, the families cooperated with each other in every aspect of life. They planned the massive move from northern Alabama to Texas, helped each other build houses and dig their fields, and later formed successful business partnerships. The men fought together in family-based units within the Texas army and formed a family militia to repel the Indian hostilities. Their leaders and commanders were their own family patriarchs. The women reproduced prodigiously, raising families of eleven to fifteen children, many of whom—as the children of brothers and sisters—were double first cousins. Mutually supportive and morally upright, they were often required to fight fiercely when threatened by Indians and war, to struggle with disease and hunger, and to face together the loss of loved ones. Extremely religious and willing to do battle, they were among the earliest Texans who dared to risk war with the Mexican military that arrived in Texas.

In addition, I look at how these two groups of families created their own cultures when they first came to the wilderness that was then Texas. I have avoided describing them as "Anglo-Texans" because that term, used today to contrast with Mexicans and Mexican Texans, does not reflect the reality of the times. The Sutherlands were called the Alabama Settlement, and the Robertsons considered themselves Tennessee Scots. Both groups retained a strong Scots character that is still evident today. What we now refer to as "Anglo-Texan" was not part of the identity of these families. Furthermore, when they arrived in Texas, they encountered a diverse population that included other Southerners, their slaves, and people from the Ohio Valley and New England, as well as different Mexican groups, including San Antonio elites, ranching *vaqueros*, soldiers, and a number of Indian societies ranging from the "civilized" Cherokee to the unpredictable Karankawa and the terrifying Comanche. Finally, there was a smattering of Europeans.

My goal here is to present, as best I can, my forebears' perspective on who they were and what they were experiencing. I do not take an Anglo-Texan identity as a given; rather, I explore how it was formed through their encounters with other groups in Texas. Their perception of the societal features of the new Texas landscape was filtered through their own cultural lenses, including preconceptions about themselves and others and a sense of their own past. They arrived, for example, with ideas about the superiority of civilization over the wild and the ownership of slaves and, for the Alabamans at least, with a strong religious ethos. I have chronicled how they carved out of the wilderness a "civilized" life for themselves through schools and camp meetings and set out to rid the country of "wildness." Moreover, I have described how the Texas Revolution became for them a rite of passage, an experience with a before-and-after quality, from which they emerged with a strong attachment to Texas as both a place and a nation.

I have also traced the lives of their children as they became men and women and produced families of their own during the years of the Republic of Texas, a time when they were always mindful that they could be invaded by Mexico at any moment. After this precarious and significant period as a separate nation, Texas gave up its sovereignty for the security of being part of the United States, only to secede fifteen years later and join the Confederacy. After having been an autonomous entity during the Mexican colonization period and its years as an independent republic, Texas was once again cut off from the United States by the Civil War. The next generation, the one that grew up after the War between the States, had to reconstruct its existence in the new reality. Stunned by the loss of their fortune in slaves, the Robertson children fiercely defended their social position. The Sutherland and Rogers families restarted their lives by migrating once again—to become ranchers in Uvalde County. Over generations, they developed origin myths and stories that defined their identity as families and as Texans.

The men and women of the Alabama Settlement were attracted to the free land in Texas, the vast amount of uncultivated space, the rich soil, and the plentiful game. Texas offered adequate land for their huge families and enabled them to live among their kin and practice their religion. Sterling Clack Robertson came to Texas as a political mover and shaker with a desire to make a fortune and a name for himself. Both groups achieved their aims, but along the way something else happened that they had not anticipated. In shaping the economy and culture of Texas, Texas in turn shaped them as well.

The book contains many unpublished documents that were not written for publication and are therefore unedited. In using the letters of John Sutherland Menefee and Lizzie Rogers Sutherland, as well as the autobiographies of Samuel Rogers, Emma Rogers, Minnie Rogers, and John Lee Sutherland, I have quoted these people in their own words. However, for the sake of comprehension and flow, I have omitted sections and sentences that are immaterial or superfluous to their narratives.

Acknowledgments

y thanks to Mary Lenn Dixon of Texas A&M University Press for her support, knowledge, editing skills, and belief in the book project and to Carol Hoke, copyeditor, for her excellent work on the manuscript.

My gratitude to Laura Ann Gibson for generously sharing her research insights and resources on the Alabama Settlement. Also to Malcolm and Marguerite McLean for enormous help with archival and biographical research on Robertson's Colony and Robertson descendants. I am grateful to Cile Robertson Ambrose for opening the Robertson house to me.

I would like to thank Jack Weatherford for ideas and inspiration on writing history and anthropology and for being a good friend. My sisters, Gayle DeGregori and Barbara Sutherland, and my friends Roberta Bondi and Susan McCombie read and edited the manuscript, and I am grateful for all of their help and advice.

All of the Robertson, Rogers, and Sutherland kin who over the years collected and preserved documents and stories of the past and present have made this book possible. I owe a special thanks to Florence Hudson for her work on reunions and kinship.

My gratitude to my father for instilling a love of Texas and writing and to my mother for true love and friendship. To Charles for always supporting my intellectual pursuits and being there for me. To my children, Frankie and Benjamin, for teaching me the most about life and love. To Phoebe, my pug, for hours of comic relief and cuddles.

THE ROBERTSONS, THE SUTHERLANDS,
AND THE MAKING OF TEXAS

CHAPTER I

Discovering My Texas Identity

was a young girl when Edna Ferber came to Texas to do research for her book on Texas, which was later made into the movie *Giant*.[1] In Texas it was a big event, at least for those of us who were preteens, when *Giant* hit the silver screen.

Ferber was eager to describe the relations between the Mexican Texans and the Anglo Texans. To help her examine the issue of prejudice against Mexican Texans, she was introduced to my father, who, at the time, was executive secretary of the Good Neighbor Commission. This was a committee that President Roosevelt created to improve interactions between the United States and Mexico. One of its major goals was to end the segregation of Mexican Americans in Texas schools and to convince the University of Texas to allow Mexican Americans access to a university education. My father was introduced to Ferber as a man with deep Texas roots who closely identified with Mexico and Mexican Texans. Enthusiastic about showing Ferber the progress that was being made on civil rights in Texas, he drove her around the state and introduced her to his friends, both Mexican and Anglo. He took her to restaurants and bars where she met Texans who were rich and Texans who were poor, both Mexican and Anglo. They spent hours talking about Texas history and Texas identity, the points of pride as well as the imperfections.

Driving Ferber across the desolate South Texas brush country, my father told her about the dismal conditions for Mexicans there. In particular he described a cause that he had personally been involved in, the Felix Longoria affair. Felix Longoria was a young Tejano patriot who went to war for his country during the dark days of World War II. Exceptionally brave, he won medals and commendations and died a hero in battle. When his body was brought home to the little town of Three Rivers, deep in the heart of South Texas, the one and only local funeral business refused to hold a wake for him, informing the Longoria family that only Anglos could hold wakes in their facilities. My father and Hector Garcia, who was president of the G. I. Forum, fought to correct this injustice. Their aim was modest: Felix Longoria had died for his country; therefore, he should be allowed a burial just like any other American. As Longoria's nonburial turned into national news, the Mexican population in South Texas became galvanized, creating a diplomatic crisis with the Mexican government. Interestingly, the local Anglos still did not budge, so the young idealistic senator Lyndon Johnson arranged for Longoria to be buried in a hero's ceremony at Arlington National Cemetery.[2]

Edna Ferber relished this story, making it into a cornerstone of her book. However, after reading the work, my father was very disappointed. In his opinion, Ferber, like so many writers before her, had ended up creating yet another caricature of Texas. She had simplified and stereotyped the Texas bluster, the cattle and oil cultures, the subtlety of relations between Texas Mexicans and Anglos, the complex tensions between rich and poor, male and female, and the deeply rewarding family ties.

When the movie came out, everyone in my family piled into our DeSoto Suburban and went to watch it. Given what my father had said about Ferber's rendition of Texas, I was taken aback that I liked the film. It was true that the movie was full of clichés and ridiculous exaggerations, but for me, at twelve years of age, it captured something I recognized in my life—the simultaneous pride and embarrassment at being Texan: embarrassment at the prejudice, the crassness of the oil rich, the way women are treated as if they do not matter, yet pride in the way that Texans can overcome prejudice, the beauty of family loyalty, and the way women are strong and capable. Watching *Giant* was a turning point for me, poised as I was on the cusp of adulthood. The movie spurred me to think about what Texas meant to me, why it is so full of contradictions, why is it so hard to understand, and why it is so maddeningly difficult to explain to others.

MY LIBERAL EDUCATION

I grew up in a family that was an integral part of the liberal political community of Austin, Texas. During the 1950s and early 1960s, I spent my childhood steeped in that liberal culture. The *Texas Observer* was our newspaper, and its editors at the time, Ronnie Dugger and then Willie Morris, were regulars at our house. Writers ate at our table and engaged my father in what seemed to me to be one continuous conversation about life, liberty, and Texas. State senator Maury Maverick Jr., writer J. Frank Dobie, Mexican American activists Hector Garcia and Ramón Guerra, historian Frank Goodwyn, television personality John Henry Faulk, U.S. representative Bob Eckhardt, economist Eastin Nelson, and writer Bill Brammer were all friends of my family and regular characters in my childhood. With few exceptions, it was an exclusively male club. Fortunately for me, one exception was my aunt Liz Carpenter, who kept in touch from her Washington bureau and later the White

House during the administration of Lyndon Baines Johnson. She gave politics a live urgency at the dinner table and showed me what a strong Texas woman can do.

Conversation at our dinner table centered on how mad the Texas liberals were at Texas Democrats for not being liberal enough. In places such as Scholz Garden, while the men talked politics at the outdoor tables and drank beer, I ran around with the other children and listened to their plotting. They planned to save the Democratic Party by expunging it of conservative members. By voting Republican, they hoped to give the poor fellows a boost in the then solidly Democratic Texas. The reasoning went that, if the Republicans had a ghost of a chance at winning anything (a laughable thought at the time), the conservative Democrats would defect to the Republican Party and leave the Democratic Party machinery to the liberals. I eavesdropped on this convoluted stratagem with its strange logic. As we now know, only part of this scheme worked out the way the liberals had hoped. Texas did eventually become a two-party state; however, it ended up more Republican than Democrat.

My upbringing on a steady dose of the purest liberalism was tempered by my parents. With deep roots in a Texas family whose traditional values he espoused, my father passed these traditions on to his children through stories about his ancestors. These tales emphasized their integrity and fierce loyalty to family and Texas, as well as their propensity for violence and excessive pride. From my father I acquired a sense of belonging to a part of Texas history, but the oblique references to murder and mayhem were disturbing.

Because of this, I would go to my mother, a blueblood from Charleston, for an outsider's eye. After graduating from the College of Charleston in mathematics and Latin, she had come to Texas to get away from Charleston and take graduate courses at the University of Texas. She arrived in Austin in 1932 and stayed in Mrs. Kirk's boardinghouse for ladies at 2100 San Antonio Street, where room and board cost her thirty dollars per month. She regaled me with stories of her first view of Texas as a "wild and woolly" place. Enjoying her newfound freedom from rule-bound Charleston society, she immediately painted her toenails cherry red, smoked a "flat fifty" tin of cigarettes a day, and threw a spitball at a gawky young man in her first class. He instantly fell in love with her. That spitball was the thunderbolt that drove him to write poems to her, follow her back to Charleston, and carry her off to Texas, much against her parents' wishes. Reared in a suffocating "proper" society, she would advise me, "Remember, Anne, rules are made to be broken. Someone made those rules. You can remake them."

At the end of the 1950s, Willie Morris and other restless liberal spirits left Texas. When I graduated from the University of Texas in 1964, I followed in their footsteps, seeking adventure in Brazil and studying in England. Buried in my anthropology books at Oxford University, mercifully I missed the home front of the Vietnam War and instead picked up some anthropology lessons. I learned what the English mean by "civilized" and how they construct the world into classes of people. In the English world of class, every object in the home, every piece of clothing on the body, every spoken word, every morsel of food, and every flower and bird in the garden has a "proper" place. English robins are middle-class birds, whereas sparrows are working-class birds. The word "bird" is middle class when referring to our feathered friends and working class when it means "woman." Catsup on the table is working class. Tea and scones are middle class, but high tea is working class. Americans, of course, live ignorantly outside this class structure, but in Oxford I was known as "the Texan," a specimen of the utmost curiosity. My best friend at Oxford was a daring English girl named Anna. I was dubbed "Texana."

Then off I went to California to do my fieldwork on the Roma Gypsies. The Roma were an important part of my early education in cultural differences and the subjects of my first ethnography. Magnificent talkers with a gusto for telling tales of life's agonies and absurdities, they taught me to grapple with everyday cultural practices and the ways in which people use their imaginations to transform the world into one they recognize as real. The lives of the Roma are a constant reminder of situated difference, the difference between their worldview and that of non-Roma, with whom they are in daily contact. One of their major goals is to mobilize group identity, to create a sense of self, to understand their experiences, and to understand who they are in relation to the outside world. Their culture is an imagined community that is constantly tested by their interactions with others; they taught me to view my own as such.

Immersed in other cultures, I returned to my native country, wiser and more patriotic, and was hit by the reality shock. I went to live in Minnesota, a state noted for an excess of niceness, sincerity, and horrendously cold winters. It is also characterized by an ironic touch of wackiness, evidenced by a Reform Party wrestler governor, Jesse "the Body" Ventura, and the oppressively serious, politically correct liberal arts college where I taught. There in the tundra I was introduced to good, earnest people, but I ended up longing for the lighter skies and livelier humor of Texas.

STORYTELLING AS A TRADITION

My parents introduced me early in life to the rare art of storytelling. Every night at dinner my large family and the many political and personal friends who dropped by to eat with us were urged to tell a good story about their lives. The next time they ate with us, they would be expected to improve on the first version, making the story even better.

Storytelling was not something I was expected to know from birth, but it was just assumed that my six sisters and I would become adept at it. We began by listening to everyone's tales, and as soon as we could speak, we were encouraged to tell our own. At night when we all piled into bed on the sleeping porch, we regaled each other with anecdotes until we fell asleep. We edited and repeated the stories so often that they changed somewhat, but we followed the dictum that any story worth telling is worth improving, so by the time these tales were handed down to me, they had gone through generations of improvement.

From my father I heard stories about Cabeza de Vaca and his experiences with the Indians, about George Sutherland bringing hundreds of his kin to Texas, about the terrible hardship of the Runaway Scrape, when my family had nothing to eat, and the fall of the Alamo, where my great-great-great-uncle Willie died when he was only seventeen. We learned about the empresario Robertson, who locked horns with Stephen F. Austin, won his battle for land, fought Indians, and had a terrible temper. And we found out that his son built a plantation house and a town and a college so his twelve children could get an education. We listened to the saga of another great-great-great-grandfather, Sam Rogers, who fought in the Texas army under George Sutherland, survived the Battle of Plum Creek against the Comanches, and outlived just about everyone he knew.

STORYTELLING AT FAMILY REUNIONS

Storytelling became an elevated art form with the Sutherland-Rogers side of my family, my father's father's relatives, who got together every year at Uvalde State Park for a family reunion. Between two and three hundred of us filled the park and spilled over into nearby motels. Most of these family members lived in the Texas Hill Country around Uvalde. This was a loyal group, but what we had most in common was a love of stories about family and Texas. The weekend of the Sutherland-Rogers reunion was the champion storytelling rodeo of my life. These kinspeople were just naturally good storytellers during the rest of the year, but when they got together, they tried to "out-storytell" each other well into the night. My great-uncle Wells Sutherland liked to tell the reunion children, in his slow-moving, understated way, the story of being treed by a cougar one day when he was riding a fence. When the "Texas lion" spooked his horse, Wells agilely jumped into the nearest tree rather than be thrown on the ground. The horse bolted, but, in a stroke of bad luck for Wells, the lion decided to take a catnap under the tree. Wells was stuck there for the night. As he told it, that night the mosquitoes were so happy they just "sang and sang," but he thought too much slapping and twitching might arouse the cat, so he sat there and got bitten. This was the all-time worst night of his life.

Then my Aunt Alice recited an anecdote I had heard many times. Just seventeen and about to go on her first date, she was showering in preparation for this historic event. Suddenly her older brother Tommy (my father) burst into the bathroom, grabbed the "go-devil" (toilet plunger), and stuck it on her wet rump so hard no one could remove it. She screamed and cried, but to no avail. They could not pry the plunger off her wet bottom, and her date had to be turned away. We children could tell she was still indignant forty years later. When she finished describing her humiliation and ire, she looked at me and said, "Your daddy is meaner than a rattlesnake. Did you know that?" I howled with pleasure at her characterization of my father and cut my eyes to him. He had sat through the whole story as he did every year, pursing his lips in mock shame, but this time he gave her a triumphant look: He was going to outdo her. He held up a poem about George Sutherland he was planning to read at the reunion's Sunday service. We quieted down while he read it:

> Our forebear was George Sutherland,
> Born seventeen eighty-eight in Old Virginny.
> At sixteen crossed the Gap at Cumberland.
> Married in Tennessee, grew strong as any,
> Led folk to Alabama, made a town,
> Was a Banker, and their leader in the House.
> He helped Old Hickory beat the British crown.
> Then Spain fell. With kith and kin and spouse
> George headed west to Texas—promised land.
> His tent was the first church of settlers here.
> The promise was denied. War was at hand,
> Our People fought and won and George was there.
> George traveled far to rich and bloody ground.
> We stand in memory of all he found.[3]

My great-aunts Mabel, Jean, and Ara wept quietly. We children did not pay much attention to them because they were always weeping. Then, from the spread of dishes everyone had brought to the table, we all ate until we were stuffed. When I flopped into bed that night, exhausted from running around all day with a bevy of cousins, I remembered my father's poem and wondered how George Sutherland had come to Texas in the first place. Before I fell asleep, I made a note to find out some day.

My sense of self as a Texan is the outcome of the hours and hours of stories told to me about the state by my numerous Texas relatives. Even at the time, I suspected that the tales I was raised on might not always be strictly accurate, but they were vivid, gripping, and full of the Texas mystique. In my mind, those anecdotes created in both the heroes and the rascals a Texas persona imbued with strength and love. They gave me a Texas identity embedded in historical memory. However, my family's storytelling tradition also got me into trouble with the literal-minded, who would mistakenly conclude that Texans are liars instead of entertainers. These same people would then be caught off guard by my frankness, even bluntness, on issues such as politics, religion, and sex, topics they considered of such great importance that it is best to lie about them. Nonetheless, I did not really pause to think about what all these personal accounts added up to until I left Texas at eighteen to see the world. My first stop was Brazil.

"Where are you from?" someone inquired.

"I'm a Texan," I replied without hesitation.

"Aren't you an American?"

"Well, yeah . . ." I stuttered reluctantly. At that moment I discovered that, although I was completely sure of my Texas identity, I had not quite acquired a strong American identity. Another important piece of information came to light while I was living in Brazil. To my surprise, I realized that Texas is famous. Amazingly, Brazilians had not only heard of Texas but also harbored all kinds of preconceptions about it and even identified with Texas in some strange way. The idea of Texas was fun. "Bang, bang!" their fingers fired at me. What a riot.

At that time, although I had found out that Texas was well known in the world and I knew I had a strong sense of self as a Texan, I still did not know what Texas was famous for or what this identity I professed to have really was. Over a lifetime of living in other places—São Paulo, Brazil; Oxford, England; Palo Alto, California; Farmington, Connecticut; St. Paul, Minnesota; Atlanta, Georgia—I grappled with the strange power the image of Texas has on others and the enigma of my own Texas identity. Out there in the rest of the world is a dizzying array of ideas about Texas, some of them romantic, many of them unflattering. It has taken me years to come to terms with them.

CHAPTER 2

Writing as a Tradition

In 1936 Texas celebrated its centenary anniversary. As part of the commemoration, the state decided to rebury its early heroes in the Texas State Cemetery in Austin. The bodies of Judge William Menefee and his wife, Agnes Sutherland Menefee, were laid to rest there,[1] and empresario Sterling Clack Robertson was transported from his lonely grave on the Brazos River in Robertson County for reburial as well. Robertson's interment was a big event, attended by numerous Robertsons. With four granddaughters, twenty-eight great-grandchildren, and countless great-great-grandchildren milling around, no one could corral everyone in one place long enough to make an accurate count. In addition, all of the members of the Sterling C. Robertson Chapter (Waco) of the Daughters of the Republic of Texas had voted to attend the service.[2] As one of the great-great-grand children, my father wrote a poem for this hundred-year anniversary of Texas:

The Texans

They fell down dead at Goliad,
Their luck ran out at Mier;
And when the Indian came and fled,
They lay in blood that turned to red
The lonely prairie here.

But who can say a man is dead
Who conquers when he dies?
The Texans took this long, sweet land
Of rivers, woods, of brush and sand
And here their domain lies.

And tall and thick their towers stand
And strong their engines go—
Six million Texans they begot
To hold a land where they were shot
A hundred years ago.

BY THOMAS SHELTON SUTHERLAND IV, 1936[3]

Home, family, and Texas were not the only topics of my father's poetry. Like all of his ancestors, he also felt strong ties to the land and often spoke about the Robertson homestead in Salado, the land and the house where he grew up. I asked him why that land was so important to him that he would never sell it. His response was another poem:

> *Here on these rolling acres of land*
> *I first looked on God's day and drank the air*
> *And did what boy alive does anywhere—*
> *All that I know is Texas dirt and sand:*
> *It is the only place I understand,*
> *And oak trees or mesquite or prickly pear*
> *Belong to me like my own sandy hair,*
> *They are the same to me as my big-jointed hand.*
>
> *This is the many-cornered piece of dirt*
> *My father sweated on and mother hurt.*
> *My mother used to look at me and tell*
> *About the first of us who wandered here;*
> *They fought to have the wild acres that year*
> *And gave me something I couldn't sell.*

THOMAS SHELTON SUTHERLAND IV, DATE UNKNOWN[4]

My father learned the practice of writing poems from his mother, Mary Elizabeth Robertson Sutherland, who also was an amateur poet. Writing was and is a long-standing family tradition that, along with storytelling, has shaped our identity. In my family, reflecting on the past has always been a way to help us grasp the present. Early in life I heard stories of Texas' painful shot in the heart at the Alamo and Goliad, culminating in the David-against-Goliath victory at San Jacinto. Tales were told of the precarious existence of my pioneering forefathers as Indian fighters, revolutionaries, merchants, and farmers. Then there were the mothers who lost their husbands and children to war and disease and suffered so terribly in the Runaway Scrape.

These chronicles often took on the narrative style of "origin myths," patterned stories that describe where people came from, what it took to get there, and who they are now. They are of course grounded in truth, but they go beyond being a report of historical events to become metaphorical accounts of identity and place. The tales of those pioneer experiences, narrated to later arrivals in Texas as origin myths, reveal a reverence for their ancestors' sacrifices. Phrases such as "the First Three Hundred," the muster rolls of every battle, and the shrine of the Alamo are all part of the process of giving meaning to the history.

Texans of the years of the republic (1836–1845) wrote the first histories of the "pioneer years," as they called them. The express purpose of their chronicles was to record the heroism and glory of those Texans who fought and suffered for independence. These first accounts were consciously myth-making, and the writers were clearly in awe of their parents' and other relatives' roles in the settling of Texas and the events of the Texas Revolution. Historians of this period include John Henry Brown, Frederick Law Olmsted, and Texas' own de Tocqueville, Frédéric Leclerc, to name just a few.[5] Moreover, ordinary citizens who were there made their own written contributions. Among my relatives, two accounts in particular stand out: John Sutherland Menefee's articles for the *Texana Clarion* and John Sutherland's "Fall of the Alamo."[6]

Texans like John Sutherland Menefee, who were either very young during the Texas Revolution or born at the end of it, glorified the years that marked the beginning of "Texas." Their experiences of Texas were entirely different from those of their fathers and mothers. The next generation's destiny was not so much to endure hardship and sacrifice life but to "civilize" Texas. For them, civilizing meant setting up schools, building churches (now that they had freedom of worship), and establishing a government that could handle the citizens' economic, political, and judicial needs. In the Texas congress, men like Sterling Robertson served the new nation by securing land titles for people, making roads, establishing courts, and forming a militia to protect Texas from invasion by Mexico and attacks by Indians.

One of the local histories written during the republic years was that of John Sutherland Menefee, one of the double first cousins of the Sutherlands and the Menefees. His lengthy diaries meticulously describe his crops and the vagaries of the weather. He wrote numerous letters to his kinfolk back in Alabama and Tennessee and eventually penned a history of the republic for the *Clarion* newspaper in Texana, a small town on Matagorda Bay that no longer exists. A well-educated lawyer and a member of the Fourth Congress (1839–1840) of the Republic of Texas, he had also participated in the war of independence. At the age of twenty-six, he was in the thick of the battle of San Jacinto. Later, when the Mexican army invaded Texas in 1840, he served as a scout for the Texas army.

As a lookout, John Menefee was frequently exposed to Indian attacks. Once, he wrote, he and two other scouts were separated from the main troops and attacked by Indian warriors on the Arenosa Creek in Jackson County. According to his report, they fought in fierce hand-to-hand combat, during which he was hit with seven arrows. At the end of the battle, he ran out of ammunition, threw his empty pistol at an Indian, hitting him between the eyes, and hid along the creek bank. Bleeding and in great pain, he pulled the seven arrows out of his body, carried them with him, and crawled to the ranch of a nearby relative.

Interestingly, John Menefee's letters to his relatives do not dwell on his amazing Indian fights or his heroism at San Jacinto. Rather, they show a more mundane preoccupation with family and religion. As the most literate Menefee, he acted as the family scribe, passing along information on relatives' whereabouts, health, and their attendance and witnessing at Methodist camp meetings. An example of his role as the conveyer of family news is this letter written from Texana on Matagorda Bay in June 1841:

Dear Aunt:

Yours of the 21st April to Father [Thomas Menefee] was duly received and as you express a desire to hear from us often he has requested me to answer your letter. Father and Uncle William are very poor correspondents—to write a letter is a task which they seldom undertake even to their best friends, [thus] you must not be surprised that a correspondence has not been commenced and kept up between you and them. You say you are desirous of hearing everything relating to each one of the family, what we are doing, how we like the country, and if we are sick or poor. I suppose from this you not only wish to know in relation to father's family but Uncle William's as well as Martha [Stanback], Elizabeth [Dever], Mary [White] and Frances [Sutherland] and to say much in relation to each one would extend this communication to a greater length than intended. Father is living on a farm [?] miles above this place, he is and ever has been well pleased with the country [Texas], is not rich although he has no right to complain, George & Susan [the writer's brother and sister] are living with him and are not married. Agnes [another sister] last summer married a Parson Hill, Frances [sister] & Mr. Peck [her husband] are now at Father's. The boys William & Thomas [youngest brothers] are all living at home. I am living in this place [Texana], was married July 1839 but death has bereaved me of a beloved and affectionate wife. She died on the 19th of February last, what a trial and O how hard it is to lose a dear companion; but I have one consolation: I believe she is happy; she is done with the trials and difficulties of this world and I hope gone to a far better; she was a member of the [Methodist] Church and lived up to her professions. We have preaching here every three weeks and sometimes oftener; sisters Susan, Frances & Agnes are members of the church, also all of my aunts and I believe all of their daughters.

Give my love to cousins Marie Brucker and Maria and Frances Menefee; tell them a letter from them would be gladly received at any time. Your affectionate nephew, John S. Menefee.[7]

Like other settlers of his generation, John Sutherland Menefee also wrote a history of the Alabama Settlement and called it "Early Jackson County Settlers" (1880), which he published in the *Texana Clarion*, a Jackson County newspaper.[8] In his dry way he faithfully recorded his family's involvement in the Mier Expedition of 1842, his attempt to set up a sugar mill, the first modern factory in Jackson County, and the vicissitudes of Texas weather—all with the same degree of feeling. His factual report provides a sense of the rhythm of life at the time:

> *In September 1842, the Mexicans, 1200 in number, entered San Antonio, and the District Court being in session, made prisoners of the Judge and lawyers, and others amounting in all to 53 prisoners. They remained in San Antonio about a week, when two or three hundred Texians under Matthew Caldwell having reached the Salado, the Mexicans 800 strong attacked them, and after fighting from 11 A.M. till near sun down, drew off with a loss of about sixty killed and as many wounded, while the Texians lost only one killed and nine wounded. About this time Capt. Dawson with 53 men from La Grange, going to join Caldwell were surrounded by the Mexicans—they got into a Musquata (firing of muskets), but the enemy kept out of reach of their rifles and raked them with grape shot, killing thirty five, only two or three making their escape, and the balance being made prisoners. The Mexicans left the next day for the Rio Grande. When the news reached here of the coming of the Mexicans, the waters were very high, and bro. George and I had to swim the sloughs to get to the bank of the Navidad, in order to let Maj. Sutherland know it, that he might send the news on east. Some volunteers collected and were camped at Wright's place beyond Victoria, and at night sent a picket on the road to Goliad, to give information in case of the approach of the enemy, but they soon returned stating that it was impossible to keep picket on account of the Musquatas. We then moved into the bottom and camped on the road, keeping up a camp-guard. Father being very sick and likely to die I returned home, and the others went on to San Antonio, but the Mexicans had left. In Oct. 1842 an expedition of 750 men, under Genl. Alexander Somervell, was gotten up to go to the Rio Grande and some of the citizens of Jackson County were on this expedition. . . . On the 19th when Genl. Somervell issued orders to march about 300 men refused to obey, and marched down the river, and elected Wm. S. Fisher to the command. They crossed the river opposite Mier and after considerable hard fighting they surrendered on terms of capitulation. The severe suffering, decimation and long imprisonment, of the Mier prisoners, are familiar with those who have read the history of Texas, and need no repetition by me, suffice it to say that*

Judge Patrick Usher, a citizen of Jackson County [and a relative], was one of the Mier prisoners who never returned.[9]

A dying town, Texana had no supply stores. Obtaining basic provisions became so difficult that residents finally abandoned the community, and the remaining families moved north to Edna and Ganado. John Sutherland Menefee described an eleven-day trip he embarked on to procure food and equipment:

Texana, from a thriving prosperous town in 1838, had gone down till very few lived in the place, and nothing was kept there for sale, consequently we had (some of us) to go to Matagorda for our dry goods and groceries. S. Addison White was living at Indian Point, and having a sail boat, I made arrangements with him to get his boat to go to Matagorda for supplies. J. M. [John Menefee] White was at Indian Point with his family, and Hugh Stapp was there. On account of rheumatism he had to go on crutches. I got them to go with me, and we started the 27 July, arriving at Palacios that night. Next day after beating round Half Moon Point against a strong wind, we reached our destination. We left Matagorda the 29, and having a bag of corn of Capt. White's, to be ground at Decrows wind Mill at Decrows Point, and having to beat down the Peninsula, we got that night about opposite Palacios, and the next day reached Decrows where we had to remain until the evening of the 31st, on account of a Norther. In the evening a light south breeze springing up, we started, but had not gone far before the wind veered around to the North East and North and increased to a fresh breeze, and night coming we had to beat up the bay; on the tack to the eastward, we would go some distance out into the bay, and on the other tack we would approach the shore till Hugh could touch bottom with his crutch. The waves beating against the bow of the boat threw the spray over us until we were wet. We reached Indian Point about midnight, wet and cold, and glad enough to stop for the balance of the night. I got home the 4th of Aug. having been gone eleven days.[10]

WRITING

In the late nineteenth century, my great-grandmother Lizzie Laura Rogers Sutherland penned many letters from Uvalde to her relatives at the "old home place" back in Jackson County. She also recorded the memoirs of her father, Samuel Rogers. My grandmother Mary Elizabeth Robertson Sutherland wrote poems and stories about her experiences growing up in the home of her Grandfather Robertson. My father continued the tradition and passed it on to me. These writings are valuable because they represent the recorded history of a family, the story of their lives over a number of generations. The written record, along with the oral traditions, provides an authenticity to their tales that would otherwise be missing. Sometimes the historical value of these accounts is greater than their literary worth, but the anthropological importance—what they say about how people thought and felt—is priceless.

CHAPTER 3

❦

The Robertson Papers

Many stories of my family history concern the life of Sterling Clack Robertson, the empresario who came to Texas in 1830. Sterling Robertson was born into a privileged family. His mother was a wealthy woman in her own right, and his father was the brother of Gen. James Robertson, known as the "father of Tennessee" for his efforts in settling the area. Unlike the devout Methodist Sutherlands and Menefees but similar to other empresarios—land agents—Robertson was not a religious man. He also lived a life that was anything but morally upright.

Sandy-haired Sterling was a hotheaded lad. Once, when still a young man, he had words with a cousin over the use of one of his mother's many slaves, lost his temper, and fatally stabbed the cousin. Amazingly, given his family's position in society, he was promptly convicted of murder, a sentence that was later changed to manslaughter. The family dictum on Sterling Robertson hinted that, because of his irascible disposition, he killed nine men during his lifetime. This first one, however, was his only conviction.

At that time, Nashville had just built its first jail, and Sterling was one of the first citizens to be given a jail sentence. What's more, he was ordered to have the letter *M* branded on the palm of one hand so that everyone would know he was a murderer.

Sterling did not take seriously either the novel idea of a jail term or the barbaric practice of branding, but, wisely deciding that Nashville needed a cooling-off period, he left for Texas to look into his prospects there as an empresario for the Mexican government. His goal was simple: If he could fulfill the conditions of an empresario contract with the Mexican government and bring eight hundred families to Texas, he would become the owner of vast tracts—some 140,000 acres—of Texas land. This bold plan he eventually accomplished, though not without facing many severe obstacles, the most daunting of which was the opposition of another empresario, Stephen F. Austin.

HISTORY OF THE ROBERTSON PAPERS

Sterling Robertson left us with an enormous number of documents, land titles, diaries, bills of lading, and correspondence that have trickled down through the family archives. Most of them are published in the massive nineteen-volume set titled *Papers concerning Robertson's Colony in Texas.*[1] These volumes present the history of Robertson's colony, which my cousin Malcolm McLean and his wife, Margaret Stoner McLean, have researched, compiled, and edited in an exacting manner and with a persistence that the empresario Robertson himself would have applauded. For fifty-seven years they collected the Robertson papers, researched and translated documents from the time, and wrote the story of the settlement, which totals 11,947 pages.[2]

The history of the survival of these papers is a heroic story in itself. Since there was no other record keeping at the time, Sterling Robertson knew that his documentation—in deeds, surveys, and the names of colonists—would be the only proof that he and the settlers would have of his efforts and his ownership of the land. He therefore spent his lifetime protecting these records. During the tumultuous days of the revolution of 1836, the American colonists fled to the Sabine River (on the border with the United States) to escape the Mexican army. To protect the precious papers, Sterling Robertson loaded them on a mule and sent his sixteen-year-old son, Elijah Sterling Clack Robertson, to take them safely across the Sabine to the United States. Then he raced to join Sam Houston's Texas militia at San Jacinto. Alone and terrified, young Elijah rode only at night, hiding by day to avoid both the Mexican troops and the hostile Indians. It was a harrowing experience for the youth, searing into his psyche forever the importance of "the papers."

The family practice of preserving these documents trickled down through the generations. In 1859 Elijah Sterling Clack Robertson built a room in his pre–Civil War mansion to store the papers, and his son, my great-grandfather Maclin Robertson, continued to preserve them in that house. Around the turn of the century, the documents were dispersed among Maclin's many siblings. According to Malcolm McLean, Alice Josephine Woods, Maclin's wife, carried many of them with her when she went to live with her daughter Mary Elizabeth Sutherland, my grandmother. Some of the papers also went with Luella Robertson Fulmore, another daughter. Still others, mostly genealogical material, went to Maj. William Curry Harllee, who, with the assistance of some long-suffering U.S. Army underlings, also spent a lifetime compiling the three-volume work *Kinfolks.*[3] Over time, Luella Robertson Fulmore and Mary Elizabeth Robertson Sutherland (both granddaughters of the empresario Robertson) supplied Malcolm McLean with copies of the papers they had acquired from the Robertson house. Some of the documents remained in the Robertson plantation house, and others passed to my father.[4]

More than a hundred years after they were written, the Robertson papers in my father's possession became an integral feature of my childhood identity. My family consisted of seven girls (the seven Sutherland sisters, we were called). Our family was poor but educated, and because my father never kept his political positions for very long, we led a seminomadic life, moving often, sometimes three times in one school year. By the time I was twelve, I stopped bothering to memorize our addresses. Before I left home at eighteen, I figured out that we had moved twenty-two times. On each move I lost something precious to me—a book, a doll, a piece of clothing. To solve the problem, my mother bought us each a salvaged World War II trunk in which to store our most valuable possessions to keep them from getting lost in transit.

Since we were strapped for cash, we did all of the moving work ourselves, lugging our few possessions and the pieces of furniture that were sturdy enough to survive. But first and foremost, my father took care to move the Robertson documents. Although I hauled those musty papers from house to house many times, amazingly I never thought to look at them, never peeked into the cumbersome trunks. They were just my father's crates of valuable papers, just as I had my chest of not-to-be-lost stuff. However, I knew that he had read each and every one of them. Without asking why or how, I took for granted the fact that they were my heritage.

As my sisters and I grew up in Austin and left home to attend the University of Texas, the documents aged, too. Generations of rats found them tasty and urinated on them before my father finally sold them to the University of Texas at Arlington, where he had taught in the latter part of his life.

The last time I saw "the papers" I was in Austin for a family visit. My father, who was very old by this time, asked me to drive him to his sister's house in the West Austin hills. We climbed into his dilapidated van, loaded down with the musty trunks of Robertson records that were to be delivered to the university archives. It was August. The temperature topped 100 degrees in the shade. Driving west was not a good idea, as we were headed straight into the setting sun. The old van's air conditioner was broken, but the heater seemed to be belching hot air on occasion. Although my father looked perfectly comfortable, I felt I was going to pass out. I stuck my head out the window in order to suck in less of the stench and, over the noise of the traffic, screamed at him, "What is that god-awful smell?"

He looked at me, shocked that I could panic so early in the trip. Slowly and deliberately he responded in his most dignified voice, "Your great-great-great-grandfather Robertson's papers, preserved in rat piss for posterity."

Mercifully, soon after this the papers went to the University of Texas at Arlington, where Malcolm McLean and his wife aired them out. Over a period of years they carefully photocopied the documents and then spent the rest of their active lives making them accessible to the world. However, true to the Robertson character, when my father died in 1991, we found that he had kept back one last trunk of papers—ones that his mother thought were too personal to make public.

CHAPTER 4

◆◆

Learning Texas History

exas history has gone through many permutations—the ironic and biased *Texas History Movies* that was used in all Texas schools during the 1940s and 1950s,[1] the early nineteenth-century written accounts that created the heroic myths about Texas, the early twentieth-century documents that note many people and deeds in the history of the counties, and the recent chronicles that try to correct the record by including groups of people who have been left out of these accounts.

This book is an ethnographic record, something that, as far as I know, has not been attempted in mainstream Texas history. An ethnographic account looks at the formation of culture over time rather than at the combination of events and biography of standard histories. It explores how people imagine themselves to be—that is, their perception of who they are and how they came to be that way. It also delves into how they perceive the world around them, including what they see and what they ignore, for it is their imagination and opinions that drive the formation of their culture. In the case of the two large families I have written about, in 1830 they adopted, rejected, and modified the new cultural forms they encountered in Texas according to how those forms fit—or did not fit—with who they were. The community they composed was the real world for them. Therefore, in this book I consider their self-perceptions in order to understand why they took certain actions and developed particular cultural practices.

Before I chronicle the "imagined community" of these two families, I want to examine the development of Texas history, or, more precisely, the writing down of that account, which is not the same as the events that took place. The recording of Texas history has played an important role in the construction of a Texas identity, in particular the dominant, stereotyped Texas distinctiveness that is portrayed in *Giant* that even people in England and Brazil recognize.

As for every child growing up in Texas at the time, my introduction to Texas history came from a small booklet called *Texas History Movies*.[2] Originally published as a serial in the *Dallas Morning News* in 1926, it is an illustrated history that was first distributed to Texas schoolchildren in 1928 by the Magnolia Petroleum Company (which later became Mobil Oil Company) and was read by every student from that time until 1961. This official account was influential in creating a Texas identity in many of us. Vivid, amusing, and biased, it made Texas history fun. Whenever I got bored during the dog days of summer, I would pick up the saucy little pamphlet and reread it. I liked it so much that I majored in history at the University of Texas, convinced that the topic would be enjoyable.

I was wrong. History is a very serious subject, and historians are quite earnest about their field. They do not always agree about what history should include, and they certainly do not see eye to eye on how to interpret it, but they do concur that it consists of information that can be found in heavy piles of documents sitting in musty archives. They have an odd suspicion of oral history and an overblown reverence for written documents. I recently taught at Rice University in Houston, where the history department offered a class in Icelandic sagas (which were, of course, oral stories until written down), but not one in Texas history. The latter subject, one Rice historian told me, is deemed so irrelevant that no one there teaches it at all. Texas historians are particularly touchy about the history of the Lone Star State, probably because it is so overwhelmed by mystique. As a regional record, Texas history is permeated by a solemn, provincial aroma. Texas history buffs pour over every word written about the state with the kind of intensity a schoolmarm feels about spelling, gleefully checking to see whether it is accurate.

The prologue of *Texas History Movies* reveals the purpose and romantic tone of the book:

> *Texas—your state and ours—is at once a land of romance and of realization; of romance because of those sturdy pioneers who more than a century ago left the older sections of America to come into a new land, to brave the terrors and the dangers of a frontier, to carve out of an uncharted wilderness the splendid empire we know as Texas today; of realization because of the vast progress that has been made since those first pioneers came, the natural resources that have been developed, the homes erected, the farms tilled, the factories built, the accumulation of the vast wealth of this state—the accomplishment of no less than a commercial miracle.*
>
> *Prompted by a desire to be of service to the pupils of the public schools of Texas and to have some small part in helping impress upon them the remarkable past of their state, its today, and its future, offering unlimited opportunities to every person in Texas, the Magnolia Petroleum Company has had prepared and printed for distribution to the schools of Texas the booklet, "Texas History Movies."*
>
> *The Magnolia Petroleum Company, organized in 1911, is itself a pioneer, for its immediate predecessors erected the first oil refinery in Texas at Corsicana in 1896 and the next in Beaumont in 1901.*[3]

In addition to impressing me with its long sentences full of semicolons and commas, this prologue sealed forever in my mind the relationship between Texas' heroic past and the Mobil Oil Company, both pioneers in producing the miracle that is Texas. On the next page a picture of the Alamo as it looked in 1956 bears this caption: "The Alamo, Shrine of Texas Liberty, San Antonio."

I already knew about the Alamo because my great-great-great-uncle died there. After the battle, his body was piled up with the bodies of the men who died with him and burned in a huge pyre that forever inflamed my relatives and spurred them to fight for their lives against the encroaching Mexican army. The book told me that the site of his heroic death had become a Texas shrine.

For effectiveness in bringing history to life, kindling a child's interest, and producing emotion and ethos along with the telling of events and deeds, no Texas history book has ever surpassed *Texas History Movies*. The drawings by artist Jack Patton are humorous and ironic, and the captions by John Rosenfield Jr. have a tongue-in-cheek quality that describes heroic deeds with a sardonic twist. This book portrays certain Texans as braggers who can laugh at themselves. The Texas history I learned from the book is gripping, intensely personal, emotionally satisfying, and, of course, deeply biased and not always accurate. It depicts heroes and antiheroes, humor and tragedy. It also recounts the importance of family ties in the creation of the Texas persona. In short, although it is in no way a full and accurate account, *Texas History Movies* tells the story of the Lone Star State always with an eye to creating or reflecting the Texas (Anglo) identity of the 1930s. That is precisely why I want to summarize it here.

TEXAS HISTORY MOVIES

Texas History Movies begins with the native inhabitants of Texas, the "tejas" Indians, who are depicted as poor, thin, and snively (figure 1).[4] It then chronicles the Spanish explorers, such as Coronado, who made a rich marriage and, using his wife's money, went to the New World and claimed Texas for the king of Spain. In this, Coronado was like all of the early adventurers who came to Texas, for in one way or another it was their families who made it possible for them to investigate new lands. The French explorer René-Robert Cavelier, Sieur de La Salle, for example, was cut out of his father's will for not being a "gay old dog." Being disinherited spurred him to go the New World to find the mouth of the Mississippi River. Mistaking Texas' Matagorda Bay for the Mississippi, he landed his ship, *La Belle,* in Texas in 1685, built a fort on Garcitas Creek, and gave the land to Louis XIV of France, convinced he had at last made his papa proud. Never mind the mistake, he spotted longhorn cows and named the river La Vache (now the Lavaca River) after them.

Hearing of La Salle's travels in Texas, the Spanish monarchy sent Alonso de León to destroy the French fort, but he found that the Karankawa Indians had already demolished it. Not to be outdone, the French sent Louis de St. Denis, a "dashing young Parisian," according to *Texas History Movies*, to set up trade routes in Texas. He succeeded, primarily because of his marriage to the daughter of the captain of Fort St. John. To keep the French out of Texas, the Spanish then set up missions and forts, called presidios, along the Old San Antonio Road. The bickering between Spain and France continued throughout the eighteenth century, with France ceding Louisiana to Spain and then Spain selling Louisiana to the United States.

Meanwhile, tiring of Spanish rule and inspired by Father Hidalgo's *grito* ("cry") for independence in 1810, the Mexicans began a protracted civil war with Spain (figure 2).[5] Around this same time, the United States was also fighting the British (the War of 1812) with the help of the notorious pirate Jean Lafitte, who made a tidy profit on the side. After the War of 1812, James Long, a medical doctor and adventurer, decided to take settlers to Texas. He got as far as the presidio at Goliad, where a battle with Indians raged for days. In Mexico, the revolution was in full force, and in 1820 Col. Augustín de Iturbide of the Spanish military set out to annihilate the Mexican rebels for the glory of Spain. In a classic *golpe* ("coup d'état"), Iturbide decided to take the country for himself instead. On May 19, 1822, he modestly proclaimed himself emperor of all Mexico, effectively ending any hope Spain had of hanging on to the Mexican colonies. Immediately, Iturbide had his own problems with Antonio López de Santa Anna, a *caudillo* ("military dictator") from Veracruz who led an uprising against the new government. Iturbide was so busy with rebellions that he could not pay attention to Texas, and this gap in oversight opened Texas to settlers and empresarios from the United States.

At this point *Texas History Movies* launches into the Anglo story of Texas, the tale intended to make Texas schoolchildren into proud Texans. The saga of Stephen F. Austin as empresario is a long account of persistence and patience as the government of Mexico seesawed on giving newcomers permission to settle Texas, each time dashing Austin's hopes of getting a firm contract. He had other troubles, too. In 1822, when he landed in Mexico City to press his case, he learned that he had competitors (figure 3).[6] Finally, through guile and impeccable Spanish, he won his contract while cleverly edging out the other land agents.

Texas History Movies now introduces Sam Houston, the model for all later larger-than-life Texans. As a young man, Houston ran away from his family to live with the Cherokee Indians and learned their agonizingly difficult language (figure 4).[7] Later he taught school, although *Texas History Movies* indicates that he used dubious teaching methods and taught certain questionable "facts" (figure 5).[8] Later, as a soldier in the War of 1812, he became a lifelong friend and political ally of Gen. Andrew Jackson. Through his ties with President Jackson, Houston was elected governor of Tennessee. However, a baffling failure in his celebrated marriage to the well-bred eighteen-year-old Eliza Allen, which remains a mystery to this day, suddenly ended in his resignation of the governorship. Houston, like others who found themselves in a socially embarrassing situation, went to Texas. There he took up with the Cherokee, who had also been exiled to Texas after the Creek War. Houston drowned his woes by embarking on a two-year drinking binge, which earned him the Cherokee nickname "the big drunk."

Having brought the schoolchildren to the Texas Revolution against Mexico, *Texas History Movies* then explains the causes of the coming insurrection. First, there was "the age old prejudice of race" (figure 6).[9] Then there was the instability of the Mexican government and the difficulty of learning the Spanish language. Finally, the state government in Saltillo, Coahuila, was too far away from Texas to govern the region effectively. In spite of these problems, Texas was being flooded with immigrants. The American colonists elected Stephen F. Austin to represent them in Saltillo and to petition for a separate governing body in Texas. The Mexicans responded by throwing Austin in jail, rightly suspecting that this petition was a first step to rebellion.

Meanwhile, Santa Anna had seized dictatorial control and was antagonistic toward the state of Texas and Coahuila because they refused to recognize him. The state government in Coahuila began speculating in land to raise money for a militia to protect itself from Santa Anna's powerful army and to make a tidy profit on the side (figure 7).[10] Santa Anna responded by sending his brother-in-law, Gen. Martín Perfecto de Cos, to Texas to quell the rebellion. Santa Anna may thus be the originator of the well-known Texas tradition of turning to one's relatives for help in a political crisis.

Taking Austin's advice, the Texans swore they were just fighting the centralist Santa Anna and not asking for independence, but because things were rapidly escalating, hardly anyone believed them. When finally released from jail in Mexico City, Austin was sent to the United States to procure aid for Texas, and Sam Houston was quickly put in charge of a ragtag Texas "army." The famous frontiersman James Bowie, ace storyteller Davy Crockett (figure 8), and hotheaded William Travis tried to defend the Alamo but failed.[11]

FIGURE 1

FIGURE 2

FIGURE 3

FIGURE 4

FIGURE 5

FIGURE 6

FIGURE 7

FIGURE 8

FIGURE 9

FIGURE IO

FIGURE II

Santa Anna ordered his troops to burn the bodies of the fallen defenders and execute the men captured at Goliad, much to the horror of even his own troops (figure 9).[12]

To put an end to the mess in Texas once and for all, Santa Anna set out with three divisions of his army to capture Houston, who was in charge of the Texas troops, such as they were. Despite the worst rains Texas had seen in decades, Houston and his men were withdrawing across swollen rivers toward the border with the United States (figure 10).[13] After retreating for weeks while the relentlessly advancing Mexican Army was destroying the Anglo settlers' homes, Houston at last decided to stand and fight at Buffalo Bayou (not coincidentally, near present-day Pasadena, where Mobil Oil erected its huge refineries) (figure 11).[14] At 3:00 P.M. on April 21, 1836, the Texans attacked, routed the Mexicans "during a siesta," captured Santa Anna, and thus secured their independence. This battle was the climax of the Texas history taught to us in *Texas History Movies*.

CREATING THE TEXAS PERSONA

Texas History Movies is a humorous and satirical story of the creation of Texas as a nation. For children like me, it was the origin myth of Texas and of ourselves as Texans. The irony, the poking fun at ourselves, the outrageousness of the characters—the adventuresome men who were heroic but rascally—were all models of the complex Texas persona. The drawings depicted pompous and unsavory men who nevertheless committed grandiose and brave deeds. Some, like Travis and Fannin, were egotistical and none too competent but stood their ground and faced their deaths with honor. Others, such as Samuel Williams (acting in partnership with Stephen Austin), were speculators who urged the state of Coahuila and Texas to donate Texas land to raise money for a militia to oppose the tyrant Santa Anna; they then sold the land for huge profits for themselves. Some of these men depicted in *Texas History Movies* came with histories of sexual scandals, drinking binges, or violence, but they were also the kind of tough survivors Texas needed. Men like Davy Crockett and Sam Houston could tell great stories of their adventures—while mocking themselves—without revealing an ounce of humility.

Although *Texas History Movies* depicts mostly a string of heroic males, it also peppers the legends with a few long-suffering females: Jane Long, who faced Indians and starvation on Galveston Island while waiting for her worthless husband; Susanna Dickenson, whose husband died at the

Alamo, delivered the news of the Alamo tragedy to her fellow Texans; Emily Morgan, the octoroon (allegedly the "Yellow Rose of Texas" celebrated in the song) who, according to legend, was in Santa Anna's bed at the decisive hour of 3:00 P.M. on April 21, 1836, thereby distracting him from the strategies of war.

Buried in these tales, however, is a much deeper sexual politics: Sam Houston's mysterious marriage-gone-awry, which led to his move to Texas and a deepening of his ties with the Cherokee; Stephen Austin's total disinterest in marriage or women; James Bowie's marriage to the daughter of the governor of the state—these were the sexual links that helped make Texas. In a more subtle way, Texas history, as portrayed in *Texas History Movies,* is the saga of political marriages and family bonds. My own family record melded so seamlessly into *Texas History Movies* that, for me at least, this comic book held a higher truth that overrode the historical mistakes and blatant prejudices against Mexicans and Indians.

Texas History Movies was written in a way that would make schoolchildren proud to be Texans. In that purpose it was highly successful—but at a price. Along with the subtext of family ties is the underlying message of deep prejudice toward Mexicans, "Negroes," women, and especially Indians. In this sense it did not resonate with all Texas children since it does not celebrate those whom it viewed as inferiors or enemies. It is the hegemonic origin myth, but it is not an all-inclusive one.

Consequently, during the 1986 sesquicentennial celebrations in Texas, when consciousness of the state's image to the outside world was at a high, the pamphlet was purged of the worst biases and blatant errors of history. The new, sanitized version by no means pleased everyone.[15] Novelist Rolando Hinojosa-Smith dubbed it still racist in its treatment of Mexicans, and Kent Biffle, in his *Dallas Morning News* column, lamented that the old version was *the* book that sparked interest in Texas history in most of the state's illustrious citizens.[16] Both assertions are probably correct. What interests me is that, although the cleaner version is certainly more palatable by today's standards, as far as I can tell, it has not had much impact on Texans, primarily because it is no longer used in schools, where drier and more serious books on the Lone Star State have replaced *Texas History Movies* in the curriculum.

A product of the times in which it was written, *Texas History Movies* is not the only account of Texas with ethnocentric and supremacist undertones. When writing about the past, all historians (and anthropologists for that matter) take into consideration the values and circumstances of the present. Furthermore, they write *for* a particular audience, a set of readers with a certain social and cultural identity. They also write *from* a unique cultural identity, usually their own. This is true of recent histories of Texas as well as my own account here. In the case of *Texas History Movies,* Anglo Texans were writing for other Anglo Texans, and their purpose was to create, reinforce, and heroize a local Anglo Texas identity.

EARLY LOCAL HISTORIES

Local histories that were written shortly after the Texas Revolution were also intended for the Anglo Texans and were consciously mythmaking. One of the classic early tomes is John Henry Brown's *History of Texas, 1685 to 1892.*[17] This account is rich in detail and marvelous for its depiction of the people who actually experienced the events. Brown's goal was not the same as that of *Texas History Movies.* He held a strong savages-versus-civilized ethos, and his two-volume narration is a testament to the superiority of civilization: "Ours is not like the history of any other State of the Union, settled and fostered by a *progressive people* and government, and aided by great interior resources and means of transportation of which practically Texas had nothing. *Wild barbarians* infested Texas, undisturbed until its settlement by Americans, and its frontiers continued subject to all the horrors, more or less extensive, of savage warfare from the beginning in 1822, to its practical cessation in 1876, a period of fifty-four years, beside[s] the period from 1835 to 1845, inclusive, of a state of war with Mexico" (italics mine).[18]

Even for the times, Brown's vision of Texas as a place at war with savage barbarians (Indians) and inferior Mexicans was an extreme position. Brown came to Texas in 1839, just after Texas' independence from Mexico. He stayed with his uncle James Kerr, a prominent early settler in the Lavaca-Navidad River area, where the Alabama Settlement was located.[19] As one of the first American settlers in the area, Kerr knew everyone and was well respected. He also enjoyed a reputation as the ugliest man in Texas. According to legend, Kerr once won the "ugliest man" prize in a contest. One day Kerr walked into a saloon at Texana and sat down at a table. He noticed a tall, homely man staring at him. The man came over to Kerr and said, "I'm going to have to kill you." Major Kerr asked why. The homely man replied, "I have always said if I ever saw a man uglier than me, I was going to shoot him." Kerr got up and asked the man to come to the window. After looking the man over, Kerr said, "Shoot away, stranger. If I'm any uglier than you, I don't care to live."[20]

John Henry Brown was a professional journalist. Through his relationship with his uncle James Kerr, Brown became an eyewitness to events after the Texas Revolution. Although he had personally missed the uprising, he was captured by its sentiment and set out to write one of the first histories of the rebellion. With access to documents and people still fresh from making history, he personally met virtually every one of my ancestors in the Alabama Settlement. Later he fought in the Civil War with the son of empresario Sterling Clack Robertson. Brown's chronicle set the standard for Texas histories in the future, espousing as it did the heroics at the Alamo, the ordinary people of the Runaway Scrape, the contributions of Stephen F. Austin, and the leadership of Samuel Houston, while condemning the "corruption and cruelty" of the Mexican government and the "savagery" of the Texas Indians.

Brown interests me partly because of a family connection with him that continued for many generations. His *History of Texas* clearly sides with the settlers, who had been eager to go to war with Mexico at the time of the Texas Revolution, a group that included all of my ancestors in the Alabama Settlement. Brown also supported to some extent Sterling Robertson's claims against Stephen F. Austin, much to the chagrin of Eugene Barker, Austin's biographer. Brown was an ardent Indian hater and a committed secessionist. In 1865 he was so devastated by the South's loss in the Civil War that he left the United States to live in Mexico for two years.[21] Apparently he begot some children there because my father ran into one of Brown's descendants in Sandborn's (a meeting place for American expatriates in the 1940s), and, as my father later recounted, they greeted each other as distant kin.

In addition to general accounts like John Henry Brown's, local counties in Texas all have their own versions of regional history, written mainly for local Anglo residents, with the same note of heroism carefully replicated. For example, *The Cavalcade of Jackson County* by I. T. Taylor declares that "The name of this book was carefully selected by the author after many hours of thought: Cavalcade means a triumphant procession of notables or historic events. No county in Texas *or the United States* has had a greater triumphant historic procession than the 'Alabama Settlement' and other early settlers of Jackson County" (italics mine).[22] As such an introduction might suggest, the book lists the names of each (Anglo) individual who participated in local history so that family members can look them up. It focuses on battles and wars, the founding of towns and churches, and specific biographies of prominent people.

Historians such as Brown and Taylor played important roles in the creation of the heroic (Anglo) Texan identity. They assumed that society and culture were the product of an evolution from savagery to civilization. Civilized white people were heroic; the savage Indians and the less evolved Mexicans were cruel and barbaric, but mostly, of course, they were invisible. Nowhere in any of these annals do we hear their voices.

TEXAS AND FRAGILITY

My interpretation of Texas history is that, far from being the gallant struggle depicted in *Texas History Movies,* John Henry Brown's *History of Texas,* and Ira Taylor's *Cavalcade of Jackson County,* the daily existence of *everyone* who lived in Texas during the early days of settlement under Spain and Mexico was extremely fragile. It was a tenuous existence for the Americans who came to Mexican Texas, and it was equally arduous for the Indian groups who migrated to Texas or were pushed into the area in the early decades of the 1800s. It was similarly trying for the Spaniards—the priests and military men who tried to penetrate this distant part of the Spanish empire—to set up Catholic missions to "civilize" the Indians and garrisons to claim the territory for Spain. When Mexico overthrew Spain and laid claim to what was the remotest region of their new country, the Spanish soldiers stationed in the military posts often remained in Texas with a new identity as Mexicans.

The unstable Mexican government was desperate to keep its hold on this outer edge of their world, and to this end they sought to encourage immigration to these wild parts. With little success at convincing Mexicans from the central plateau to migrate to the outer edge of Mexico, they turned to the Americans, who were very interested in the Texas frontier.

The Americans who arrived in 1820 and 1821 found a sparsely occupied territory. Mexicans were living in three pockets of Texas—the Nacogdoches area along the Louisiana border, the surrounds of the fort at Bexar in San Antonio, and the ranching south. In each region, distinctive Mexican communities had produced their own particular cultures.[23] The ranching areas in the south, for example, had already developed a new way of life, a vaquero tradition based on taming the abundant wild horses and cattle left by the Spaniards. The population of the ranching south was very small, but its influence on Texas history and identity has been enormous. The arriving Americans imitated their style of riding horses—sit heavy, reins up, feet out—and quickly picked up the vaquero culture and technology. They adopted the Mexican saddles, bridles, whips, spurs, and methods of rounding up and breaking animals. They learned the vaquero vocabulary, and soon Mexican words such as rodeo, riata, canyon, lasso, cinch (*cincha*), cowboy, and buckaroo (from "vaquero") became part of everyday Texas English. They adopted the vaqueros' clothing—the tight pants, vests, chaps (*chaparejos*), ponchos, and sombreros (large brim). They collected herds of longhorn cattle, which they cooked as barbecue (*barbacoa*) in deep pits as the Mexicans did.[24]

Some Indians also lived in Texas before the American settlers came. For example, the Caddo in the Nacogdoches area were situated on the edge of their former sophisticated, complex city-state civilization along the Mississippi. The Karankawa, who were foragers, fished and gathered food along the several rivers that fed into the Gulf of Mexico. There were also Indians who had recently migrated to Texas. Pushed from the United States into Texas, bands of Choctaw and Cherokee were trying to find a niche for themselves just as the Americans were. Both groups had to deal with the fierce Comanche hunters who periodically came to the central and western parts of Texas to hunt.

The Texas the American colonists entered was, at the time, so sparsely populated (when it was populated at all) that it was, in terms of culture construction, an open, unformed, fluid situation. In a very short time, from 1821 to 1836, the Texas population exploded with immigrants from the United States and, a short time later, from Germany and Ireland (although groups of Irish immigrants were already in Texas before the revolution). Between 1830 and 1836, a mere six years, the population of Texas increased more than sevenfold, with Anglo Americans accounting for half of the populace and Indians as the second largest group. In 1834 Col. Juan Almonte, the illegitimate son of Morelos, the hero of the Mexican revolt against Spain, estimated that Texas had 21,000 people (not counting Indians) distributed in three pockets (4,000 around San Antonio; 8,000 around Austin's colony; and 9,000 in Nacogdoches).[25] By 1836 the population of the republic had exploded to an estimated 52,970.

Like the Mexican colonies established earlier in Texas, early American settlements formed specific, discrete enclaves. Each one had its own particular character created from the cultural context its inhabitants brought with them and adapted to the conditions they encountered. These situations included the influence of Indians living or traveling through the settlement, the particular makeup of the colonists who came with them or followed later, the social and cultural life they created in Texas, and the nature of their relations with empresarios, who acted as their local leader. Then there were the colonists' own struggles with illness, growing crops, acquiring goods, forming religious associations, organizing a social life, and educating their children.

These mundane activities took place in a context of wider, more dramatic processes and events. In the global arena, Mexico's independence from Spain denied Spain access to one of the largest and most profitable parts of the Spanish empire, but it had an equally dramatic effect on local conditions. Mexico experienced a period of political instability expressed in violent revolutionary activity—golpes and civil war. Like the fledgling United States,

ETHNIC DISTRIBUTION OF POPULATION, C. 1836

Slaves	5,000[1]
Mexican	3,470[2]
Indian	14,500
American	30,000

1. Estimate based on county tax rolls.
2. Tijerina (1994, 22) gives 6,000; Randolph Campbell (2003, 159).

Mexico had to worry for a long time about European intervention in its lo-cal affairs. Moreover, Mexico was quickly plunged into shaky relations with its neighbor to the north, whose citizens were arriving daily. In a desperate attempt to end that encroachment, the president of Mexico sent troops to Texas to quell the rebellious murmurings. Then Santa Anna himself led a huge force into Texas, a step the Texans saw as daunting but which in fact was riddled with problems ranging from inadequate supplies to mistakes in strategy. Fresh from having "brutally crushed" civil war in the states of Za-catecas and Yucatán, Santa Anna set out to destroy the Texan settlements, only this time he was humiliated and defeated.

In 1836 Texas became a republic but sought all along to join the United States as a slaveholding state, only to be thwarted by the Yankee abolitionists, whose champion was Pres. John Quincy Adams. Those years of the republic, when Texas was an independent nation, were the years in which Texas so-lidified its identity, learned to govern itself, established "civilization" in the form of churches, schools, and local government, and rid itself of "wildness," namely Indians. However, this postwar period was not so good for the Mexi-can Texans, who lost their land and suffered intense discrimination. At the end of nearly a decade as a republic, Texas had transformed itself. With the Texas identity now firmly established, it became a state of the United States, only to be thrown into turmoil fifteen years later, when it seceded from the Union and went to war with the North.

These events exacted a toll on Texas both economically and culturally. The state arrived at the end of the nineteenth century primarily as a poor agricul-tural region with few resources, on the edge of the main events in the United States and the rest of the world. Cotton and cattle were the economy's pri-mary resources until the discovery of oil in 1901 at Spindletop in Beaumont, a moment that changed Texas' economic fortunes forever and created the Magnolia Oil Company.

A NOTE ABOUT HISTORY AND ANTHROPOLOGY

Like all histories, those about Texas are temporally specific, that is, products of their times. What is more, they are written in a format that is specific to the cultures of modern Europe and the United States.[26] This narrative style, developed in Western Europe and the United States, tells history as a series of events supplemented by the biographies of the people who shaped those events.[27] Utilizing a structure of "event and biography" is only one of many ways to write history, however. In the Middle East, for example, the narrative structure is poetry, with meaning embedded poetically through metaphor and symbol.

History, as I see it, is not so much a narrative progression of incidents and biographies from one time period to another; rather, it is a shift in *meaning structures* through time. These changes in meaning may be affected by cataclysmic events, but in general they occur incrementally in prosaic microevents, personal experiences, and everyday cultural practices.[28] In this way people create and transform culture. It is history as agency in creating both culture and, more specifically, identity that I want to discuss. As an anthropologist, I am interested in cultural meaning, meaning that is both local and embodied in people and places. Meaning speaks to identity—our sense of self as well as an understanding of our difference from others.

In this book my question is, how did Texans mobilize these feelings of identity into a "Texan" group identity in such a short time after arriving in the region? I want to cull from the archive of a particular group of Texas families in the nineteenth century a narrative that illustrates how their experiences and imaginations created and reproduced, generation after generation, their Texas selves.

In creating this kind of local history from family documents, it is also important to place the local context within the wider framework of the region. The culture of regions within the United States has become a hot topic in these times of globalization and supposed homogenization of culture. Scholars today are concerned with how regional differences persist in the face of the broader forces pushing us toward a homogeneous national— or even global—culture.[29] We know that U.S. history began with a number of regional accounts that were eclipsed by the writing of a national history during the nineteenth century. Ironically, the rise of mass culture (after national culture), rather than further diluting regionalism, has seen an increase in the recognition of regional cultures and a renewed concern with preserving local histories. It has been suggested that this rekindled focus on regional culture has come about as a counterbalance to the homogenizing effects of mass culture.

However, those assertions are not true of Texas. National culture has never diluted the regional culture of the Lone Star State, which has always remained strong. In modern times, partly through the influence of the news media and film, Texas has become perhaps the most immediately recognizable local identity in the States, as I found out in Brazil. In this book I explore the way in which that Texas identity was created and sustained for one particular group of people.

CHAPTER 5

Sterling Clack Robertson, Empresario

exas history may not be accurately portrayed either in the cartoon book *Texas History Movies,* in early county histories, or in movies like *Giant,* but all of these venues were powerful producers of a Texas identity. For me and many other Texans with ancestors on Texas soil, our Texas identity was acquired through family stories. Sometimes these tales conflicted with the "official" history; sometimes they corroborated it. Although my family occupied a number of niches of Texas colonization, we never quite made it into the central story of our history books. My fore-bears seemed somehow to remain in the margins and footnotes of Texas his-tory, and this has given me a particular slant on the central narrative, not just from their point of view but also with a skeptical eye on the production of the canon. I consider my position on the sidelines to be a great advantage, a diagonal counterpoint from which to view the rest of Texas history.

The story of my great-great-great-grandfather Sterling Clack Robertson's efforts to start a colony in Texas has never quite made it into mainstream Texas history, partly because it brought him into direct competition with the great empresario Stephen Austin, the most important colonizer of Texas. Austin's biographers Eugene Barker and Gregg Cantrell have focused on Austin's many accomplishments in the settling of Texas and in general have developed bio-graphical material that supports Sam Houston's pronouncement upon Aus-tin's death that he was "the father of Texas." Both Barker and Cantrell portray Austin as a true statesman in the Anglo settling of Texas, and they dismiss Robertson as something of a rogue. My story is not a biographical assessment of either Austin or Robertson. Rather, I am interested in the perspectives of the settlers involved in the controversy at the time, as well as Austin's and Rob-ertson's actions, in order to understand the meaning of the friction between them and the emotional impact on the subjects of my story.

The intertwined lives of these two men are intrinsically interesting. By all accounts, Robertson was irascible and Austin overly cautious. Willing to bend the rules to advantage, neither one was above manipulating others for political ends. I contend that the story of the competition between Aus-tin and Robertson was much more than a rivalry between two men. In the nineteenth century, it was indicative of the wheeling and dealing going on in one of the biggest land grabs in the United States. The struggle and animosity between these two men was not just a private fight; rather it was a battle fought in the public arena of the Mexican legal and political system. Robertson represented an obstacle in Austin's plans for expanding colonization to the area of contract that Robertson held. He and Austin threw scurrilous accusations at one another. A number of settlers sided with Robertson, others with Austin. Their clash of wills is a soap opera of deception, one that resulted in an animosity not only between these two men but also for generations of historians of Texas, who even now tend to take one side or the other. The story of their conflict has been generally confined to a footnote of Texas history. I propose that it be viewed not as a sidebar but as a key example of the political practices and economic stakes of the times. Theirs was not the only empresario battle; other adventurers also tried to make their fortunes in Texas and to shape its future. But Robertson's and Austin's actions set the tone of politics in Texas, and it is unmistakable in Texas political culture even today.

The American colonization of Mexican Texas, which began in 1821, was a period of intense competition for land under the empresario system. An empresario was someone who contracted with the Mexican government to bring settlers to a specific region, survey a certain amount of land, and deed it to them in return for the right to acquire fees from the settlers. Empresarios were responsible for organizing and even financing the colonization of the area of their contract, but they also had enormous legal and moral authority over the region and stood a good chance of becoming some of the largest landowners of the times. In short, what was at stake in an empresario contract was no less than a large personal empire in Texas and a great deal of power over people's lives. For this reason, the long battle, both legal and moral, between Sterling Robertson, empresario of Robertson's colony, and Stephen Austin, empresario of Austin's colony, is significant. This protracted confrontation is a story of a high-level intrigue, one that had a huge impact on the political formation of Texas, on the telling of Texas history, and of course on the lives of the colonists themselves.

Robertson's colony spanned an enormous area of Central Texas, 100 miles wide and 200 miles long. The wide swath started where the Old San Antonio Road crossed the Brazos River northwest of Houston and ran northward to the outskirts of Fort Worth. Today this broad strip of land is one of the poorest and most undeveloped parts of the state. Located in the heart of Texas, it is surrounded now by the major cities, the dynamic hubs of Texas commerce and learning, but does not encompass them. The entire region is

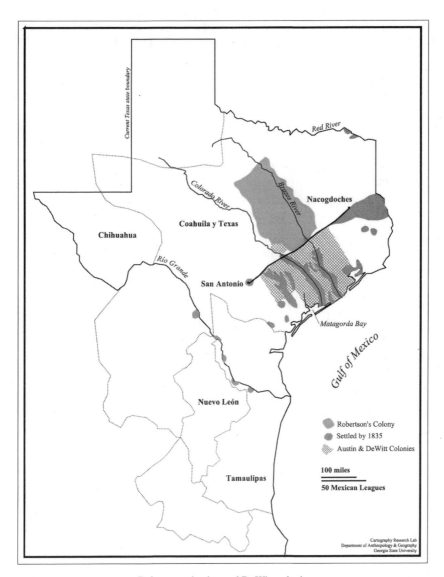

Robertson, Austin, and DeWitt colonies

composed of small towns that still have a 1950s' ethos and decor. The country-side consists of pretty but unspectacular rolling hills dotted with oak and pine trees but with poor soil for agriculture. This huge piece of the state is sparsely populated partly because of the toll the Austin-Robertson controversy exacted on it.

Robertson's Colony and Sterling Clack Robertson's efforts to colonize the area of his empresario contract are intertwined with Austin's efforts in Mexican Texas; it is thus particularly interesting to look at the juxtaposition of these two colonies to see how the Texas identity began to come about. Other settlements, such as DeWitt's (very closely linked in fortune to Austin's) and the Galveston Bay Company (associated with Lorenzo de Zavala), which also struggled and floundered amid the wild speculations, are part of the whole story of Mexican Texas colonization. But it is Robertson's and Austin's painful clash of wills that is the main strand in the tale of Texas colonization up to the revolt against Mexico.

Although much has now been written on the controversy, many conflicting claims and confusing interpretations of the records still remain. Historians know that every document is written with some purpose in mind—to proclaim one's innocence, to condemn an enemy's actions, to gain privilege, to avoid punishment, to record claims. Determining the purpose and the position of the author of the document often helps readers to understand the accuracy of the content. Many of the issues in this discussion may never be resolved. What is clear, however, is that something large was at stake, and it is perhaps more fruitful to establish what that might have been than to become mired in the often murky details of the accusations of perfidy and revenge, greed and subterfuge, and vicious character assassination.[1]

HISTORY OF THE ROBERTSON COLONY

For those who choose not to read the monumental nineteen-volume *Papers concerning Robertson's Colony in Texas,* this brief synopsis peppered with my own interpretation might suffice.[2] The idea for the colony was born on March 2, 1821. Seventy men came together in Nashville, Tennessee, drafted a letter to Mexico's newly independent government, congratulated it on winning independence from Spain, and asked for permission to settle in Texas.[3] The seventy Tennesseans who bought stock in this newly formed "Texas Association" included prominent men from prestigious families, such as Nelson Patteson and his son James (just returned from prison in Mexico), William Campbell, Ira Ingram, Robert Leftwich, and Sam Houston (who later became governor of Tennessee). A passel of Robertsons also took part: Felix, William, and John Robertson, all sons of Gen. James Robertson; James Randolph Robertson, a grandson of Gen. James Robertson; Sterling Clack Robertson, son of Elijah Robertson, a brother of Gen. James Robertson; and Samuel Marshall (married to Robertson's niece, Jane Childress).

Andrew Erwin, another member of the Texas Association, was designated to deliver the letter to the newly minted Mexican government. In 1822 such a task was not for the fainthearted. Erwin took a boat down the Mississippi River to New Orleans, boarded a ship bound for the port of Veracruz at the bottom of the Gulf of Mexico. There he had to climb up through the mountains on horseback to Jalapa, the beautiful bougainvillea-covered capital of Veracruz, before making the final climb to Mexico City in the central plateau. The journey took almost two months.

In Mexico City, Erwin met up with Robert Leftwich, another member of the Texas Association. Together they placed their petition to bring families to Texas before the Colonization Commission of the new Mexican congress. They naively expected it to be approved in a matter of days.

In 1822 Mexico City was teeming with petitioners for the coveted Texas land contracts, including daring young men such as Ben Milam (later a hero in the Texas War of Independence), the Baron de Bastrop (the Dutch adventurer who had been very helpful to Moses Austin), Hayden Edwards (who was looking for a contract to settle the Nacogdoches area and an instigator of one of the early rebellions against Mexico), and several Europeans who were hoping to bring in Catholic Irish and German immigrants. Finally, there was Stephen Austin, who had taken over the now defunct empresario contract his father, Moses Austin, had obtained from Spain. Austin arrived in Mexico City in April of 1822, almost a year after his father died and a few days after Erwin and Leftwich arrived. There he met the other petitioners, including Leftwich, with whom he roomed for a while.

Contrary to their expectations, empresario contracts proved extremely hard to obtain for a number of reasons. First, the early days of Mexico's independence from Spain were tumultuous times with Balkanesque intrigues, sudden shifts in power, and changes in laws that followed the political winds and buffeted people's fortunes. The sheer flux and the degree of changeability were frustrating to the petitioners, and only the most persistent would succeed. Moreover, it was necessary to know the Spanish language and Mexican customs. Finally and perhaps most important, they had to learn how to present a bribe with the utmost delicacy.

Still, the contracts were potentially very lucrative and therefore worth the fight. Austin, because his father had made valuable contacts in high places earlier than anyone else and because he was fluent in Spanish, was able to get the first Mexican government contract on February 17, 1823. The agreement allowed him to bring settlers into Texas and to provide them with deeds for the land. In return for surveying the land and providing deeds and his services as empresario, he could charge each immigrant $12.50 per hundred acres, potentially a fortune since he would be distributing thousands of acres. In addition, for each two hundred families he introduced, Austin was to receive some sixty-seven thousand acres for his services.[4] According to his biographer Eugene C. Barker, Austin also knew that the value of his contract was as much at risk from "the encroachment of new grantees as from any other cause."[5]

Austin's stay in Mexico City from April 1822 to April 1823 proved valuable to him over the next ten years. He perfected his Spanish, made solid personal ties with government officials, acquired a deep knowledge of Mexican society and culture, and, most important, became friends with key people in vital political positions. An able negotiator with the personal skills to work within the Mexican system, he was clearly in his element.

Robert Leftwich, acting for the Texas Association, kept a diary of his two years in Mexico while he negotiated with the Mexican government. He often spoke of the fruitless efforts of those who were trying to obtain empresario contracts and the constant frustration of working in such a chaotic environment.[6] The Mexican government initially dealt with each petitioner individually. However, so many of them were clamoring at the door that the government decided to implement a general policy that would cover all of the applications. To this end it passed the Imperial Colonization Law on January 7, 1823, only to revoke it nearly three months later, on April 8. The frustration of the applicants was palpable. In his diary Leftwich complained that he and two others (Haden Edwards and Daniel Stewart) finally resorted to the payment of a bribe of ten thousand dollars (in pesos) each to acquire their contracts:

> *I confess it would have been far more congenial to my feelings could a grant have been obtained in [an]other way than the above. In the United States it would be called bribery and would be considered by me dishonorable in the person offering as well as the person accepting, in Mexico it is more elastically called paying a man for his trouble and probably has been the custom of the country for three hundred years from the Viceroy down to the lowest officer in it. They have thrown off a Royal yoke after a struggle of thirteen years but to divest themselves of former habits may yet take a century to come. From my acquaintance with the Spanish character I find that the use of a golden key is not only necessary but that it is indispensable to unlock the door to any object that you wish to obtain—you will perceive the length of time that had elapsed between my arrival and resorting to it.[7]*

When the law changed yet again, imagine Leftwich's feelings after finally overcoming his distaste for the maneuver. A national colonization law was passed that referred colonization contracts to the states, and at the same time the state of Coahuila and Texas was formed. Leftwich had to start over. He traveled to Saltillo, then the capital of the new state, to petition under the new state colonization law (March 24, 1825) for his contract. This time he put the petition in his own name (he was by now working on money borrowed from Haden Edwards), and it was granted on April 15, 1825, by the state government of Coahuila and Texas.[8] On that same date other empresarios—Green DeWitt, Haden Edwards, and Frost Thorn—were also given contracts. Leftwich went back to Tennessee after an absence of slightly more than three years and sold the contract to the Texas Association for eight thousand dollars. He died shortly after.

Once the Texas Association obtained Leftwich's grant, Felix Robertson, a medical doctor and the uncle of Sterling Robertson, was selected to organize the first expedition to the territory covered by the contract. Felix set out for Texas with thirty-one men, leaving Nashville on a keel boat at 3:00 P.M. on November 21, 1825, just seven months after Leftwich had returned from Mexico City.[9] Excited by the prospect of their leading citizens setting up a new colony, a crowd of Nashville residents gathered on the banks of the Cumberland River to see them off, firing guns to mark the moment. It took a month to float down the Cumberland and then the Ohio River to Natchez. From there they went on to the mouth of the Red River and then traveled by horse to Nacogdoches, arriving at the Brazos River in February 1826. The Robertson family members on this expedition—Felix, James R., Peyton, Henry V., Sterling C., and Mark Robertson Cockrill—each had their leagues surveyed around the area of Cow Creek on the Brazos in present-day McLennan County.[10]

In June, Felix Robertson sent a report back to Nashville that spoke glowingly of the rich river bottom of the Brazos, which was excellent for growing cotton and sugarcane. The land that was not suitable for agriculture, he contended, was wonderful grazing for buffalo, deer, wild horses, and cows. With trade winds blowing from the south, it was a healthy region, he noted, removed from the marshes and fevers of the South and the rheumatism, apoplexy, and consumption prevalent in the North. The Nashville newspaper claimed the report spoke of a "promised land."[11] News of the beauty, healthfulness, and promise of this area of Texas was greatly exaggerated, however; nevertheless, the citizens of Nashville caught the immigration fever in no time.

Sterling Clack Robertson

Felix's nephew Sterling was greatly captivated by the suggestion of adventure in Texas and the smell of enormous tracts of land. However, he might not have felt so drawn to the idea of immigrating were it not for his unfortunate hotheaded stabbing of his cousin. Robertson had a bad temper, and these were times of fights to the death in questions of honor and impassioned disagreements. His predicament was not all that unusual for the times; nevertheless, it gave him a good reason to strike out for Texas.

Sterling Robertson was born in 1785 into one of the finest, wealthiest, and most politically connected families in Nashville. As a member of a prominent clan, he was given a liberal education under the direction of Judge John McNairy, who was related to Robertson by marriage.[12] Sterling was handsome, five feet ten inches tall, sandy haired, with penetrating gray eyes and an aquiline nose. He was known as something of a ladies' man although there is no record of his marriage to anyone. However, he fathered one son with Frances King before leaving Tennessee for Texas.

Robertson's quick temper sometimes led him to take a man aside for a private conversation. As his agitation mounted, he would start shouting, drawing a crowd. He dressed well in linen shirts, black pants, a black vest topped with a frock coat, and a large, white, low-crown brimmed hat. His boots sported long-necked spurs. On each hip he wore a percussion-lock pistol in a leather holster, the straps crossing over his abdomen. Each handmade holster had a small pocket for a black-handled knife (a knife was often a better weapon than a gun with percussion locks). He always rode a superb Tennessee Arabian horse.[13] In short, he was well dressed, well mounted, and well armed.

Sterling Robertson was forty-four years old when he assembled, financed, and led twenty to thirty families on the long trek to Texas. On October 25, 1830, they arrived in Tenoxtitlán, the Mexican garrison on the border with Louisiana. Robertson presented the commandant with the Nashville contract that had been granted on April 15, 1825, well within its six-year deadline. But they were still too late. The Mexican government, nervous about the many American colonists that were pouring into Texas and in fear of losing the region to them, on April 6, 1830, had passed a new law to restrict further immigration from the United States. Furthermore, the government sent Gen. Manuel de Mier y Terán to Texas to set up a number of forts—at Lipantitlán, Tenoxtitlán, and Anáhuac—to enforce this law.[14]

Ignoring this legal snag and aware that he still had a valid contract, Robertson did not turn back at Tenoxtitlán and return to Tennessee. Instead, he took the families back up the road a bit and then in the dead of the night cut a new road that circled the town and continued down to San Felipe, where he hoped to get permission for his colonists to join Austin's colony. This tactic shows the kind of resourcefulness—or winking at the letter of the law—for

which Texans are still well known. The new road was soon used by other immigrants and eventually became known as the "Tennesseans' Road."[15]

When Robertson arrived in San Felipe, he found Hosea League, the appointed agent for the Nashville contract, chained to a cabin wall awaiting trial
on a charge of accessory to murder. Robertson obtained a power of attorney
from the unfortunate League to become the empresario himself and went to
see Stephen Austin to discuss a way to circumvent the 1830 law.

Like all the other land agents, Austin was vehemently against this new
law, but he never dealt with legal setbacks by flouting the law as Robertson
had. Instead, he hoped to wangle an "interpretation" of the law that would
allow existing contracts to be completed if a certain number of families had
already been settled *before* the passage of the April 6, 1830, law. Austin himself could claim to come under this interpretation, and, judging from his
actions, it seems Robertson fully intended to "extend" the interpretation to
his own advantage as well.

Then, at the end of December 1830, Austin, the newly elected deputy from
Texas to the state congress of Coahuila and Texas, set off for the conven-
ing of the new assembly in Saltillo. Before he left, Robertson asked Austin,
as his elected representative, to make an appeal to the state government on
his behalf. Robertson wanted to appoint a land commissioner for the Nashville Company who would be empowered to grant legal possession of their
land to the families who had arrived.[16] He also wanted Austin to request an
extension of the contract so that Robertson would have more time to fulfill
it. According to Robertson, Austin assured him that he would try to help.
Confident in Austin's ability, Robertson then returned to Nashville, where
he learned that part of his sentence for manslaughter—that he be branded
with an *M* on the palm of one hand—had been pardoned due to a petition
circulated by the ladies of Nashville, who denounced the practice as barba-
rous and disfiguring, especially on a handsome and presumably eligible man.
He was, however, still expected to serve nine months in jail. Consumed with
the Texas immigration fever, he instead sold some of his property in Nashville and loaded another group of settlers on the steamboat *Criterion*, which
left on March 29, 1831.

While Sterling Robertson was in Nashville gathering up his second group
of colonists, he of course hoped that, in Saltillo, Austin was arranging for
an extension of the time period for colonization. Instead, Austin had applied to the congress, of which he was a member, for the Nashville contract
for himself and his partner, Samuel Williams. While this kind of action by
an elected representative would be considered perfidy today, Austin's letters
readily provide an explanation for his astonishing conduct. In the first place,

Austin noted, he had been planning all along to apply for a league of land for Samuel Williams. Then he heard that a French company called Villevèques was seeking an empresario contract in Texas. Austin viewed the French as dangerous interlopers in *affaires americaines.* So, in order to "save" Texas from the French, he decided to apply for the whole area of the Nashville contract for himself. He reasoned that he was doing so for the good of Texas, which was always uppermost in his mind and best guided by his hands alone, in his opinion. Robertson did not buy this argument, however. Feeling betrayed, he devoted the rest of his life to the recovery of the empresario contract from Austin.

The contract for the Robertson colony was granted to Austin and Williams on February 4, 1831. Austin had indeed figured out how to bypass the law of 1830 halting American immigration, but only for his own advantage. He quickly wrote his partner, Williams, urging him to keep quiet about their contract for the "upper colony" (that is, upper in relation to Austin's lower colonies) at least until May—when the Nashville Company contract would expire. When it was made public that he and Williams had grabbed such a huge area for themselves, Austin knew there would be repercussions from Robertson.[17]

He was right. Robertson was apoplectic at the betrayal by his elected representative, but, as Gregg Cantrell, an Austin biographer, has noted, "Austin might have handled Robertson with greater care if he had known more about him."[18] Having killed a man for less perfidy, Robertson did not hesitate to jump into a fight that would last for most of the rest of his life. He also knew he was taking on the most powerful man in Texas, a man with the best contacts in the Mexican government and a close personal friend of Mexican general Mier y Terán, who was in charge of the Texas garrisons.

The betrayal by Austin was galling, but Robertson knew that, to move through the maze of Mexican bureaucracy, he needed the help of a lawyer who was familiar with Mexican law and fluent in Spanish. He found that combination in Thomas Jefferson Chambers and quickly hired Chambers to present his appeal. The crux of the petition was that Robertson wanted an opportunity to qualify for the "Austin interpretation" of the 1830 law by providing proof that he had introduced one hundred settlers before April 6, 1830.[19] Although we know that he brought his first group of settlers six months after the law, he intended to provide depositions that stated otherwise.

His right to appeal approved, he returned to Tennessee to serve his sentence of manslaughter from April 6, 1832, to September 1, a total of five months. In December 1832, Robertson went back to Texas, this time bringing his twelve-year-old son by Frances King, also called Sterling Clack Robertson.

They made the trip entirely on horseback, riding the outstanding Tennessee Arabian horses Robertson favored. To collect depositions from his settlers to present to the congress in Saltillo, Robertson went to San Felipe. He wanted to show that he had brought in a total of 146 colonists, many of whom he had financed personally, and that they had been forced by the April 6, 1830, law to settle in Austin's colony instead.[20]

Before Robertson finished collecting the depositions, he decided to accompany Sam Houston (whom he had known in Tennessee), James Bowie, and a man with the improbable name of Caiaphas Ham on a trip to San Antonio. There is no doubt that both Houston and Bowie were influential men who could be of help to Robertson, and Robertson needed all the political help he could get.

Once in San Antonio, Robertson put his son into the Catholic mission school with instructions to teach the boy Spanish, a very desirable skill for Robertson, who desperately needed the land deeds of his settlers translated into Spanish so they could be recorded with the Mexican government. He wanted his son to be that translator. In San Antonio, Robertson met Juan Martín de Veramendi, the father of Bowie's wife and also, as of January, the acting governor of the state of Coahuila and Texas. Although Sam Houston went back to the United States, the rest of the party, along with Governor Veramendi and his other son-in-law, A. B. Sterrett, set out for Saltillo.[21]

Arriving in Saltillo on February 7, 1833, they found the city in an uproar. In Mexico, Generalissimo Santa Anna had started a revolution and declared himself el presidente, abolishing the legislature of Coahuila and Texas. Neither the people of Saltillo nor the state government knew what action to take, but Veramendi and Bowie suggested to the deposed congress that, for safety's sake, they move the entire capital to the town of Monclova, Veramendi's hometown. Fearing for their safety, the state congress voted to declare Monclova the state capital, and on March 9, 1833, the entire congress and its staff loaded up the state government's papers and made the momentous journey across the desert in north Mexico to the remote town of Monclova. Robertson did not stay with the slow oxcarts and burros laden with the state archives but rode ahead on his Tennessee steed with Governor Veramendi. Arriving in the new capital, he presented his documents and settlers' depositions to Governor Veramendi. Robertson was clearly learning to play the same it's-who-you-know game as Austin. He returned to San Felipe in June 1833 to find that the intrigues and counterintrigues with Austin were just beginning.[22]

In July, General Mier y Terán, Austin's special friend, despondent over the uprisings in Mexico and his own failing health, dressed himself in his military uniform and eviscerated himself with his sword at the wall of the church of San Antonio de Padilla.[23] Within three months of his suicide, Mexican forces were withdrawn from Texas, and Austin and Williams began giving out eleven-league grants from the upper colony to nonresident speculators, while Robertson tried desperately to get the *ayuntamiento* (town council) in San Felipe to hear the case regarding his empresario contract. To express the sentiments of some of the colonists about Austin's actions, Ira Ingram wrote a letter to Hosea League in Matagorda in July 1833: "Where, let me ask, will the art of this half Mexican, half American Jesuit, this trans-atlantic Fouché, finally land us?" (Fouché was the French minister of police from 1799 to 1810 and is regarded as the creator of political espionage).[24] Finally, on February 5, 1834, the ayuntamiento accepted Robertson's depositions and decided in his favor. This was a curious decision since it was a direct repudiation of Austin by key men in his own seat of government, the starched William Barrett Travis and the colorful "Three-legged Willie" Williamson. Moreover, either they did not know that Robertson had arrived in Texas with his first colonists six months after the April 1830 law or they decided for some reason to support him anyway.

Samuel Williams immediately went into high gear and sent his agent, Thomas McQueen, to Monclova to press Williams and Austin's case for the upper colony. However, just after leaving San Antonio, McQueen was attacked by Tawakoni Indians and died of his wounds.[25] At the same time, Robertson and his companion, William Steele, were also on their way to Monclova to counter Williams and Austin and present their own case to the governor. To keep their journey under wraps, they took a different route from McQueen's. Riding fast Arabian horses, they were well armed and accompanied by a manservant. The story of this ride is a wild one.

As empresario Robertson told it, he was joined on the trip by a Mexican companion on horseback. When the Mexican kept falling behind, Robertson scuffled with him and forced him to admit that Austin had sent him to assassinate Robertson and prevent him from reclaiming his contract.[26] After eliciting this confession, he let the man go rather than killing him. This family story has passed down through five generations. Although there is no written evidence for the tale, its longevity is a testament of the family's belief in its veracity.

Robertson made it to Monclova with the settlers' depositions and satisfied the Mexican government that he had brought one hundred families to Texas before the law of 1830. According to Cantrell, Austin's biographer, this was a terrible lie. He maintains that Robertson perjured himself and that some of the deposed must have lied, too.[27] Actually, quite a few of the deposed colonists would have had to lie, but if they did, Robertson would certainly not be the first land agent to present false evidence to the Mexican government. It would also be interesting to know why the colonists were willing to perjure themselves for Robertson. In any case, the Mexican government accepted the evidence, and Robertson's contract was reinstated on April 29, 1834. He was given a four-year extension to complete his contract by bringing in the requisite number of colonists.

Samuel Williams quickly countered by hiring a new agent, Juan Antonio Padilla, who was dispatched to Monclova a short time afterward. Padilla presented to the legally constituted authorities of the country a letter accusing Robertson of insulting them and creating unrest in the municipality of San Felipe.[28] Robertson was immediately arrested and thrown into prison in Monclova. It was two months before he could answer the charges, which he did by accusing Williams of having come to Texas under an assumed name to flee criminal accusations in the United States and having brought a wife and children whom he later abandoned (these allegations were true, for whatever that is worth).[29] After convincing the authorities of the falseness of the accusations against him, Robertson was released from jail. One of the stories he later told of his jail time was that the Mexican who had been sent as his assassin—and whose life he spared—in an ironic twist of fate came to the jail and brought him food.

Once out of lockup and with his contract securely in hand, Robertson appointed his friend William Steele land commissioner, and they began issuing land titles to the families Robertson had already brought to the colony.[30] By this time, the poisonous relationship between Austin and Robertson had reached a peak.

While all of these machinations give us a classic case of early Texas mythmaking at the empresario level, this story has yet several more layers, and we may never discover the whole truth about the case. I am not convinced it matters much, but this much is incontrovertible: Robertson had the Nashville contract, and Austin had it transferred to his name while acting as a member of the state congress. Robertson fought to reacquire it. The Mexican government decided Robertson's claim was valid, and he went on to colonize the area. Did a number of colonists lie under oath in their statements supporting his claim? They may have, but that in itself would indicate they supported Robertson rather than Austin. Did Austin grab Robertson's contract to eliminate a competitor and profit by speculating on the land? I think those may have been his motives. The result was an enmity between the two that affected the colonization of Texas for years to come.

Other events then overtook the hostility between the two men. In October the Mexican constitution of 1824 was abolished. Santa Anna declared himself dictator for life, and the states of Zacatecas and Yucatán immediately revolted against the centralist despot, declaring their loyalty to the federal-ist constitution of 1824. These were volatile, dangerous times. Also refusing to obey the centralists, the state congress of Coahuila and Texas moved to Monclova. In this period of immense confusion and unsettled government, Samuel Williams successfully introduced a state law authorizing the gover-nor to sell four hundred leagues of public land in Texas to raise a militia to oppose Santa Anna. This directive unleashed a massive speculation on land grants that many Texans and others grabbed (and ran back to Texas to sell at a profit). According to Barker, "this act was one of a series of laws that opened the way to gigantic speculations," speculations that were extremely unpopular with the Texian settlers.[31] Williams went on to charge fifty dol-lars per league for the location of large claims ranging from three to eleven leagues, and in the end he and John Durst (who also sponsored the law) were the main financial beneficiaries of the act.

The eleven-league grants covered 1.5 million acres taken from the public domain and sold to speculators who would never colonize them but only sell them for a higher price.[32] According to Barker, the speculation of the grants "brought great bitterness on Austin's memory. They became, in time, the basis of much litigation extending over many years, and in general the courts sustained them. The losers in these suits, frequently small holders, blamed Austin as the original cause of their losses and gave full sway to a sense of wrong and injury, the consequences of which have survived to the present day."[33] Because of the uncertain legal status of the land, the litigation that followed the eleven-league law (some of it went to the U.S. Supreme Court) delayed the settling of Central Texas by forty years.

Given such bitterness against Austin and Williams, it is no surprise that many citizens believed Robertson when he said that Austin had cheated him. They knew small landholders who had been pushed off of their land so that Williams and Austin could profit by selling large tracts for a fee. In the end, it is no wonder they did not vote for Austin to be the first president of the repub-lic. They had seen him use his office not just to represent his constituents but also to enrich himself. Apparently they were not persuaded as Barker hoped to convince later generations when he argued "that [although] his [Austin's] personal interests were bound up in the public interest[, this] does not neces-sarily weaken the sincerity of his belief or the cleanness of his motives."[34]

Austin's unpopularity among his own colonists at this time can also partly be accounted for by his unswerving loyalty to Mexico. His wily manipulation of the Mexican government, which he considered so necessary to his effec-tiveness, began to backfire on him. He was also opposed to Texas' becoming a part of the United States. Col. Anthony Butler, a U.S. government agent in

Mexico City who was trying to purchase Texas for the United States, wrote the following in a dispatch to Washington: "He [Austin] is unquestionably one of the bitterest foes of our government and people that is to be found in Mexico, and has done more to embarrass our negotiations upon a certain subject [the U.S. purchase of Texas] than all the rest put together; and I am very sure that he was the principal cause of my being defeated in the last effort made to obtain a secession of Texas."[35] Why did Austin oppose this purchase? It is hard to determine, but with Texas as a state of Mexico, Austin had a political edge as intermediary between the colonists and the Mexican government, an advantage he would no longer have if Texas became part of the United States.

Ironically, despite his loyalty to Mexico, Austin was getting flak from his adopted country as well, a fate that often befalls those who play both sides. The Mexican authorities were distrustful of Austin's efforts to make Texas a state separate from Coahuila because they saw this as a possible first step toward independence. They suspected that Austin might be secretly supporting the Anglo settlers, who were already clamoring for freedom from Mexico.

In the summer of 1833, Austin went to Mexico City to file an application for Texas to become a separate state under the federal system. Frustrated with the snail's pace at which the Mexican government operated, on October 2 he wrote to the ayuntamiento in San Antonio, urging it, along with other ayuntamientos in Texas, to organize a state government independent of Coahuila even though Mexico had not consented to a separate state for Texas. Austin wrote, "[T]here is no doubt but that the fate of Texas depends upon itself and not upon this government; nor that that country [Texas] is lost if its inhabitants do not take its affairs into their own hands."[36] Unfortunately for Austin, his letter was intercepted and interpreted as a bid for independence from Mexico. He was thrown in jail for sedition.

During the crucial months before the Texas Revolution, Austin was in prison in Mexico City and was thus unable to influence the events in Texas that were rapidly heating up. He was also distressed that his fellow Texans did not appear to be working for his release. Languishing in confinement, he was upset by the report that members of the "war party" (of which the Alabama Settlement was a large part), including Thomas Jefferson Chambers (Robertson's lawyer) and William Wharton (of Brazoria), were actively hostile to Austin. He also knew that Robertson was adding to his woes by fanning the flames with accusations. Austin recognized that the Mexican officials may have been exaggerating the reports of his enemies' activities in order to wrest a large bribe from him in return for his freedom, but he was deeply dismayed that his friends were making such little effort to get him released from jail.[37]

The Mexican government was also furious at the congress of Coahuila and Texas for giving away so much prime Mexican land in Texas (400 leagues) in order to raise a militia to oppose Santa Anna. When Samuel Williams applied to Gov. Agustín Viesca of the state of Texas and Coahuila for 400 leagues of public domain, he agreed to raise and equip one thousand men in return. The next day Gen. Martín Perfecto de Cos stated that if they did this, he would use arms against them and arrest the speculators, including Samuel Williams, James Bowie, Ben Milam, Francis Johnson, William B. Travis, and Lorenzo de Zavala. In the absence of the imprisoned Stephen Austin, Texas' agitation with the Mexican government reached its peak, and the colonists vowed not to let the Mexican government arrest anyone.

When Austin finally arrived back in Texas in September of 1835, he was welcomed at Velasco at the mouth of the Brazoria River. At a dinner celebrating his release from prison and his return to Texas, in a famous speech he told the assembled men that the federalist constitution of 1824 had been abolished and that a new central government had formed under Santa Anna. He urged the people of Texas to elect representatives who could pressure the new administration to give them a state government friendly to the "education, habits and situation of the people of Texas." This speech, which John Henry Brown has called "the essence of simplicity"—since Austin had just been imprisoned for doing exactly that—raised more suspicions that he was not only the consummate loyal subject of Mexico but also, in suggesting such a ridiculous course of action, sorely out of touch with the sentiments of the people in Texas.

Austin soon realized his folly. Eleven days later he declared that Texans must defend their rights by force of arms. Once again, however, he oscillated, urging men to band together, not to form an army but to appeal to the Mexican government to grant them statehood, and he accused the members of the "war party" of being "political jugglers and base political intriguers" and of trying to take control of "public affairs to promote their own aims of ambition and personal aggrandizement." [38] Trying to gauge the winds of war, Austin, a sophisticated and manipulative leader, had become unsteady at the helm.

On January 7, 1836, Austin finally declared in favor of Texas independence, unfortunately well after a declaration of autonomy had been written by George Childress, Robertson's nephew. A brilliant orator, Childress presented the colonists' grievances in a logical manner, thereby articulating their feelings and creating a burst of patriotism around the state. He also suffered from periodic depression. Not long after writing the statement, Childress returned to Galveston, where, in a bout of hopelessness, he eviscerated himself and slowly bled to death while holding a bedside conversation with his doctor.

The declaration of independence was signed by Texas representatives elected as delegates to the March 1, 1836, convention and voted on by the colonists in the different municipalities. Thus, in spite of clear evidence of their desires as well as his own treatment by Mexican authorities, Austin had to be dragged into the movement for self-government. Because he declared himself in favor of Texas independence at the last minute and only when the effort was already in full swing, Austin's leadership role was discredited.

After acting as commander of the Texas army at the siege of Bexar, Stephen Austin was dispatched to the United States to rustle up support for the ragtag Texas troops. When the war was suddenly over after the battle of San Jacinto, Austin returned to Texas, too late to be a hero, thereby conceding that role to Sam Houston, who led the Texas army to a decisive victory.

While Austin was absent from Texas, Robertson was deeply immersed in the swirl of events. Along with his nephew Childress, Robertson was elected a delegate to the convention of 1836 and signed the declaration of independence. After the fall of the Alamo, he joined the Texas army with Sam Houston and was stationed at Harrisburg to guard army equipment and the wounded during the battle of San Jacinto. In a letter to his mother in Tennessee on May 26, 1836, he wrote that he had ridden with a detachment of mounted men in pursuit of the fleeing Mexican troops commanded by General Cos, whom Santa Anna had ordered to retreat. He described the Mexicans as nearly frightened to death, shucking their arms and cannon as well as the plunder they had acquired during their advance through the settlers' abandoned homes. Robertson found mules with the packs still on their backs left by the roadside. When he and the others caught up with the fleeing troops, he concluded that they could have taken at least a thousand of the Mexicans if they had had orders to do so, but they had been directed not to molest them even though "our men were all anxious for the contest; flushed with victory, and full of resentment against the Mexicans." [39]

Sam Houston was elected the first president of the Republic of Texas in a resounding vote. Although Stephen F. Austin had lost his credibility with his fellow Texans because of the land speculations and his reluctance to support Texas independence, Houston took the statesman's approach and eulogized Austin, naming him the "father of Texas" in recognition of his efforts to bring settlers to Texas. Texas was Austin's only beloved child, but the territory had now reached its rebellious teens, and Austin was no longer to be a major player in its governing, nor would he live to see it burst into adulthood. Sadly, two months after Houston appointed Austin secretary of state, Austin died. [40]

Sterling Robertson joined the government of the new republic of Texas on September 5, 1836, when he was elected senator from the district of Milam. He served in the first and second congresses of the republic from October 1836 to May 1838 and was instrumental in laying the foundation of its laws. In the senate he was chairman of the committee on Indian affairs and the committee on roads, bridges, and ferries, which organized revenue for roads. He also served on the military committee, the finance and land claims committee, and the naval affairs committee. Because his passion was ensuring people's rights to their land, he sponsored the bill that created a general land office to handle all issues of land and water rights in Texas.

Robertson was fiercely stubborn and hotheaded to the end. Francis Lubbock, a governor of Texas, described Robertson's time in the senate: "He was quick, earnest and positive in speech and action, not particularly observant of parliamentary law and rules. I remember happening in the Senate in the midst of some discussion, when a senator quite vociferously called Senator Robertson to order. He paid no attention to the call. The senator continued to interrupt his speech by cries of 'Order! Order!' He [Robertson] stopped his speech but continued to address the president of the Senate, saying: 'Mr. President, I am called to order. I do not know that I am out of order, but this I do know, I will not come to order at the command of the gentleman. But, Mr. President, if you will just knock that little hammer down on me, I will squat like a partridge.'"[41] Sterling Robertson's portrait sits in the senate chamber in the capitol building in Austin.

In 1838 Robertson retired to Robertson County near Nashville on the Brazos and the home of his cousin Randle Robertson. There he built his first home, a double log cabin, two stories high, made of squared cedar logs, and spent the rest of his days raising thoroughbred racehorses. He had brought high-quality Arabians to Texas for some time. One of his horses was Black Douglas, whose pedigree reached back to the Godolphin Arabian, a stallion owned by the king of England. Robertson recorded his breeding efforts in a horse book, and he kept papers on all of his horses.[42] An ardent Scot, he named them after characters in Sir Walter Scott's novels, the same ones my grandmother read to my father in the Robertson home in Salado many years later. I grew up with stories of Black Douglas's speed and powerful gait, and when I was ten, my father brought back from that home a descendant of Black Douglas, named Chief Cloud. As a teenager, I rode Chief Cloud's colt Friday during the endless hot summer days in Texas. Friday was my companion and most immediate warm-blooded link with my great-great-great-grandfather Sterling Robertson.

At his place near Nashville, Texas, Sterling Robertson died from pneumonia on March 4, 1842, after swimming the swollen Brazos River to get an important letter. He was fifty-seven. His son wrote this florid epitaph:

No man ever led a more eventful and trying life. Ever on the border, he was subjugated to all those hardships and trials attendant on a life-time contact with savage Indians. He was naturally daring, bold, progressive—a love of country was with him a prominent trait handed down through generations. He was humane to a fault, a man of great moral courage, fidelity, chivalry and an indomitable will power and perseverance. He was possessed of a good liberal education and a speaker of much eloquence. In conversation he was interesting and entertaining. His fondness for music and art was well known, he played well on the violin and some hunting scenes in oils attested a talent in art. He was an active participant in every struggle of his countrymen from the campaigns of 1812 to the time of his death in 1842. He made as great an effort for the colonization of Texas and her greatness and glory as any man who came to Texas from the days of La Salle to the day of his death.[43]

The Robertson–Austin controversy is merely one example of the politics that developed at the time of Texas' colonization, one characterized by conspiracy, slippery truths, manipulative devices, and greed. Situated on the outskirts of the Mexican republic, Texas was so far from the centers of power and government that, in the minds of the colonists, Mexican law had little authority. They realized that the ayuntamientos and presidios were only weakly able to enforce Mexican control in this vast frontier. They also saw that the empresarios, the wheelers and dealers of Texas land, accomplished almost everything through personal favors and bribes to Mexican officials. They viewed such dubious practices as necessary.

Elites such as Sterling Robertson and Stephen Austin learned to work in this environment of intrigue; otherwise, they would not have prevailed. It was a high-stakes game, one that has been repeated many times throughout Texas history with other resources: cotton, cattle, and oil in the next hundred years, and the Texas Rangers baseball team, Dell Computers, and Enron later on. From the beginning, it was a game that required entrepreneurs with colossal egos, friends who were less than totally ethical, bribable administrators, and determined Machiavellian leaders. Not a whole lot has changed since then.

CHAPTER 6

The Alabama Settlement

T he preceding chapter outlines the battle of the empresarios as they scrambled for land and power. Nevertheless, that story gives us pitifully little to go on if we want to understand how Texas culture was cut from the bedrock of people's daily lives. We still want to know about the settlers who scratched a living from the Texas soil, enduring blazing heat and numbing cold, terrible deprivations, and endless hard work. Most histories of Texas emphasize the individual men who came to Texas to seek adventure and fortune, as well as perhaps to escape an unfortunate transgression committed in their past, political wheelers and dealers like Sterling Robertson, Stephen Austin, and Sam Houston. In this chapter I want to convey a sense of the families who came to Texas to create a new home, the hardworking, down-to-earth yeoman farmers more interested in family ties than sudden fortune. The men and women of the Alabama Settlement were such folk.

The Alabama Settlement came to Austin's colony in 1830 and put down roots near where the Brazos and Navidad rivers meet and flow into Matagorda Bay at the Gulf of Mexico. Because this large group of kith and kin came from northern Alabama and settled together in one area, historian John Henry Brown early on dubbed them the Alabama Settlement of Austin's colony.[1] These law-abiding Christians were not among those who, in coming to Texas, were fleeing the law or interested in making a fortune. Rather, they came to make a new home on land they could get for free. Closely related through kinship and marriage, they were a tightly knit group led by senior kinsmen experienced in organizing life on the frontier. Theirs was no spur-of-the-moment migration; it was deliberately planned over several years.[2] The size of the group alone—around three hundred people—would have made such a move unusual, but it did not seem out of the ordinary to them. The relocation to Texas was not their first migration.

The men and women of the Alabama Settlement were stout, devout Methodists, fiercely loyal to and protective of their family. According to my father, as good Methodists they brought to Texas their eighteenth-century notions of reason, but as clannish Scots they also embraced that century's romanticism. When they shouted "Damn the king!" they meant George III.[3]

Most of the older adults of the Alabama Settlement were born in Virginia in the late eighteenth century to parents who came there from the Highlands of Scotland. These Highland Scots had been subjected to "the Clearances" during the earlier part of the eighteenth century, when English landlords forced the Scottish crofters off land they had lived on for generations. During the eighteenth century, the clearances ignited a massive migration first to Ireland and then to America, and the Sutherland clan was part of this exodus. They landed in Virginia and settled west of the tidewater area, where the English elites had received the earlier land grants. One member of the clan was a young man named John Sutherland, who was married to Agnes Shelton. He, his father, and a brother all fought in the Revolutionary War, at the same time providing beef to the Revolutionary Army. When the Cumberland Gap opened up the Tennessee Valley for settlement some time in 1800, the next generation—the American-born Sutherlands—took their families to Knoxville, Tennessee. There they cleared land for farms, built communities, and raised their children. In Knoxville, three of John Sutherland's offspring married three children of John Menefee and Frances Rhodes. When these three families of sibling marriages relocated to Alabama, John Sutherland joined them there in 1822.[4]

During the early 1800s Tennessee was flush with settlers who had ideas about the freedom of the frontier. Riding this tide of grassroots democracy and individualism, Andrew Jackson led a populist democracy movement and, to the horror of the Eastern establishment, moved into the White House. At the same time that the "west" moved into government in the east, goods from the industrial revolution moved in the opposite direction, sweeping through the western United States, particularly Tennessee. New opportunities for merchants who could ferry such desirable commodities to remote areas were created by this expansion. The Sutherlands and Menefees, although they had large stakes in their communities in Alabama, were swept up in this period of economic change and democracy. They also hoped to live together as one large clan without the interference of the state or local elites. Gathering their families together, they moved en masse to the wilds of Texas.

These early settlers did not expect Texas to be their last destination. Because they had never felt enough allegiance to any particular place to stay for very long, they had for generations chosen to migrate west to less settled areas. This time, however, they had within a few years become Texans and fierce defenders of Texas independence. The development of a strong

Texas identity was not unique to the families of the Alabama Settlement. Many early Anglo Texans had similar experiences and ended up with the same powerful feelings. But the story of this particular family's experience with identity formation was passed down through stories told and retold to the present generation. It illustrates how and why the Texas identity came to be so intense.

FAMILY TIES

In 1830 the families of the Alabama Settlement were led by men who were married to or brothers of a group of sisters. George Sutherland, James Dever, and Stephen Heard had all married Menefee sisters. Agnes and Lucy, two of George Sutherland's sisters, were married to two of the Menefee brothers, William and Thomas respectively. In addition, Jesse White was married to George Sutherland's sister Mary. This tight group of siblings, brothers-in-law, and sisters-in-law lived side by side and reproduced prodigiously, raising their forty children as if they too were siblings—not so strange when twenty of those youngsters were double first cousins and therefore genetically the equivalent of siblings.

In addition to being inextricably intertwined through marriage, this huge family replicated to some degree the clan structure of eighteenth-century Scotland. They reserved their strongest feelings and loyalties for one another and provided each other with aid, food, and military support at a moment's notice. Their world was divided into "family" and "others," with most of their lives spent in the company of the former. As one large clannish group, they had converted to Methodism at the beginning of the nineteenth century. And as one family they migrated together to Texas in 1830.

George Sutherland, Jesse White, and William Menefee were the leaders and coordinators of the migration. In 1830 Sutherland, born in Virginia in 1788, was forty-two. He was a large energetic man, six feet four inches tall, weighing almost three hundred pounds. Having already served in both the Tennessee and Alabama legislatures in his former home states, he was a natural clan leader because of his organizational abilities and sharp intelligence. At thirty-four, William Menefee was much younger than George, but he was smart, tough, and disciplined. Married to George's sister Agnes, he was the brother that the Menefee sisters respected most. Jesse White was forty-seven, the eldest of the three men, and married to George Sutherland's sister Mary. He was also an experienced leader though somewhat less charismatic than George and William.

Menefee/Sutherland families who migrated to Texas

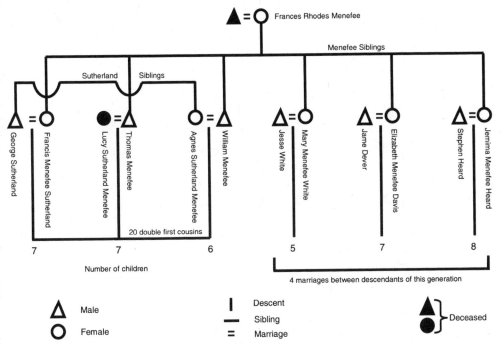

Genealogy of the Menefee/Sutherland marriages.

All three of these men knew from experience what migration entailed. Not only had they spent their lives breaking ground along the American frontier, they were also skilled militiamen who had fought against Britain in the War of 1812 and against Indians numerous times. They knew how to plan such a massive move and how to form a company of men into a fighting unit should they be attacked. Furthermore, they enjoyed the full confidence of their kin and could count on unquestioned cooperation and loyalty in conquering fear of the unknown and accepting tragedy. Physically and emotionally tough, they held family allegiance to be a paramount value.

THE MIGRATION TO TEXAS

In the fall of 1829 this large group of relatives selected George Sutherland, Anthony Winston, and Jesse White to make a contract for land in Texas with Stephen Austin, whom they had known in Tennessee. The men set out for Texas on horseback, using a compass to plot their journey. Each carried a blanket behind his saddle, a flint, spunk and steel or knife in his saddlebag, and a flintlock gun that was kept close to hand. They swam rivers on their horses, killed game for food as they moved westward, and slept on their blankets under the open skies.

Stephen Austin had just secured his third colony contract with the Mexican government, opening up the land around the Lavaca, Navidad, and Mustang rivers with the Lavaca as the western boundary. When the three men arrived, George Sutherland sat down with Austin and signed a contract for the families of John Sutherland, William Menefee, William Heard, Joseph Rector, William Pride, Jessie White, Benjamin White, Samuel Rogers, and Robert Crozier. The contract with Austin also granted Austin a piece of land at the junction of the Lavaca and the Navidad on the eastern side. Sutherland paid Austin in advance $15 per league for the surveying, $15 for Commissioner Samuel Williams's fee, $10 for Austin's fee, $5 for the office fee, and $2 for the stamp paper. Later he would have to pay the government $30 and a balance of $40 to Austin for his fee when the land was surveyed, the balance on the surveying fees, and another $5 office fee. Should any of the would-be settlers fail to emigrate, they would forfeit the fees, and the land would then be distributed to other families.[5] *Stephen F. Austin's Register of Families* shows that land certificates were issued on January 24, 1830, to George Sutherland, his brother John Sutherland (who claimed his land certificate later), brothers William and Thomas Menefee, William H. Heard, Joseph Rector, brothers Jesse and Benjamin White, Samuel Rogers, and others from Alabama (W. Pride, R. Crosier, W. Haskins, P. Dudley, J. Smith, M. Smith, R. Royall, T. Winter, J. Caldwell, and W. Cockrill) who were only distantly connected to the family group.[6] Austin wrote the following in the land register: "These gentlemen have designated their land on Arroyo Karankahuas and Arroyo Navidad. George Sutherland is promised the land at the junction of the Mustang Creek and Navidad River." Anthony Winston decided not to immigrate and returned to Alabama to stay, writing Stephen F. Austin that he could not dispense with his business in Alabama.

Sutherland and White selected their land and made claims for themselves and all of their relatives. Once this was done, the committee went back to Alabama to tell the others what they had arranged, excitedly describing how they would be able to live where laws were unnecessary. Since they would be surrounded only by family, they expected to have the freedom to practice their Methodism and their business without the interference of neighbors.

Hoping to be in Texas in time to plant crops in the spring of 1831, the group decided to move quickly. Preparations for the migration thus began in the spring of 1830. The first task was to sell their property and businesses and complete all of their personal and business affairs. With that accomplished, by summer it was time to gather supplies for the trip and arrange for transportation. It was decided that some of them would travel overland while others would go down the Mississippi to the Gulf and then enter the Navidad River through Matagorda Bay. Since there were few ferries and no bridges, those who were planning to go by land would need to build wagons and carts and be prepared to ford rivers. They would float their wagons on logs or small boats and then swim the livestock and horses.[7]

The confidence they felt was based on their long association with one another, a kinship that reached back to when their families had landed in Virginia. This self-assurance was cemented through their childhood experiences of migrating through the Cumberland Gap with their families. They knew how to organize a migration and how to prepare for the first years in a new land by sending a first wave to break ground and put in the first crops. This group would then be followed by a second. The full relocation was expected to take place over a period of three years.

The first wave, led by George Sutherland, departed from Decatur on October 3, 1830, and included the following people:

- William Menefee (34); his wife, Agnes (36), who was a sister of George Sutherland; their four sons and two daughters, ranging in age from twelve years to two months
- Thomas Menefee (51), the widower of Lucy (another of George Sutherland's sisters; she had died in 1829); their seven children, ranging in age from seventeen years to thirteen months
- Frances Rhodes Menefee, the seventy-year-old mother, mother-in-law, or grandmother to almost everyone in the group
- George Sutherland (42); his wife, Frances Menefee (41), sister to Thomas and William Menefee; their two sons, also called William and Thomas (a third son remained in Alabama and died there in 1832); three daughters, ranging in age from twelve years to eight months
- Jemima Menefee Heard (48), another Menefee sister; Jemima's son W. J. E. Heard (29) and his pregnant wife, America (22), whose mother was George Sutherland's sister Mary White; their two-year-old child; Jemima's pregnant daughter Martha (18); Martha's husband, Thomas J. Read (21) (their child was the first offspring of this migration to be born in Texas)

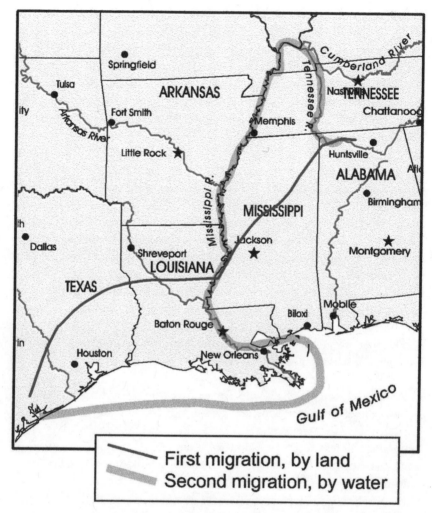

Map of the first and second migrations of the Alabama Settlement

- Jemima's son John Heard (27); his wife, Maria Dever (24); their two children (ages 3 and 1); four other Heard children (ages 8 to 2)[8]

They went overland by oxcart and wagon and on horseback, heading south by southwest through the Choctaw nation to Natchez, on the banks of the Mississippi River at the eastern border of Louisiana. Turning west, they traveled to the Sabine River at the westernmost border of Louisiana and the United States. Before making the arduous river crossing, they camped among the thick piney woods there and held a camp meeting, at which they prayed for safe passage. When they went across into Mexican Texas, they were entering a strange new country with unknown dangers.

The next day they crossed the Sabine at Gaines Ferry on the Old San Antonio Road and slowly filed down the route to Nacogdoches. Next they forded the Trinity River at Robbins's Ferry (in what is now northeastern Madison County). River crossings were arduous affairs that took several days. For each trip, the ferry had to be loaded with wagons and oxen, horses and household goods, and women and children and then unloaded on the other side.

On December 9, 1830, this first wave arrived in San Felipe, the capital of Austin's colony, and wrote claims to their land. Each family head received a "league and a labor" of land (4,605 acres).[9] After recording their land claims and paying the survey fees, they crossed the Colorado River at Beason's Ferry (just below Columbus today). Following the Atascosito Road, they forded the Navidad River at Hardy's Ferry, their last ferry crossing. The wagons and carts then continued overland to Major Kerr's place on the Lavaca and followed F. G. Keller's wagon tracks to Keller's Creek. Both Kerr and Keller had been among the earliest settlers in the area. Around nightfall the group reached its destination farther south on the Navidad River. There they camped among the elms on the west bank just below the mouth of Mustang Creek.[10] The journey had taken a little more than two months.

The second wave left Alabama in December. Because they had bales of cotton to sell in New Orleans, they took two flatboats down the Tennessee, Ohio, and Mississippi rivers to New Orleans, rather than make the overland journey. The only vessels that could transport so many people and goods on the thousand-mile trip to New Orleans were flatboats. These were wide, boxlike structures with a flat bottom made of rough oak planks caulked with pitch. Steered by a board at the back end, flatboats were 20 by 100 feet in length and could carry wagons, teams, and up to four hundred bales of cotton. Although not particularly livable, they allowed the settlers to bring a great many supplies. The second group of migrants took a long, roundabout, and dangerous course marked by river hazards. One area of eddies was known as "the Suck," and farther downstream was the dreaded "Mussel Shoals." In 1830 the Tennessee River could take steamboats upriver as far as Tuscumbia, but several shoals prevented them from going any farther.[11]

This second wave included the following people:

- George Sutherland's sister Mary (46) and her husband, Gen. Jesse White (47); their five children, ranging in age from twenty-one to eight;

two sons-in-law, one of whom was Samuel Rogers (20)

- Jesse White's younger brother Ben White (37); Ben's wife, Mary; their children; as well as Jesse and Ben White's sister Lydia Glasgow
- Morgan Rector (50, a Menefee cousin); his wife, Amelia (51); their eight children
- Joseph Rector (28), and his wife and cousin, Harriett Heard Rector (23)
- Thomas H. P. Heard (25), and his wife and cousin, Nancy Heard Kellett (21); their three-day-old child
- Mrs. Elizabeth Dever (53; another Menefee sister); her five children, ranging in age from twenty to twelve
- John Davis (33); his wife, Louisiana (33; an adult daughter of Elizabeth Dever); their two children; John's siblings Samuel and Mary Davis
- Richard Carter (41); a cousin and his wife and eight children (ranging in age from twenty to infant)
- Thomas Winston (26), a relative of the Menefees and brother of Anthony Winston, who had decided not to migrate; Thomas's wife; their four children[12]

In New Orleans they chartered a steamer named the *Emblem*. Given the size of the group, the *Emblem* could not carry everyone, so some stayed there to await the steamer's return. The first voyage of the *Emblem* arrived at Cox's Point at Matagorda Bay on February 12, 1831. There they were met by members of the first wave, who had built a small flatboat to transport the arriving families and their goods up the Navidad.[13] While members of the first and second groups of immigrants planted corn and built houses, the group that had waited in New Orleans came on the second voyage of the *Emblem*. In all, there were about two hundred Alabamans who made this trek, of which ninety-three were close relatives, and the rest were in-laws and more distant cousins. These new immigrants included twenty-seven slaves, who were owned by the elderly Frances Menefee and the older men, Joseph Rector, Thomas Winston, George Sutherland, and Jesse White.

Samuel Rogers, the son-in-law of Jesse White, was a young man of twenty at the time of the journey. A good-looking, six-foot-tall slender man with masculine features, long arms and legs, and large muscular hands, he was a prototype for the Texans of the movies we have all seen. Friendly, lovable, well spoken, and cordial, Samuel was one of thirteen children born in Virginia of a wealthy family.[14] His father had died en route to Alabama, and his French mother moved into an enormous plantation in Alabama purchased by his father just before his death. They owned one hundred slaves. His mother was soon defrauded of her wealth by a dishonest man who administered the estate, and the poverty-stricken children had to make their own way in the world.

In 1828, when Sam Rogers was eighteen, his mother sent him to see a dying neighbor, George's brother Thomas Sutherland. On that day he saw George's fourteen-year-old niece, Mary White, and was "struck by the thunderbolt." They married, but so young and innocent were they that, when they traveled from Decatur to Tuscumbia to visit the Sutherland relatives, their hosts invariably thought they were brother and sister and gave them two beds in a room. In the morning, Mary would make up both beds so that no one would know the difference, and they moved on in the morning without telling them. Two years later Sam and Mary migrated to Texas with the Alabama settlement. Later in life he became one of the best storytellers in the state, even though he ended up stone deaf and, as he described it, "much afflicted." Because he lived longer than most of his contemporaries, his memoirs provide us with one of the best descriptions of the early days of the Alabama Settlement:

> *We started from Decatur on the Tennessee River on the night of Dec 2, at 11 o'clock. The entire inhabitants of the town stayed up to bid us good-bye.*
>
> *The sadness of departing from mother, brothers and sisters I will say nothing about, as parting is one of the conditions of our existence here. I never saw but two of my brothers, Henry and Franklin, again.*
>
> *General White had two flat bottomed cotton boats, one was loaded with cotton, the other was the residence of the family. In passing the Mussol [sic] Shoals the cotton boat was partly wrecked, but we had it repaired so that we reached New Orleans with it. We reached New Orleans in safety but had to wait there over a week to get a vessel to transport us to Texas. General White obtained "The Emblem" owned by Captain Baker.*
>
> *The day after we passed through the mouth of the Mississippi a storm struck us and everybody gave up hope as lost, even the captain and the mate. The captain put all the passengers down the hole of the vessel and nailed us up. It was the gloomiest night and day that ever mortals passed. There were between 180 and 200 passengers aboard, of that number Judge Frank White, Samuel Rogers, Mrs. Betty McFarland and two Negroes are all that are now living. We landed at Cox's Point on Feb. 12.*
>
> *We constructed a boat at Cox's point and brought the baggage up the Navidad to General White's league of land. I there built me a cabin for a home.*[15]

The Alabama settlers had arrived in the wilds of Texas without much knowledge of what to expect there. They did not know what living in the Mexican nation would entail or how it would change their lives. They were not privy to the history of Spanish colonization and the laws and customs that had been established there. They were not particularly aware of the instability of the new Mexican government or the sets of relationships that one needed to operate effectively in Mexico. They expected to be left alone to take care of themselves and fashion their own ways of living.

The settlers did come with a great deal of previous cultural knowledge of their own, however. They knew how to make a living as farmers, and, although they brought slaves with them, they were yeoman farmers, not plantation owners. They carried their mixture of Scottish clan structure and Virginia culture to Texas, modified by their experiences in Tennessee with the Andrew Jackson democracy movement of the frontier. They had technical skills in fighting both the British and the Indians, building houses, bringing in goods from afar, and starting new fields for planting. In Tennessee they had also undergone important spiritual experiences when they became part of the Methodist revival movement. Their religious conversion was more than a life-changing personal moment; it provided the mortar for the solid family ties that were the bedrock of their unique family culture.

CHAPTER 7

The Prayer on the Sabine

Before they came to Texas, the men and women of the Alabama Settlement were swept up in a Methodist revival movement known as "the Methodist Excitement" or "the Second Great Awakening," which arrived in Tennessee at the beginning of the 1800s. The Methodist Excitement was inspired by Bishop Francis Asbury, who was sent to America in 1771, just before the American Revolution, by Englishman John Wesley, the founder of Methodism. Asbury stayed through the American Revolution and eventually established a Methodist church on American soil. Known as the "horseback apostle of Methodism" because of his willingness to ride into Tennessee in search of new converts, he ended up in the Tennessee Valley early in the nineteenth century.

The core of the Methodist revival movement was a massive gathering of people in spiritually inspired camp meetings.[1] People from all over the Tennessee area gathered together their wagons at a revival site in the woods, which were cleared for the occasion. They spent the first day setting up tents. Everyone brought enough provisions to spend several days living on the grounds, visiting kinfolk, and expressing their religious feelings.[2] The camp meetings opened and closed each day with family prayers in the individual tents, followed by a general prayer meeting at eight and then preaching at ten, two, and six o'clock, finishing at midnight.[3] These were emotional "love fests" in which sinners would raise their hands to receive the grace of God and then "suddenly fall as if struck by a thunderbolt into an ecstasy of bliss."[4] There is little doubt that people at the prayer meetings were experiencing something close to a religious trance. The Sutherland and Menefee men and women were drawn to this movement and delivered into spiritual ecstasy by the inspired preaching of Francis Asbury. The women in particular voiced their convictions in loud shouts of joy, bursting into songs such as "How Great Thou Art."

John Menefee, the head of a large and influential east Tennessee family, most of whom were Methodist, became a trustee of the church that Bishop Asbury set up in the home of John Heyne. When the church moved to Knoxville in 1816, it was built on a lot given by Hugh Lawton White, a relative of John Menefee and John Sutherland, who were both church trustees.[5] In the 1820s Heyne and John Sutherland, along with George Sutherland and the Menefee brothers, Thomas and William, moved to Tuscumbia, Alabama, a frontier town in the southern part of the Tennessee Valley. Around the new communities of Tuscumbia and Decatur they farmed, set up banks, and brought their newfound religion. The Menefees built the first Methodist church in the area.[6]

When the Menefee, White, and Sutherland families decided to migrate to Texas, they knew that Mexican law prohibited the open practice of their religion. As the migration progressed and they reached the border with Texas, John Burruss, a traveling Methodist preacher, joined their camp on the Sabine. Burruss was well known along the frontier for "inspired praying." Quietly the relatives all gathered in George Sutherland's tent for their last camp meeting as an openly Methodist congregation. Aware that they were about to enter a foreign land where they would be required to swear allegiance to the Catholic Church, Burruss began by speaking of Jacob's flight from his brother and his vision at Bethel. He then invoked the image of Abraham journeying to a strange land, and he asked God to direct these "pilgrims" to their new homes. Deeply moved, the women and men in Sutherland's tent broke into exclamations of religious passion. Pausing to take a deep breath, Burruss then invoked God's grace so that these Christians might eventually establish their own churches. For years afterward, Burruss's prayer was one of their most vivid recollections, marking as it did the journey from their former lives into their new ones. Stories about the prayer, about crossing the Sabine River from their native country into a foreign one, and about going from one religion to another became fixed in the mythology of their migration.[7] The camp meeting on the Sabine was the last time they all prayed together as one family. When they arrived and claimed their tracts of land from Stephen Austin, they spread out over a wide area.

After four years in Texas, W. J. E. Heard, along with his mother, Jemima Menefee Heard, and grandmother Frances Menefee, moved to Egypt, a town on the Colorado River just above Wharton, so named for its "fruitfulness." Other relatives—Eli Mercer and his family, A. H. Sutherland (son of John Sutherland) and his family, T. H. P. Heard and his family, and T. J. Reed and his family—soon followed. Even before the Texas Revolution, at a time when the Mexican government strictly forbade Protestant religions, the Heards had a secret Methodist mission in their home.[8] The Mercers, who had also moved to Egypt, were Baptists, but since five of the six Mercer children were married to Menefees and Heards, they too attended the Methodist camp meetings and put up the Methodist "saddlebag preachers" in their homes.

One of the earliest saddlebag preachers to come to Texas was Martin Ruter, who arrived in 1828. In 1833 a camp meeting was held in Texana with people from all over the Navidad River area, and by 1834 a number of traveling Methodist preachers were turning up, including Homer S. Thrall, who wrote *History of Methodism in Texas* in 1872, and John Wesley Kenney, a relative of the founder of Methodism.[9]

Traveling preachers had a tough time getting from one camp meeting to another. Traveling alone, often in bad weather, assailed by Indians and illness, they had a very short life span in Texas in those days. Because of the possibility of Indian attack, people generally traveled in groups of five or six armed men when going west toward San Antonio, but the traveling preachers did not have this protection. Some of them even refused to carry arms. Martin Ruter, for example, insisted on riding no matter what the weather and also declared that he would carry no weapons "made with hands."[10] They traveled through forests and immense prairies, wending their way through flocks of geese and turkeys, passing deer, wolves, and wild horses without seeing another person or a place to take shelter. The often severe and long-lasting storms on the prairies took a toll on their physical stamina. Undeterred by such conditions, Martin Ruter described Texas as a new country of rich soil and mild climate, a land that presented great opportunities to industrious immigrants. He noted that since the country was recently ravaged by the Mexican army, people were suffering from the burning of their fields and houses. The territory also attracted a number of imposters who came, professing to be ministers, so the settlers were cautious of preachers of the gospel. Ruter learned that the colonists were also good at figuring out who was a phony and who was a person of good standing in the community.[11]

Homer S. Thrall wrote a biography of another preacher, J. W. DeVilbiss, who had a circuit at Egypt. There he described the Heard, Menefee, Hodges, Sutherland, Reed, and Mercer families as "well-to-do in worldly matters" and noted that Egypt was well named because of the abundance of corn raised, enough to supply the new settlements farther west on the Navidad. Thrall's circuit included sixteen "appointments" in Colorado, Lavaca, Jackson, Wharton, and Matagorda counties, areas populated by the Alabama Settlement. The circuit meant four hundred miles of travel and took four weeks to complete.

After the Texas Revolution, an open mission was established at the home of Jemima Heard. At its first quarterly conference meeting, according to Thrall, there was "a gracious outpouring of the Spirit." Among the converts were two daughters of Colonel Hodges. His eldest daughter, with the unfortunate nickname of "Puss," married George Sutherland's son T. S. Sutherland. The youngest, who followed the family propensity for being pegged to an animal, was called "Duck." Another strict member of the church was William Kerr, who lived eight miles below Egypt and owned the mill where lumber was sawed and corn was ground. Martin Ruter stayed with William Menefee and organized classes for the women—Martha Higginbothan; Martha's sister, who was married to William Kerr; and Tilithia Ann, daughter of Agnes Sutherland and William Menefee and wife of J. W. DeVilbiss.[12]

After the revolution, when the Texas Methodists were finally free to build a place of worship, the first Methodist church was organized at Texana. A lot in town was deeded to the building by Francis F. Wells. The Menefee, Gayle, and Rogers families were early trustees. The church was large for the time, about forty by sixty feet, and faced west, with the pulpit on the east side and pews down the center. To the right of the pulpit was the amen corner, two pews running the length of the building and reserved for the older men. In the left corner was the organ. The church was lit by a chandelier with four lights and four bracket lamps on each wall with bright reflectors. It was considered the very latest in illumination.

Following an unwritten rule, men sat on the north side of the church, couples (whether married or still single) in the center, and women on the south wall. Only one man defied this rule and always sat in the women's section with his wife. No one said anything about it, though it was the subject of much tsk-tsking. No woman dared join her husband on the men's side. Mrs. McIver, a lonely widow, always arrived last, taking a place in the very back pew. She was then the first to leave, thus avoiding contact with the congregation. She had become a bit odd, according to the pastor of the Texana church, after the slaying of her husband, Sheriff McIver, in a famous unsolved murder case. With these sitting customs in place, it was only necessary to glance at the congregation to know anyone's religious standing. Those in good standing sat in the front, sinners in the rear.[13]

When the town of Texana died, the church building was moved to Edna, and another house of worship, called the Rogers Chapel, was built in Ganado for the Sutherland and Rogers families. A twenty-by-thirty-foot log cabin built between the Sutherland and Mercer homes, the Rogers Chapel doubled as the Sutherland schoolhouse. Samuel Rogers preached for the Methodists, and the Baptist Mercers had their own preachers there as well.

Even after the churches were built, people continued to hold camp meetings because these were powerful events where the spirit of the Lord entered people's bodies and minds. The preacher was Sterling Fisher, whose mother, Mary Susan Simons, was born in Texana and whose father, O. E. Fisher, was also a preacher. Fourteen slaves attended the meetings, too. One of the Menefee slaves, "Aunt Ora," described a camp meeting held in July 1849, when she was ten years old. It looked like a "white village on the river," she said. "They had a large arbor covered with brush in which they held their services. The woods would fairly ring, the white folks on the inside, and the colored ones on the outside. We sang 'Old Time Religion.'"[14] According to John Sutherland Menefee's diary, eighteen conversions took place that year. He records at least one and sometimes two camp meetings near Texana every year after that. Later, across the Navidad on William Menefee's place, the Methodist families formed a permanent arbor covered with boards and seats made of split logs, with pegs for legs stuck in them. For many years they held services in this arbor led by traveling Methodist preachers and elders such as Sam Rogers.

George Simons described a camp meeting that took place as late as 1893 or 1894.[15] It was held in a "brush arbor" with seats made of one-by-twelve-inch planks placed on logs cut for that purpose. The area was lit by lanterns, and the ground was covered with six inches of hay so that babies and small children could sleep while the adults prayed. Six groups camped near the arbor—the Gayles, the Menefees, Mrs. Francis Flournoy, Judge Francis Menefee White, George and M. T. Simons, and the W. P. Laughter family.

The meeting began on a Wednesday and continued for ten days. By Saturday night the woods were full of people, and everyone who arrived was taken into one of the five camps and fed. All were welcome. The Simons camp had three forty-foot tables on Sunday to feed the crowd. The entire meeting was devoted to spirituality, with men and women giving their hearts to God; when they did, they burst out with shouts of "Victory!" Then the congregation would sing "I'm Bound for the Promised Land" or "I'm a Soldier of the Cross" with great enthusiasm.

By 1840 Martin Ruter, who had been in Texas for twelve years, convinced the Texas congress to donate land to finance buildings and teachers for a Methodist college. The first president of Rutersville College was Chauncey Richardson, with Homer Thrall and both their wives as teachers. The Heard, Sutherland, and Menefee families sent their children there for many years.[16]

Religious expression in the Alabama Settlement began in clandestine camp meetings in Mexican Texas and moved to open gatherings during the republic years, finally culminating in a Methodist church in Texana, the building of the Rogers Chapel in Ganado, and a Methodist college. Passionately religious, these families prayed, read the Bible to their children, and sang Methodist hymns with gusto. These emotional religious experiences are still shared today as an integral part of the family culture.

The family reunions I went to as a child were modeled after the Methodist camp meetings. After gathering on Friday afternoon to become reacquainted with close and distant relatives, we all held hands and prayed before eating together from a huge table covered with dishes each family had brought. The next day the men began the long, slow process of barbecuing massive quantities of meat while telling humorous stories to each other. The women gathered in groups to catch up on family news—marriages, births, and deaths—while the children ran in and around these adult gatherings. Then, on Sunday morning, my great-aunts read passages from the Bible and in their creaky voices led the singing of "Rock of Ages" and "Amazing Grace." To this day, although I myself am not a believer, I cannot hear Methodist hymns such as "How Great Thou Art" without becoming tearful.

❧

CHAPTER 8

Making a Living

The first years in Texas were bound to be difficult for the Alabama Settlement, consumed as they were with the basic necessities—building houses and planting their first crops. The summer before the settlers arrived, the prairie between the Navidad and Karankawa rivers had burned, driving thousands of animals to relocate in the Lavaca and Navidad river bottoms. Even without the burn, the Lavaca River area of Texas had been known as a grazing ground for buffalo and wild longhorn cattle. Longhorns were so abundant that the area was ripe to become ranching country later on. The settlers had brought ample provisions and clothing from New Orleans, but they also learned to live on the wild deer and longhorns they hunted. Game was plentiful. Until their crops grew, the settlers depended on the hundreds of deer that wandered the prairies between the rivers. During the first year in their new homeland, they were able to plant only a few acres of river bottom land in corn, using an axe to clear the ground and a hoe to cultivate the soil.[1] Even with this backbreaking labor, Francis Menefee White declared that he was able to grow enough corn for a year's supply of bread.

Illness posed a more serious problem. During the first summer everyone was sick with the "rounds" (diarrhea) and "fevers" (malaria and possibly dengue fever and typhoid), and ten to twelve people in the party died. Benjamin White's daughter Lydia died within a few days of arriving. Martha Dever and Mary Davis (Elizabeth Dever's daughter and granddaughter respectively) died of "fevers," and Joseph Rector (Jemima Heard's son-in-law) was killed by lightning.

The rest of the time was spent building houses and preparing and fencing fields. The houses followed the basic style common in the American frontier. A small family built a one-room cabin, but a larger family built two rooms, one for the parents and one for the children, with a "dog run" between them to catch the breezes. A separate cookhouse was built in the yard behind the house, and beyond the kitchen was an outhouse.

The weather in Texas was harsh. After a cloudburst, the rivers have a terrifying propensity to rise rapidly and flood. Even as a young girl, whenever

I went out for a walk in the country, my parents would remind me, "Watch out for flash floods," just as today one might tell a child, "Look before you cross the street." The Lavaca and Navidad rivers are entirely fed by rains and therefore have some of the most destructive flooding in the state, roaring through a mile-wide floodplain, uprooting trees and cutting down banks.[2] Some of the biggest rains in Texas history fell during 1832 and 1833. Sometimes it rained for whole months, and once it poured for forty-four hours straight.[3] During these deluges the rivers were impassable, and houses were sometimes three to four feet deep in water, cut off from others in the middle of a huge swollen floodplain. Even without the flooding, this part of Texas— a mosquito-infested, searingly hot lowland—did not foster a particularly healthy climate. Surprisingly, after the first year in Texas, when everyone became sick with the rounds and the fevers, and the cholera epidemic of 1833, which spread as a result of so much flooding, the settlers enjoyed reasonably good health. They had been "seasoned," as they put it, to the Texas climate.

The newly tilled land was rich, and crops thrived, but if anyone ran short of corn, the settlers took the road from the Sutherland land to League's Ferry on the Colorado River, where their relative Eli Mercer had settled. He gave them enough corn to make it through the next growing season. For a cash crop, the members of the Alabama Settlement planted cotton, which they knew well from cultivating it back in Alabama. Several cotton gins sprang up. Millican's gin was the first to be built in the area, but several others soon followed. Once ginned and baled, the cotton was floated on rafts down the Navidad to the Mills brothers' warehouse in Brazoria. The river was navigable from Matagorda Bay to George Sutherland's land at the meeting of the Navidad River and Mustang Creek. It was also relatively easy to bring goods upriver to Sutherland's place and then transport them by oxcart down the road to other relatives and members of the colony.

All in all, the settlers viewed this early period—before the political turmoil of the Texas Revolution but after the crops were planted and the houses built—as an auspicious time. John Sutherland Menefee, George Sutherland's nephew, later described it in quite romantic and nostalgic terms: "From this time, 1832, till the latter part of 1835, we lived in peace and quiet, no taxes or duties to pay, no law but a law unto ourselves, all friendly, sociably [sic], sober, honest, and moral, good crops and prosperous times; no courts, no suing, fighting or quarreling, no sheriff, no constable, no justice of the peace, no serving on juries or working on roads; no lawyers fees or costs to pay, and very little doctors bills; no branding yearling, no killing hogs in the wrong mark, no riding another's horse without permission; no worms to eat the cotton, plenty of corn, bacon and beef. Those were happy days, the like of which we never expect to see again in this world, unless the millennium should happen to come."[4] Those idyllic cultural circumstances were possible only where everyone was one big family.[5]

COMMERCE AND AGRICULTURE

Soon after arriving in Texas, George Sutherland renewed his commercial ties from Alabama and joined the firm of A. G. and R. Mills Bros., which was already shipping goods from New York to New Orleans. The most important merchants in Texas at the time, the Mills Brothers distributed goods imported from New York and New Orleans throughout coastal Texas and Mexico. They actively exported both cotton and sugar and advanced money to sugar plantations to develop the sugar industry. Later they made the currency for the Republic of Texas. At one time they were reported to have been worth five million dollars.[5]

By 1831 George Sutherland had laid out a road between his plantation and Hosea League's ferry on the lower Colorado River in present-day Matagorda County.[6] He then built a warehouse at Cox's Point on Matagorda Bay to house the commodities the Mills brothers sent by boat. On a flatboat, Sutherland hauled the supplies up to his house and redistributed them to the families living along the Mustang and the Navidad. From Cox's Point, Sutherland also handled the export of the settlers' goods — corn, cotton, cattle hides, pecans, beeswax, horses, mules, and beef cattle. Cox's Point was a good location not only because of its access to Matagorda Bay (and therefore to New Orleans) but also because of the salt beds that lay between Cox Creek and the Point. For many years people from all over Texas came to get their annual supply of salt. They cut out salt cakes, transported them home, and ground them into fine salt.[7] Business in goods and salt was so prosperous that in 1835 John Sutherland Menefee joined his uncle George Sutherland in the mercantile business.

Through the Mills brothers, Sutherland had quick and direct access to all of the necessary goods for a lively social life. The brothers imported brogans, pantaloons, gloves, silk shawls, scarlet hose, velvet and fine blue satinet, flannel, Swiss muslin, and duck shirting as well as Jew's harps, violins and violin strings, sets of cutlery, plates, tumblers, coffeepots, gridirons, frying pans, spices such as nutmeg and mustard, coffee, tea, sugar, whiskey and lots of brandy, shaving soap, calomel, castor oil, opium (presumably as a painkiller), pocketknives, gun locks, quills, pens, tobacco, spelling books, sheet music, and books. They also provided spades, handsaw files, flints, nails, tacks, screws, log and trace chains to drag logs, baling wire, rope, and twine, as well as equipment for horses and cattle—plow lines, bridle fillings, snaffle bridles, spurs, stirrup leather, saddlebags, and cowbells.[8]

In addition, the kinds of household necessities that George Sutherland brought in indicate that they had access to the spices and drinks that were available elsewhere in the United States. They did not lack in items for personal use and comfort, for treating illness, and for hunting, writing, and learning. Finally, the settlers also had the tools and building supplies they needed as well as paraphernalia for the horse and cattle business.

Trade with the United States—the export of cotton and later sugar for cash, which was used to buy the manufactured goods the colonists needed— was a key factor in the success of the Alabama Settlement. The colonists may have lived on the edge of "civilization," as then defined, but through George Sutherland's mercantile business, they were plugged into the global economy and had access to the technology available at that time. Sutherland's role as a merchant served as the economic base for his position as the family patriarch. The combination of his business enterprise and military experience was to prove pivotal in the difficult times that lay ahead. The Sutherland and Menefee plantations relied on a staple crop of corn to feed their families, but they also grew tobacco, potatoes, oats, millet, and peas for personal use. Cotton was the primary commercial crop, and they were very successful with it. José Enrique de la Peña, a captain in Santa Anna's army, which swept through the area of the Alabama Settlement during the war of 1836, reported with amazement the bales of cotton and the (burned) fields of corn, marveling at the settlement's productivity. He wrote the following in his diary: "All along the road we found dwellings of frame construction, some were well built; there were several barns full of cotton, a great deal of it already ginned and carded; spinning wheels for weaving and coffee grinders were found in most of these houses. Everything found in them was unequivocal testimony to the industry and diligence of the unfortunate families who had abandoned them."[9]

John Sutherland Menefee kept meticulous records of his agricultural activities and recorded the exact dates for planting and harvesting. His yield was 700–800 bushels of corn the first year they broke the ground, and the Alabama Settlement pioneers were among the earliest in Texas to produce cotton in large amounts. By 1836 George Sutherland had his own cotton gin, which he operated throughout the Texas Revolution, and was the major shipper of cotton bales to the United States, which brought much-needed cash to the settlement.

Texas longhorn cattle wandered the prairies between rivers and were easily rounded up. Almost as soon as they arrived, the Alabamans began raising livestock on a very large scale, borrowing from nearby Tejano Mexican ranchers their know-how and technology in herding the cattle and taming the wild horses. During the revolution their cattle were killed by the Mexican army as it swept though the settlement, and George Sutherland lost all of his livestock.[10] However, three or four years later, George Sutherland, with his vast rangeland, again became a major cattle rancher. His livestock increased steadily, with herds of 400 in 1843, 1,000 in 1849, and 1,800 until his death in 1853. He also owned a large number of horses. Roundups and other cattle work thus became increasingly important economic activities.

As the settlers' assets increased, their houses also expanded to accommodate their growing families. From the first one- and two-room cabins, the colonists added a living room and extra bedrooms. In these larger houses the colonists put in fireplaces and chimneys made with bricks from an abandoned brick kiln that the Mexican army had built on the Lavaca. The kiln produced bricks for the construction of a fortress that would control Matagorda Bay. At the time the garrison was built, 200–250 soldiers were stationed there, but in 1833 the project was suddenly halted, and the soldiers and laborers returned to Mexico, leaving behind a brickyard that the settlers raided.[11] The fireplaces greatly improved the cooking facilities and provided heat in the winter when a norther blew in.

In 1833 George Sutherland and another relative, Eli Mercer, who had settled on the Colorado River, developed a sugar evaporator for processing sugarcane. Although such production was a new enterprise for the Alabamans, they began experimenting with it soon after their arrival in Texas and for a long time regularly produced sugar and molasses for themselves. John Sutherland Menefee soon followed suit with a mill and an evaporator of his own. The extensive records he kept on his sugar business, in which he boasted that he made the "best sugar in Texas," show that slave labor was crucial to the enterprise, although extra workers were hired as well. Of John Sutherland Menefee's various farming ventures, the most innovative were his attempts at making sugar and molasses. He made enough of both to supply all of his relatives in the Alabama Settlement and had a sufficient amount left over to export to the United States. His meticulous diary details these efforts and shows how laborious and complicated sugar production was:

> As a good many are going into the syrup and sugar business on a small scale, and as ours was the first sugar made in this section of country, and the first good sugar made in Texas, I propose to give my experience on the subject. We had to start at the beginning, and had no money or means to operate with, but we had credit and friends, which in many cases answer the purpose of money. The

Mill Kettles costing four hundred dollars, were bought for us by Col. Owen. The rollers 26 inches in diameter, 4 kettles from 40 to 66 inches across, furnace mouth, grate bars and fifteen hundred fire brick, cost of $400 and $50 freight, and the setting the kettles cost $50 besides a hand to wait on the man who set them. Commenced getting boards Aug. 16, and kept the Negro men, most of the time afterwards, preparing to make sugar, besides hiring several other hands at different times.

Commenced firing the brick kiln Aug. 23rd. Built a shelter 16 by 50, picketed in with puncheons, and divided it into two parts, one for the furnace and the other for the cooling room and sugar house, in the latter was a cemented brick cistern 15 feet long and 10 feet wide, and 4 feet deep, to hold molasses; adjoining the furnace room there was a two story frame house, the lower part for the sugar mill and cane, and the upper story for the team that pulled the mill, the floor of which was puncheons pinned to the sills and girders. Perry commenced the furnace Oct. 16 and finished Nov. 11, and we commenced making sugar Mon. the 15th, but the cement around the kettles not being dry enough, boiled off, and had to blow out, and put wood around the kettles. It took about thirty six hands to run the mill night and day, about 20 of which I had to hire; for all the night work I had two sets of hands, and worked them six hours at a time, changing at six and twelve o'clock, I thought it was better to hire more hands and have a double set for the night work than to do as they did on the Brazos and in Louisiana, that is, work their hands all day & half the night—there was another particular in which I differed from them—I did not work on Sunday, and I don't think I ever lost anything by stopping from Saturday night till Monday morning.

The first season six horses and mules to the team kept the furnace going without any difficulty, but after the first year it took eight to each team, and it was as much as they could do to keep the kettles boiling rapidly, which is important in order to make a good nice article. We made about two hogsheads in twenty-four hours. Previous to this time, not real good sugar had been made in Texas, but I got a sugar maker [McMillan] who came from Barbados in the West Indies, and told him I would rather have a good article and less of it, than the ordinary kind—he did make good sugar, and the molasses was fine—the sugar was as good as the best of Louisiana sugar, better than a great deal. [12]

Making sugar required sophisticated technology and organization of labor. In style of production, the mill was an early factory modeled after the Caribbean sugar factories, with a steady production line and continuous shifts of workers. It was also a successful business for John Sutherland Menefee, Eli Mercer, and George Sutherland. The most successful entrepreneur by far was the latter. According to Freeman, "A survey of his property and an account of goods he ordered in 1837 reveals [George] Sutherland to have been one of the most prosperous individuals in Jackson County, owning, in fact, more land than any other person on the tax list. His 35,397 acres were evaluated at $40,407. In addition, he owned four town lots, probably in Texana, worth $400; six Negroes worth $2,400; ninety-seven horned cattle worth $810; four horses at $400; two mules at $200; and miscellaneous property evaluated at $2000."[13] By 1844, seven years later, his land holdings had increased to a total of 53,023 acres, and he had acquired cattle herds ranging from 500 to 700 head. From six slaves in 1837, he now had fourteen:

Various inventories and appraisals of George Sutherland's property reveal that he was a wealthy man, and Spring Hill a prosperous plantation until his death on April 22, 1853. . . . [H]e retained large acreage in Bexar, Fayette, Bastrop, Refugio and Victoria Counties, as well as half of the Jemima Heard League which adjoined his league on the south; one house and two half and two quarter lots in Texana. His livestock included 2,400 head of cattle (one-third interest belonging to his son Thomas), 57 horses, 20 mules, 100 sheep, one jackass, and two carriage horses.

Farm implements were a two-thirds interest in seven ploughs and sets of gear, two cram ploughs, two coulters [V-shaped plough blades] two sweeps, four cultivators, one large harrow [plow blade with teeth], seven ox chains, twelve weeding hoes, six axes, two grubbing hoes and one mattock [chopping hoe], three spades, one cross cut saw, one broad axe, various planes and augers, one cradle with two blades, and one set of blacksmith's tools. Household items included three feather beds and bedding, five mattresses, nine bedsteads, one old secretary [probably the same one buried before the Runaway Scrape], one bookcase with lots of books, six cane-bottomed chairs, one common chair, one broken looking glass, one stove and cooking utensils, one clock, three small tables, one dining table, one washstand and one candle stand, one lantern, and one cupboard with cupboard ware, jugs, jars, etc.

Slaves included men Will, Flemming, Pompey, and George and women Dinah, Sylvia, Ann and her two children, Tamer (?) and her two children, and Celia. Total value of this vast estate was $67,739.17.[14]

When George Sutherland died, his widow, Frances, and son Thomas Shelton Sutherland, who became the head of the family, moved more and more into the cattle business. They continued to live in the house at Spring Hill until Thomas married Puss Hodges in 1848 and built a large house for her. The home was surrounded by a separate kitchen, slave cabins, a barn, an abandoned sugar mill, a smokehouse, a cotton gin, and a blacksmith shop. The family cemetery was close by in a copse of oak trees. According to Freeman, Thomas Sutherland, George and Frances's only male heir and surviving son,

> *inherited not only considerable property but also his father's money making ability and sterling integrity. Returning to Jackson County after his marriage he built his home across the Branch from the home plantation. The house of two and a half stories was built on the brow of a hill and was fronted by magnificent live oak trees which still stand as sentinel, recalling the grandeur of a by gone day The house was typical of that of the landed proprietor of that day and many of those living now [1930] recall the old Sutherland home which was razed several years ago. Thomas Sutherland carried on the life of his father as a planter and head of family. He raised large herds of horses and drove herds to San Antonio with his sons. He is pictured as having been a man of strong convictions and of undoubted integrity. It was said in the countryside that Thomas Sutherland's word was a good as his bond.* [15]

The land and slaves belonged to Thomas's mother, Frances Menefee Sutherland, but, as the only male heir, Thomas became the owner of the homestead. Frances and her son Thomas also operated a blacksmithing shop that forged horseshoes, metal hoops to make tubs, and branding irons as well as repairing metal wagon wheels and farm equipment. In addition, mother and son continued growing and ginning cotton on the five thousand acres they owned, farmed by thirteen slaves.[16] Frances took in boarders as she had done when George was alive. By 1855 they had only a modest cattle ranch with 240 cattle and 62 horses.

Thomas Shelton Sutherland and his wife, Mary Elizabeth Hodges Sutherland, eventually had twelve children: six boys and six girls. His offspring continued the tradition of marrying with other Alabama Settlement members, and the pattern of close kinship-based relationships in the community was reproduced in the next generation. When Benjamin Ward, an outsider to the Alabama Settlement, married Frances Evans, the granddaughter of Samuel Rogers, Sam Rogers turned to him and said, "Now, Ben, you are kin to Jackson County." It was that simple. However, mostly they did not marry outsiders. Thomas Shelton Sutherland's oldest daughter, Talitha Morton, married her cousin Frank M. White, son of Francis White. The next daughter, Frances, married Judge Lucky Francis Wells, son of Francis F. Wells, who had been Stephen F. Austin's doctor. A double wedding, one of the largest social affairs of the county, was held at the Sutherland house. The event started with an enormous breakfast and ended with a fabulous dance in the evening. The next daughter, Elizabeth Margaret, married Judge Wells's younger brother, Robert. When Elizabeth Margaret ("Bettie") died, Robert married the next sister, Mary Hodges.[17]

As in Thomas's father's generation, the males of the family did not fare as well. Thomas's son George was mentally retarded from birth. Another son, John Wiley, was killed by a runaway team of horses and buried in the family cemetery. A third son died in infancy. The three youngest sons, Thomas Shelton II, William DePriest, and Robert, married the three youngest daughters of Sam Rogers. They produced a whole new set of thirty-four double first cousins and moved west to the Hill Country of Texas, where they became ranchers. Only one Sutherland child remained in Jackson County: their sister Lillian Bell Faires. When Thomas died, he was no longer a wealthy man, but he left an estate of 2,980 acres of land, forty horses and mules, and three cattle. This was divided equally among his children.[18]

In the short space of six years—from their arrival in 1830 until the war with Mexico in 1836—the group of families who composed the Alabama Settlement established homes, raised subsistence and cash crops, and set up a mercantile business that gave them access to a wide variety of goods from the United States and Europe. They were prospering, having babies, and becoming attached to their new home in Texas, only to see it begin to unravel before their eyes. They faced what they felt was an increasingly unjust, hostile government that took tariffs without providing roads and schools. They needed a legal system that could deal with the problems that arose over land rights and personal safety in a bursting Texas immigrant population of thirty thousand. In the circumstances they faced, they were not afraid to fight for their chosen home. The Sutherland clan motto, *Sans Peur* (without fear), had been their guiding principle since before the clearances in Scotland. They would depend on their fearlessness in Texas, too.

Sterling C. Robertson and the families of the Alabama Settlement—the Sutherlands, Menefees, Heards, Whites, Devers, and others—represent two different settlements in Texas. Sterling Robertson wanted to make a fortune in land by orchestrating the colonization of Texas through the Mexican empresario system. The farmers and merchants of the Alabama Settlement hoped to make a new life in Texas by planting crops and building businesses. In both cases the war with Mexico changed their lives. For Robertson, it ended the empresario system but catapulted him into the governing of the new nation of Texas. For the families in the Alabama Settlement, it destroyed their farms and businesses but gave them the freedom to govern themselves and practice their religion.

CHAPTER 9

The Comanche, Karankawa, Lipan Apache, and Tonkawa

n the mid-nineteenth century, the world and its people were conceptually divided into the civilized and the uncivilized. Texans, starting with Austin, wanted to create a civilization out of a wilderness by replacing Indians and Mexicans with "civilized" people: Americans. This was how they viewed the world. They saw what they did as progress, as the right order of things. Just as schools and churches were considered the outward signs of "civilization," an equally important step to civilizing Texas was getting rid of everything they considered "wild." It is important to remember just what "wildness" the colonists were trying to expel from Texas.

The Comanche, Lipan Apache, Kiowa, Kiowa Apache, Waco, and other Plains Indians who made periodic forays into southeast Texas to hunt game were viewed as barbaric savages who did not belong in a civilized world. Originally Plains hunters and gatherers, they became formidable warriors as soon as the Spaniards brought horses to the New World. By the time the settlers arrived in Texas from the United States, the Comanche had already been tested by one hundred years of conflict with the Spaniards and other Indian tribes and emerged as victors. Anglo-American settlers were no match for them. Consummate warriors, the Comanche were intelligent, skilled, and courageous. They could outride and outshoot with bow and arrow any frontiersman. The flintlock gun was of little help in protecting the colonists. What's more, the Comanche fought only when and where they chose, used hit-and-run tactics, riding in small groups of warriors, attacking suddenly, taking women and children as prisoners, then retreating and disappearing. Texans came to regard them with hatred and terror. In their view the Comanche were a threat that had to be eliminated.[1]

The Karankawa were nomadic foragers. They lived along the southeast coastal prairie and marshes from Galveston Bay to Corpus Christi Bay. They were fierce fighters, having had bad experiences with the Spanish expedition of Cabeza de Vaca and the French explorer René-Robert Cavelier, Sieur de La Salle, as well as with other French and Spanish invasions in the region. By 1825 Stephen Austin had led a campaign against the Karankawa in the DeWitt and De Leon colonies west of Austin's, pursued them to the coast of

Matagorda Bay, and defeated them decisively. His success was partly due to the effect of European diseases, which had by this time severely reduced the number of Karankawa. By 1830, when the Alabama Settlement arrived, the Karankawa were a "nuisance" but not a threat to colonization, having only scattered small groups, remnants of a once large and powerful nation.

To the colonists, the physical appearance of the Karankawa was striking but disgusting. Karankawa men were very tall; some were six feet in height, strong, and muscular. They strode through the woods stark naked, nipples pierced, bodies rubbed with alligator grease to protect against mosquitoes, and faces painted half red and half black. Although awed by their height and physical prowess, the Texans considered them hopelessly "primitive" people who begged and stole goods, savages who, in spite of being exposed to civilization, never gave up their rudimentary foraging lifestyle. Rumors that the Karankawa had been cannibals only made them more repugnant to the American settlers.

The Tonkawa, formed from a number of smaller groups of southern Plains Indians, owned few horses and searched along the lower Lavaca and Navidad river bottoms for wild grapes, pecans, berries, plums, and persimmons. They also fished the rivers and traveled up and down in canoes searching for new foraging areas. The men wore buckskin leggings and breechclouts. The women wore skirts, and both men and women painted their bodies in black stripes with concentric circles of black paint around the nipples. Many were tattooed as well. The Tonkawa did not usually attack the colonists, but their lives were based on principles of reciprocity rather than ownership of goods. At night they sometimes came to the settlers' cabins and "borrowed" ropes, axes, bridles, knives, firearms, and livestock.[2] The settlers disliked the Tonkawa, having no anthropological sympathy for their loose notions of private property, especially in light of the precariousness of the settlers' own hold on survival. Moreover, the Tonkawa were known to practice ritualistic cannabilism.[3]

A bigger threat were the Lipan Apache, who sometimes rode down from their habitat in the northwestern plains of Texas to the rich hunting grounds on the Gulf Coast, where deer and longhorn cattle were plentiful. The Apache were hunters and experts at riding horses and shooting arrows at the same time. Although they were fierce fighters, they had been no match for the Comanche, who continually defeated them, driving them out of the West Texas bison lands into eastern Texas. Although already decimated by both the Comanche and the Mexicans by the time the settlers came to Texas, the Apache still instilled fear in the new arrivals. My great-great-grandfather told a story about a close call with a group of Lipan Apache who had suddenly arrived in the area on a hunting expedition. My father told the tale to my sisters and me: "One of the young boys with his sister had gone out to pick berries or some such on a fast mare, when a band of Indians rode in sight. Children were heroes then as well as the grown people. The boy was on his horse in a second, pulled up his sister and barely outran the Indians to the settlement. When he arrived they took him down from his horse with a cluster of arrows in his back, which speaks well for the Indian marksmanship if not for the strength of the bow. The women of the settlement bathed him in salt water and dressed his wounds and he was not too much the worse for it."[4]

Although the young men could not do much about the Comanche and Apache incursions into their settlement, on one occasion they felt brave enough to launch an expedition to chase the Tonkawa out of their area. The group, all brothers or cousins, gathered together and formed two squads, one positioned on the east side of the Lavaca River and the other on the west side. Then they advanced upriver to flush out the Tonkawa at their camps. In a rash, youthful moment, John Sutherland Menefee decided to play a trick on the men on the other side and shouted, "Indians! Charge!" The men across the river hurtled through the thick brush, vines, and briers and shot a hog who had haplessly wandered in front of the charge, only to realize they had been deceived. Furious, torn, and bleeding, they drew guns on the men on the opposite bank, who replied by drawing their own guns. This prank might have come to a tragic end with brothers and cousins killing each other except that, hungry from the excitement, everyone soon calmed down. Some of the men cut up the dead hog and threw him into a stew pot they had brought along, adding potatoes and salt. By the time they ate, darkness had fallen. Samuel Rogers thought the stew a bit unsavory. In the morning he looked into the pot and saw that it was full of hog hairs, dirt, and sand. In their haste, the hog had not been stripped of hair, the potatoes had not been washed, and the salt was spilled in the sand and then scooped into the pot. In spite of the gritty meal, the raid was declared a success.[5]

According to Rogers and John Sutherland Menefee, the young men were still not sure that they had flushed out all of the Indians, so they continued the pursuit along both banks of the river. Eventually they found the Tonkawa and quickly fired on them, killing a few, while the rest fled. Sam Rogers was on this expedition and claimed that he had fired the first shot that killed one of the Tonkawa. Rogers was quite a storyteller, one who naturally embellished his tales from time to time, and in those days killing a cannibalistic Tonkawa was something to brag about even for a religious Methodist such as Rogers. The Tonkawa were sufficiently frightened and decided to forage elsewhere. Years later, Rogers found the bones of the unfortunate Tonkawa he had shot. He brought home the skull, which he kept on his desk for many years as a kind of macabre memento.[6]

Farther north in Robertson's colony, the situation was entirely different. For decades the Indians had had the upper hand. The colony was unfortunately situated in the Comanche hunting grounds. The Comanche created havoc and fear among the settlers by hunting their scalps and gathering their women. The Comanche were so famous for taking white women as "wives" that the Comanche LaDonna Harris once said, "If you meet a full blooded Indian, he is not a Comanche."[7] The Comanche were a serious deterrent to the success of Robertson's colony.

In a number of spectacular raids in which hundreds and hundreds of Comanche warriors swept into the area, whole families and settlements in Robertson's colony were wiped out, the survivors fleeing east to Nacogdoches for safety. Even more disturbing for the colonists was the Comanche penchant for capturing and keeping women and children, trading them among different groups. Over a period of time this Comanche custom created a strange sexual politics between the colonists and the Indians. Families beseeched the Texas Rangers and Indian traders to search for captured women and children, with only mixed success. The quest to find and return the captives to civilization took on an emotional intensity that went beyond the ache to find a loved one. It became a vital imperative not to let wildness win and particularly not to allow the women and girls to become "squaws."

The most notorious Comanche (and Kiowa) raid in Texas was the one on Fort Parker on May 19, 1836, just weeks after the battle of San Jacinto. Fort Parker was built on the western edge of the inhabited part of Robertson's colony by the multigenerational Parker family. The Parkers, including several grown sons and their families, were "Hardshell" Baptists led by seventy-nine-year-old Elder John Parker. Since they lived on the edge of the colony, well inside Comanche territory, they built a formidable fort with cabins within a stockade, block houses on the corners for fighting, and bulletproof walls. During the Runaway Scrape, the Parkers fled the Mexican army, going as far as the Trinity River, but after the battle of San Jacinto they returned to the stronghold.

On the day of the raid, most of the men were busy planting a new crop because the Mexican army had destroyed their fields. Riding in from the west, 500–700 Comanche and Kiowa appeared at the fort. Most accounts state that the attack was totally unexpected, but others have indicated that Elder John Parker had known of the Comanche presence in the area and had stolen horses from them. The Indians attacked the fort and quickly overwhelmed and killed the few men there, while the women, children, and elders ran to hide in the river bottom. Of the thirty-six members of the Parker family present when the fort was attacked, twenty-three escaped, five were killed, three were badly wounded, and five were captured. The prisoners included Rachel Parker Plummer; her eighteen-month-old son, James; Mrs. Kellogg (a Parker daughter-in-law); and nine-year-old Cynthia Ann Parker and her six-year-old brother, John. After recovering from the raid, the surviving Parkers set out to find the captured women and children, who eventually became the objects of a long search to wrest them from the heathens and return them to civilization and godly ways. Although the Parkers enlisted Indian traders and other men who went into Comanche territory to help find the captives, success was a long time coming.

Mrs. Kellogg was killed early on in captivity, but James Parker's search for his married daughter, Rachel Parker Plummer, was finally successful a year and a half later. When she wrote the story of her time with the Comanche, she related that, when first captured, she was beaten, tied up so tightly her arms had permanent scars, denied water and food, and forced to witness the killing of her newborn baby.[8] The two children, Cynthia Ann and John, were traded to a different group of Comanche and were not found until they were well into adulthood, when they had already "become Indians."[9] John married a woman in Mexico, with whom he lived the rest of his life; all attempts to retrieve him were unsuccessful. When Cynthia Ann was finally discovered, the battle between the Comanche and the colonists was already coming to a close. She had become the wife of Pete Nocona and the mother of Quanah Parker, an important Comanche chief. Cynthia Ann was brought back to "civilization" against her will. With her daughter, Prairie Flower, she stayed with relatives but was never able to adjust to life among the whites. When her daughter died, Cynthia Ann soon died, too.

As I was growing up, my father told me the story of the Comanche raid on Fort Parker and the capture of Cynthia Ann. Many of the documents on the attack were in the Robertson papers, and he maintained a special interest in the incident. This tale was more vivid to me than "Little Red Riding Hood" and more real since it took place close to home. Cynthia Ann's was to me the most terrifying fate any child could endure. When I saw this tragedy depicted in the film *The Searchers*, I imagined the horror of being ripped from my family by "wild" Indians.[10]

Based on the Cynthia Ann Parker case, *The Searchers* stars John Wayne as Ethan Edwards, the uncle of a girl stolen by the Comanche. Determined to bring her back, Ethan devotes his life to an agonizing search for her. He knows that the hunt is a race against time because, as she grows up, she will certainly become the wife of a "buck." Ethan's hatred of the Indians is so intense that he plans to kill his niece when he finds her, on the grounds that, if she has become an Indian, it is better for her to be dead. He is prevented from doing so only by an adopted nephew, who is a half-breed himself, the offspring of an Indian mother (the subtext is that, while the son of a white man and an Indian woman is somewhat acceptable, a white woman who becomes the wife of an Indian is no longer part of the civilized world). This very anti-Indian film, highly praised by film critics, portrays the sexual politics of settler-Indian relationships in a complex, emotionally powerful way.

From a historical point of view, the attack on Fort Parker was just one of many such raids that threw settlers into a panic about the capture of women. From a cultural point of view, the Cynthia Ann Parker saga raised the question of whether a girl who has had sexual relations with an Indian man would be suitable for reentry into the "civilized" world. The Fort Parker story is about cultural practices and how people imagined that women fit into the civilized world; that is, they were not allowed to become sexually or ethnically contaminated. The incident has so resonated with the Robertson family, a family very concerned with its place in civilized life, that it is still talked about today.

CHAPTER 10

Political Rumblings in the
Alabama Settlement

he Alabama Settlement arrived in Austin's colony just when the Mexican law of 1830 forbade further emigration except in that outpost. This law, however, was no more enforceable than the Mexican law forbidding slavery, which the settlers circumvented by registering their slaves as "indentured servants." The political structure of Texas at this time consisted of weak local governments (ayuntamientos) in towns such as San Antonio and San Felipe and a distant state government in Saltillo, Coahuila. Bringing grievances to the attention of the state government meant several weeks of travel by horseback just to reach the capital. The Mexican military who were stationed in scattered garrisons in Texas were responsible for the enforcement of the 1830 law and the collection of tariffs. In Texas there was no authority beyond the ayuntamientos that could handle crimes or disputes over land, and no government existed to take care of roads or schools.

Many of the settlers chafed at being subject to military rule and viewed the presence of the garrisons as a threat. As early as 1832, disagreements between the settlers and the Mexican soldiers were becoming more common. On June 26, 1832, a fight broke out between a group of Texans and the soldiers at the Velasco garrison.[1] Samuel Addison White, from the Alabama Settlement, participated in this skirmish and reported the event to his relatives in the Lavaca-Navidad area. Things worsened when Mexican soldiers tried to enforce the 1830 law by preventing land surveys, thereby halting the issuing of land deeds. Another sore point was the military's attempt to collect tariffs from the colonists, who had until then been exempt from duties on the goods they brought into Texas. Incensed by these actions and the corruption and high-handedness of the Mexican commander John (Juan) Davis Bradburn at Anáhuac (the easternmost Mexican garrison in Texas), a number of colonists presented a set of grievances to Bradburn. In these complaints, they protested his order to close all ports of entry other than the one at Anáhuac (where he alone could impose tariffs on the importation of goods) and the abrupt cancellation of further work on land titles.

By all accounts Bradburn was a corrupt official who used his position to enrich himself, but he did have the law on his side. He responded to the written allegations by arresting the protesters, one of whom was William Travis. When news of the arrests reached the Alabama Settlement, the colonists were enraged. George Sutherland called a meeting of the settlement's leading men at Thomas Menefee's house. Their complaints, which they put into a series of resolutions, continued to fester even after the Anáhuac situation calmed down and Travis and the others were released.

Some Texas historians today would argue that Mexico was more accommodating to the settlers than it has been given credit for by their counterparts in the past. While it may be true that the settlers had an inflamed sense of injustice and were provincial, even prejudicial, in their opinions, it is just such a perspective that is important to identity formation. Identity is often constructed around a perceived injustice or enemy. The view that Mexico was unfair and hostile was very much the opinion of these (though not all) settlers, and this outlook affected their cultural practices and identity formation.

George Sutherland, like others in the area, also had a commercial stake in these issues. He knew that the Mexican authorities could shut down his mercantile business at Cox's Point at any time. The imposition of tariffs (often little more than bribes to the officials) would add a huge cost to the import and export of goods. Furthermore, the families and farms of the Alabama Settlement were directly in the path of the Mexican garrisons. Thus, the Alabama Settlement was galvanized by the arrests at Anáhuac and began to think in terms of political involvement in a rebellion.[2]

Later that year George Sutherland and William Menefee were elected as delegates of the settlement and the municipality of Matagorda at the convention of 1832. This was the first public gathering of representatives from every community in Texas to address the issue of governance. The only exception was the Tejano community in San Antonio, which refused to participate. The delegates wrote a petition requesting a state government for Texas separate from Coahuila, the liberalization of the ban on immigration as set out in the law of April 6, 1830, a reduction in tariffs, and the regulation of customs officials (whom they deemed corrupt). Finally, they asked for permission to form a militia to protect themselves from Indian attacks.

Knowing that all of these matters would be viewed as explosive by the Mexican government, which feared any separation of Texas from Coahuila, and on the advice of Stephen Austin, the delegates waited until the resolution was confirmed at the convention of 1833 (at which both Menefee and Sutherland were also present as representatives) before submitting it to the Mexican government. Austin was selected to take the petition to Mexico City, where Santa Anna had only recently assumed the presidency.[3] For six months Austin pressed the Texans' case with the Mexican government, and although the immigration law was repealed, the request for separate statehood was denied, leaving the colonists with virtually no local government to handle the administration of justice and disputes over land titles.

Then, in January 1834, the Mexican authorities intercepted a letter from Austin to the Texas colonists, in which he argued that eventually a separate state for Texas was inevitable. Austin was arrested while returning to Texas and taken back to Mexico City. He languished in prison for almost a year before being released on bail but was still required to stay in the city until July 1835. During this eighteen-month period, the colonists were without an effective local government, a court system, and their primary leader. In the meantime, the population of Texas had increased to more than thirty thousand, of which only one-tenth were Mexicans, who lived mostly southeast of San Antonio toward the Gulf of Mexico, separated from the Anglo population by 25–75 miles.[4] This huge population of Anglo Texans had also become commercial farmers and ranchers with agricultural exports and a thriving livestock export business—75,000 head of cattle, 100,000 head of hogs, and 10,000 sheep.[5]

The lack of an effective day-to-day government to deal with political and judicial issues was becoming critical. The Mexican government was uninterested in developing (or simply unable to develop) any of the much-needed social institutions (such as schools) or the infrastructure needed for commerce (such as roads and ports in Mexico for the export of goods). The final straw was the passing of a series of land laws (the one-hundred-league grants) introduced by Samuel Williams, acting in partnership with Austin. These laws meant that massive land grants were given to speculators (in return for a huge profit to Williams and partners); the speculators then sold the grants at a higher price to ordinary farmers. Land that before the law had been given free to honest farmers was now going for a high price from the speculators. Furthermore, land that settlers were already living on, without yet being able to survey and get title to, was also sold to speculators. The colonists were outraged.

The first group of settlers to gather and protest these conditions met on July 17, 1835, at Millican's cotton gin. William Millican was a Robertson colonist who had relocated to Austin's colony when the fate of the former outpost became uncertain. Present at this meeting were some forty men of the Lavaca-Navidad area, including the men of the Alabama Settlement. Samuel Rogers was appointed secretary of the meeting. Thomas Menefee came with his two sons, George and John Sutherland Menefee. Jesse White, Sam Rogers's father-in-law, and Archibald White and his sons Addison, John, and James were there. The men of other families married to Menefees and Sutherlands who were there that day included James Dever, Steven and J. E. Heard, Francis Menefee White, and Francis F. Wells. George Sutherland brought his only adult son, seventeen-year-old William DePriest.

Sentiments at the meeting must have been strong because, in the end, the participants wrote a statement describing the injustices committed by the Mexican government and declared their intention to obtain independence from Mexico. *The Handbook of Texas Online* states that they "drew up a formal statement that Santa Anna was a threat to stable sovereignty and the state constitution; that they would oppose any military force that entered Texas for any other than constitutional purposes; that, as there were 200 Mexican infantrymen on the march from Goliad to reinforce the Centralist garrison at San Antonio de Bexar, the political chief should intercept them and take steps to hold San Antonio as a guarantee against invasion; that they supported a general consultation of delegates from all the municipalities of Texas; and that the militia of Jackson Municipality stood ready to march at a moment's warning."[6]

This was an inflammatory document, written seven months before the official declaration of independence was written at Washington-on-the-Brazos by Sterling Robertson's nephew, John Childress. The Mexican authorities instantly noted the signers' names and targeted the men for arrest and execution. Sam Rogers, who took the minutes at this meeting, later wrote the following: "Gen. Austin had given us to understand that war was inevitable, that we had to conquer the Mexicans or leave our homes. The people met in convention to discuss what was best to do. At one of these meetings [Millican's gin] I was appointed Secretary and the Declaration of the Independence of Texas was declared and we sent the proceedings of the meeting to Gov. Smith [Lizzie Rogers, Sam's daughter and my great-grandmother, adds a handwritten note that these papers were lost]. The political chief of San Antonio demanded of the citizens to give up to the law those who participated in the meeting. Strange as it may seem, some were willing to give us up."[7] Obviously not all of the settlers were happy with this precipitous step. John Henry Brown has described the meeting this way:

> *[The settlement's] members lived in a territory twenty miles wide by fifty in length, in which there was no town. They were all farmers and not a politician or professional man among them. Major James Kerr, the oldest inhabitant, was elected president, and Samuel C. A. Rogers (in 1891 living in the same vicinity)*

was made secretary. There never was on the soil of Texas a better average popu-
lation. George Sutherland, who afterwards led a company in storming Bexar,
and had a horse killed under him at San Jacinto (and his son William, then also
present, killed in the Alamo), who had been in the legislatures of both Tennessee
and Alabama and in the Texas conventions of 1832 and 1833, was there.

These facts are stated because of the unjust assertion of more than one con-
tributor to the history of that momentous period that the War Party, or as some-
times stigmatized, the "demagogues," "agitators," and "fanatics," were found in
the towns, while the farmers generally composed what was inappropriately called
the Peace Party.

On the contrary, the farmers most exposed geographically to Mexican ven-
geance — as those on the Navidad, Lavaca, Guadalupe and west side of the Colo-
rado — generally belonged to or sympathized with the War Party, while the most
conspicuous advocates of the other element in the country resided in the towns.[8]

In October 1835, the 1824 Mexican constitution, a federalist document that
gave the states considerable autonomy, was abolished. A new national congress was set up to consolidate the government under the control of centralist Mexico. The states of Zacatecas and Yucatán immediately revolted, and
Santa Anna personally led his army to brutally crush these rebellions. Once
the uprisings were quashed, only the state of Coahuila and Texas stood in
opposition to Santa Anna's abolition of the constitution of 1824. The congress of the state of Coahuila and Texas moved its capital farther away —
from Saltillo to Monclova — and quickly sold four hundred leagues of Texas
land in the ill-fated speculations, hoping to raise a militia capable of fighting
Santa Anna, who would certainly come after them. In the meantime, Santa
Anna sent his brother-in-law Martín Perfecto de Cos with a large number of
troops to reinforce the garrison at Bexar, the town with the largest Mexican
population.

The arrival of new troops in Texas triggered a series of frantic actions and
reactions among the colonists.[9] In what is now called the consultation of 1835,
a meeting of delegates from all of the settlements was held in San Felipe to discuss how to deal with the threat of Santa Anna. Although he had been elected
a delegate, George Sutherland could not attend because, by this time, he was
already involved in military action.[10] Nonetheless, the delegates officially put
him in charge of organizing a full militia for the municipality of Jackson.[11] The
final resolution was to throw in their lot with liberal Mexicans, remain part of
Mexico, and fight for the restoration of the constitution of 1824. They also decided to establish a provisional government for the state of Texas within the
Mexican nation.

These political rumblings were drawing the Alabama Settlement toward war. Following the leadership of George Sutherland and the Menefee brothers, the settlers supported a revolt against Santa Anna's government. In some parts of Texas, colonists were reluctant to confront the Mexican government since many of them agreed with Austin's opposition to conflict. But in these closely connected, clan-structured families, if one went to war, they all went to war.

The Alabama Settlement at War

I n 1836, war with Mexico began. Lying directly in the path of the advancing Mexican army, the Alabama Settlement began to organize the defense of its families and homes. Having heard how brutally Santa Anna dealt with the uprisings in Yucatán and Zacatecas, the colonists feared that they would be similarly treated. They also were intimidated by the size of the Mexican army with its cannons, fine cavalry, and uniformed soldiers. Historians today would argue that the Mexican army was not as formidable as the settlers supposed. José Enrique de la Peña documents the many strategic and, in his opinion, stupid errors made by the officers that contributed to the downfall of the army.[1] Since dissension about tactical procedure also cropped up among the officers, the Mexican army had problems of its own making. However, the families in the Alabama Settlement were aware of what had happened to their relatives at the Alamo and thus viewed the Mexican army as a fearsome force bearing down on them.

The organization of the defense of the settlement fell to George Sutherland, family patriarch and the man with the most experience of battle. The young males immediately formed a company under his command. They did not need to be trained or instructed to follow their leader's orders. They all had grown up together and migrated to Texas as a unit under Sutherland's direction. They had worked together in their fields and helped each other's families build their first cabins. Their families gave one another aid and comfort when food was short or people were sick. They shared the same religious beliefs and had all gone through the transforming experience of the Methodist Excitement in Tennessee. They were already a solidly united, mutually supportive clan. Forming a disciplined fighting regiment was merely a matter of extending family practice into military practice.

Because of Sutherland's shipping business at Cox's Point in Matagorda Bay, his company was assigned to help supply the Texas army, which, at the time, was under the command of Stephen Austin. Their job was to highjack Mexican ships bringing supplies for the Mexican garrisons in Texas. The Mexican army had a fort on the Lavaca River, but as hostilities became imminent, this defense force was moved to the Velasco garrison to reinforce the troops there. As soon as they left, George Sutherland and his men outfitted a private ship to attack any arriving Mexican supply vessels that would be unaware that the troops had suddenly left.

The first ship to arrive from Mexico was immediately boarded and overtaken by Sutherland's company. They confiscated the supplies—bacon, flour, and coffee—intended for the Mexican stronghold. However, they did not take the vessel itself, returning it to its captain because this was not a war against the ship's owners. Some of the provisions were distributed among the men to send to their families, and the rest was kept to feed the crew of the Texas ship. Hugh L. White (nephew of George Sutherland) was one of the relatives in Sutherland's company. His portion of the booty was half a sack of flour, half a side of pork, and a pound or two of green coffee beans. In a dugout he paddled these supplies the eighteen miles upriver to his family, who, in his absence, were scraping by with very little to eat.[2]

Soon afterward, the citizens of Gonzales, who were in even greater danger since they were close to the garrison at Bexar, decided to oust the Mexican soldiers stationed in their town and capture their cannon. During this period of fighting, the people of Gonzales requested help from the Alabama Settlement. On September 3 and again on October 1, William Wharton, a leader in the DeWitt colony, sent messages to George Sutherland, urging him to send reinforcements. Men from the Alabama Settlement responded and joined the volunteers at Gonzales. On October 2, the day after the action at Gonzales, George Sutherland, F. T. Wells (another relative in the Alabama Settlement), and others wrote to the colony from the "camp of volunteers," pleading for more men to join them "armed and equipped for war even to the knife."[3]

After the Mexican forces were ousted from Gonzales, Sutherland and his company, again because of their links to the port at Matagorda Bay, were put in charge of supplying goods to the Texas army, which was still under the command of Stephen Austin. Getting supplies from the ships at Matagorda Bay and hauling them to the Texas army were daunting tasks and a crucial operation if the ill-equipped army were to have any chance of success. The Texans faced a Mexican army that was in general better trained, well equipped, and adequately supplied. No time could be lost in trying to organize their own equipment.

On October 26, 1835, Austin instructed Sutherland and twenty men to transport materials to the ranch of don Erasmo Seguín, whom Stephen Austin had authorized to organize his own militia to fight Mexico.[4] Two days later, Major Sutherland, as he was now addressed in army dispatches, loaded twelve teams of oxen and, with twenty-five men, delivered supplies to the provisional Texas government, who were camped on the Salado River north of present-day Austin.[5] These provisions included forty-three barrels of flour, six sacks of salt, three dozen bags of coffee, two boxes of sugar, a cask of claret, one barrel of gin, one dozen bottles of rum, one dozen bottles of cordial, three boxes of wine, four dozen bars of soap, two dozen sperm candles, three bales of tobacco, and two dozen each of iron kettles, tin pans, cups, frying pans, and powder horns.[6] The provisional government of Texas was certainly well stocked with liquor and tobacco even in the midst of the revolution.

Much has been written about this time of general confusion in Texas. My account of the period is from the perspective of the family participants and, of course, is not a full account of the war. The Alabama settlers' knowledge of the conflict was patchy. As actors in this saga, they knew only pieces of it. I examine their experiences in relation to the way in which they were transformed by the events. Many of the men spent the war riding back and forth on horseback across Texas from their homes to the garrisons at Gonzales and Goliad to halt the Mexican advance at Bexar. The men of the Alabama Settlement rode in groups—family units, under family leaders—but in so doing they left the women and children in a precarious position, unprotected from Indian attack and required to find food and shelter on their own.

The slaves were also left behind during this period. With the adult men riding off to battle in Gonzales and San Antonio, the slaves in the Alabama Settlement seized the opportunity to revolt. Because Mexico did not allow slavery per se, they knew they held some prospect for freedom under Mexico but not in an independent Texas; therefore, they saw the beginning of hostilities with Mexico as a chance to break out of bondage. The Karankawa also used the opportunity of war—and the absence of the men who had driven them out—to return to their foraging area on the Lavaca and Navidad rivers. Benjamin White, a nephew of George Sutherland, wrote Stephen Austin from Goliad on October 17, 1835. In this dispatch he related the news of the slave revolt and the Karankawa attacks: "Negroes on the Brazos made an attempt to rise. Major Sutherland came on here for a few men to take back, he [Sutherland] told me [that]—John Davis returned from Brazoria bringing the news that near 100 [Negroes] had been taken up, many whipped nearly to death, some hung etc. R. H. Williams had nearly Kilt [sic] one of his. The carancawa [sic] Indians is in the Navidad country killing, stealing etc."[7] This terse note, so shocking to us today, indicates that the crisis of the times presented a window of opportunity to both the slaves and the Karankawa to revolt against their situations. By the end of October, it was reported that the Karankawa pillage had been stopped. The slave revolt was also brutally subdued.

In the first week of November, Stephen Austin resigned his command of the Texas army, and the Texas government quickly replaced him with Houston. The defense force, however, was hardly an army. Men frequently left to help their fleeing families, and those who stayed were neither disciplined nor trained. Operations were hampered because the troops were poorly equipped and supplied. In this context, Sutherland's unit was one of the more disciplined groups since it was led by a family patriarch and consisted of kinsmen with a long history of working together. In addition, they were better equipped and armed because of Sutherland's access to goods through his shipping business at Cox's Point. Throughout the war, George Sutherland was one of the few officers in the Texas army who had continuous access to supplies and delivered them not only to his own soldiers but also to the Texas army.

Sutherland's eldest son, William DePriest, had gone to San Antonio to attend school. There he stayed with José Navarro, local land commissioner and friend of Texas patriot Juan Seguín.[8] With Santa Anna's army approaching, on February 2 William, his uncle John Sutherland, William Wells, and two Kerr brothers, all from the Alabama Settlement, joined those at the Alamo who hoped to hold the garrison. From Goliad, George Sutherland rode back to the Navidad to move the rest of the family out of the line of the impending Mexican advance.

As we all know, those who defended the Alamo died fighting or were shot after being captured, their bodies piled high and burned. The bones of the cremated men lay in the open air for months, a testament to the horror of the event. William died at the Alamo, but his uncle John, according to his own account, was crippled when his horse fell on him while John was scouting for the commander of the Alamo, William Travis, during the siege. Travis then sent Capt. William Patton and John Sutherland to Gonzales on February 23 to try to "rally the settlers" and bring more men to defend the fort.[9] According to Sutherland's own account, he attempted to return with a small group of volunteers but did not reach the Alamo until after it fell on March 6.[10] Because Sutherland lived to write his version of that event, it is one of a very few surviving firsthand accounts.

Another narrative of the Alamo, perhaps more reliable because the author was actually there in the heat of the battle, is that of José Enrique de la Peña, a lieutenant in the Mexican army who witnessed the entire debacle.[11] De la Peña's description of the badly orchestrated military campaign in Texas and his disgust with the unnecessary carnage and the destruction of the houses, farms, businesses, and livestock make great reading. But what has shocked the San Antonio Chapter of the Daughters of the Texas Republic is de la Peña's claim that Davy Crockett did not die fighting as a hero should but was captured and summarily shot.

After the Alamo and the executions of the Texans at Goliad, for the rest of the war, the ragged Texas army kept up a dreary eastward retreat across Texas, their families fleeing just ahead of them. George Sutherland was at this point a member of the Texas Volunteers (1st Regiment, Company D) under Capt. Moseley Baker, whose unit was trying to slow the advance of the Mexican forces by means of small skirmishes. They briefly fought the Mexicans at the crossing of the Colorado River at Egypt, where George Sutherland had many relatives, including his wife's family (Jemima Heard), and again at the Brazos River. While Houston gathered at Jared Groce's plantation to organize and train his motley forces, Moseley Baker's regiment faced the eleven-hundred-man Mexican army in hit-and-run fashion. Even when they camped under the oak trees where the San Jacinto River meets the inlets and marshes of Galveston Bay, the Texas volunteers skirmished with the Mexicans on April 20. In that clash, George Sutherland's horse was shot from under him. According to John Sutherland Menefee, who was also in the conflict, Major Sutherland had to run a long stretch of the field to get back to the Texas line and arrived "much fatigued."[12]

THE FAMILIES IN THE RUNAWAY SCRAPE

While the men in Texas formed the makeshift Texas army that engaged the enemy in attack-and-retreat tactics, the families in the Alabama Settlement, along with the entire population of southeast Texas (some twenty thousand people, mainly women and children), set off in panic on foot, in oxcarts, and on the few horses not put into military service. For hundreds of miles on their six-week flight, they were drenched by torrential rains, lived in daily fear of Indians attacks, and received nothing but gloomy news—the fall of the Alamo, the executions at Goliad, and the continuous retreat of the Texas army. With no shelter from the rain, not only were they constantly cold and wet, but they could not even light a fire for warmth or cooking lest the smoke alert the Mexican forces to their whereabouts. With only the food they brought with them or were able to find along the way to sustain them, everyone went hungry.

Fifteen-year-old Thomas Shelton Sutherland, George Sutherland's only surviving son after the death of William at the Alamo, accompanied his mother, Frances Menefee Sutherland; his three younger sisters, Frances, Elizabeth, and Georgia Ann; and a few slaves on the Runaway Scrape. Having buried as many of their possessions as they could, they joined their relatives on the getaway. As the eldest white male in the family during that ordeal, Thomas was responsible for finding food for his group by hunting deer as they traveled. Terrified for their lives and worried about their men fighting the Mexican army, they felt their situation was hopeless—until word arrived of the miraculous outcome of the battle of San Jacinto.

Men from the Alabama Settlement were of course anxious about their families during this time. Periodically they sent someone to check on them or went themselves. Francis Menefee White, a nephew of George Sutherland and a lieutenant in the Texas army, left the militia during its flight from the Brazos because his wife's pregnancy was too far advanced for her to join the Runaway Scrape. They hid in bushes along the Brazos river bottom while the Mexican army passed by them. With the help of her husband and a slave, Francis's wife gave birth in the reeds along the riverbank, but the baby died soon afterward.[13] Samuel Rogers also tried to deliver his young wife and two children to safety and was never able to join Houston's army.

Finally, on April 21 Houston decided to attack the part of Santa Anna's army that had pursued him to San Jacinto. George Sutherland, now horseless, joined the infantry and ran across the grassy stretch between the Texan and the Mexican camps to take part in the massacre and the defeat of Santa Anna's troops. He left no written memoirs about this day. He knew that his son had been killed with all of those who were at the Alamo, his body burned on Santa Anna's orders. He knew that the rest of his family was living out in the open, wet and hungry, suffering from exposure and unknown dangers. Family legend has it that George Sutherland, normally a calm, measured man who had always supported Sam Houston, confronted Houston, as did others, just before San Jacinto. They were angry and fed up with the continuous retreat. It is not hard to imagine his feelings when, at the cry of "Remember the Alamo!" he charged toward the army that had killed his son.[14]

As soon as the battle of San Jacinto was over (some say it lasted eighteen minutes), George Sutherland rushed to find his family and take them home. When he, his wife and children, and his slave, Uncle Jeff Parsons, returned to their land, they found their houses, cotton fields, sugarcane factory, and herds of longhorn cattle destroyed. Jeff Parsons described this moment:

> *Before we started on the runaway to the Sabine, we buried the wash tubs, pots, kettles, cooking utensils, and the old master's secretary, the same one which his*

*grandson George S. Gayle had in his possession for a number of years. The Mex-
ican army never found them, but they swept the country of poultry, sheep, hogs
and horses. On our return we found nothing but the wild animals on the prairies, and hard times met us at home. We had to live there months on game and
without the taste of bread. We built scaffolds for drying the meat. We ate it dried,
fried, boiled, broiled, stewed, baked and roasted, but we had to live on it so long
we became tired of it, any way we could cook it. Finally at the end of three months
we heard a cannon fire on the bay, and it was a joyful sound. It was the signal
telling the people that the vessel had arrived and they could come get supplies. Old
master was not long in getting off. He bought ten barrels of flour, three barrels of
pickled pork, one hogshead of rice and sugar and coffee. There was a feast on his
place when these supplies came. I know the president never smacked his lips with
more relish over a Thanksgiving dinner than we did over the first meal we ate
after the groceries came.*[15]

Samuel Rogers also described his family's return from the Runaway
Scrape:

*[I] shall never forget the privation and actual suffering that my family and all
had to endure. We had but little to eat and it rained all the time. I had thought
when I left home of taking my family some place east where they could care for
themselves and join General Houston's command but that I could not do as they
depended on me entirely for something to subsist on. . . . We returned home at
last but found nothing as the Mexicans had carried off everything. Of about a
hundred head of cattle they had taken all but one. . . . When returning home, almost naked for want of clothing we came upon old Black Head, one of our milch
cows. Never will I forget the joy and gladness expressed by Lucinda and Catherine. Catherine clapped her little hands while the tears of gladness rolled down
her little cheeks and said, "Papa, now we will have milk."*[16]

For serving in the Texas army, Rogers received a land certificate of 120 acres,
which he sold for fifty dollars in Texas money. With the cash he bought a little
more than half a barrel of flour, which he described as "sour but better than no
bread."

At the end of the war, George Sutherland, at age forty-nine, had lost all
but one of his sons. His eldest son, George, died in Alabama at age fifteen;
his youngest son died at age five in 1827, before they made the journey to
Texas; and now his second son, William, had perished at the Alamo, leaving
their last remaining son, Thomas Shelton Sutherland, only fifteen years old,
to carry on the family name and produce progeny such as me. His bereaved

mother, Frances, wrote to her sister back in Alabama one of the most heart-rending letters in Texas history:

June 5, 1836
Dear Sister,
I received your kind letter of some time in March, but never had it been my power to answer it til now, and now what I must say, O, God support me. Yes, sister, I must say it to you, I have lost my William. O, he is gone, my poor boy is gone, gone from me. The sixth day of March in the morning, he is slain in the Alamo in San Antonio. Then his poor body committed to the flames. Oh, Sally, can you sympathize with and pray for me that I may have grace to help in this great time of trouble. He was there a volunteer, when the Mexican army came there. At the approach of thousands of enemies they had to retreat in the Alamo where they were quickly surrounded by the enemy. Poor fellows. The Mexicans kept nearly continual firing on them for thirteen days. Then scaled the walls and killed every man in the fort but two black men.

Dear Sister, I think the situation a sufficient excuse for not answering your letter sooner. Since I received your letter I had been away from home with a distracted mind and had got back to our house where we found nothing in the world worth speaking of—not one mouthful of anything to eat, but a little we brought home with us. God only knows how we will make out. I will try to compose my mind while I give you a short history of a few months back: The American army was on our frontier. We thought prudent to stay at home and did so until the General [Sam Houston] thought proper to retreat. We, being on the frontier, were compelled to go—I speak for all. We went to the Colorado, forty miles, but after some time, the General thought proper to retreat farther and of course we had to go, too. We proceeded to the Brazos River. There stopped a few days, but dread and fear caused another start. There Mr. Sutherland quit us and joined the army. William Heard was in, also, with a good many more of our citizens, however, we went on for several miles and again stopped, hoping we would not have to go farther, but someone over there that week brought in the early news the Mexican army was crossing the Brazos not more than forty miles behind. I wish you could know how the people did as they kept going about trying to get somewhere, but no person knew where they were going to get to. Several weeks passed on without any certain account from the army. All this time you could hardly guess my feelings. My poor William gone, Sutherland in the army, me with my three little daughters and my poor Thomas wandering about, not knowing what to do or where to go. You will guess my feelings were dreadful, but ever the Lord supported me, and was on our side for I think I may boldly say the Lord fought our battles. Only to think how many thousands of musket and cannon balls were flying over our army and so few touched. I think seven was all that died of their wounds. Some say our army fought double their number and who dares say that the Lord was not on our side. Mr. Sutherland's horse was killed under him, but the Lord preserved his life and brought him back to his family. He found us at the mouth of the Sabine from thence we all returned home. I pray that God will still continue our friend and bless us with peace again.

I will now say that our relations are only in tolerable health, tho' none very sick. Poor mother [Frances Menefee, aged 75; she died that year] went the rounds [diarrhea] not very well all the time. I was afraid she would not hold out to get back again, but she is much better. She stopped at Brother Williams's [Menefee], and I expect she will stay there all summer. Sister Martha [Menefee Stanback] lives there. We are still trying to raise something to eat, but I fear we will miss it. Brother Thomas' [Menefee] house was burnt with stable and corn crib. Mr. Sutherland's warehouse [at Cox's Point]was burnt, also his houses on the Bay. But if we can have peace and can have preaching I won't care for the loss of what property is gone.[17]

REBUILDING THEIR LIVES

The war of independence in Texas exacted an enormous price from its inhabitants. The death of their eldest son devastated George and Frances Menefee Sutherland. Francis Menefee White and his wife lost their first child, and Samuel Rogers lost two children and his wife not long afterward from the starvation and exposure they experienced. The Karankawas' last attempt to keep their place along the Navidad River was a failure, and they soon left the area and faded from human history. The slaves who revolted were beaten into submission and, under the Republic of Texas, lost all hope of emancipation. In spite of all of the hardships they endured, the Sutherlands and the Menefees set about rebuilding in the years after the Runaway Scrape. With their strong family ties and the strength they derived from their Methodist religion, they again prospered.

THE NEXT GENERATION

From the fall of 1835 through the spring of 1836 the events of the revolution dominated the Alabama Settlement. Their businesses were destroyed by the Mexican army during the Runaway Scrape, and their cotton bales and warehouses were burned. The Sutherlands and the Menefees still managed to receive goods through Matagorda Bay, which the Texas army purchased at one-third of their face value and sometimes less. On one occasion, powder kegs, horses, and other goods were taken off the schooner *Henry* at Galveston by an officer and never paid for, which further caused their fortunes to suffer. However, by August 1836, soon after the battle of San Jacinto, the Sutherlands and the Menefees were baling cotton again. They rebuilt a cotton gin and warehouse at Cox's Point and once more began to ship their cotton to New Orleans. George Sutherland had to build a new house, and this time he constructed a large manor that he called Spring Hill.

At Spring Hill the Sutherlands lived for many years, turning it into a hub of neighborly activity and a center of hospitality for travelers and kinfolk, of which there now were many. Spring Hill was known for welcoming, housing, and feeding anyone who passed through. In 1838 Mary Maverick stayed there for four months with her two sons and her slaves, while her husband, Samuel Maverick, determined whether it was safe to settle in San Antonio (the possibility of an attack from Mexico was still a threat):

February 4 we reached "Spring Hill," Major Sutherland's on the Navidad, where we all, except Mr. Maverick, remained until 2ⁿᵈ of June. Mr. Maverick went on to see if it was safe to take us to San Antonio. He also visited Cox's point on Matagorda Bay, opposite Lavaca, with a view to possibly locating there. There he owned land, but he decided in favor of San Antonio. In February, at Sutherland's, two of our horses froze to death in a norther. April 18ᵗʰ, Mr. Maverick went to New Orleans to purchase furniture, clothing, provisions, etc., for beginning housekeeping, and returned to us in May.

At Spring Hill boarded a young widow with her son—also Captain Sylvester, from Ohio, who had captured Santa Anna after the battle of San Jacinto and Captain [Barton] Peck of the Louisiana Greys [one of the volunteer companies from the United States during the war], who was engaged to be married to a niece of Mrs. Sutherland, Miss Fannie Menefee, who lived beyond the Navidad and was the belle of Jackson County. Fannie and I attended a San Jacinto ball at Texana, on April 21ˢᵗ. Her nephew, John [Sutherland] Menefee, one of the heroes of that battle, escorted us, and there was quite a gathering. Miss Fannie received great attention.

In April, Major Sutherland's corn gave out, and he went over to Egypt for a supply. Egypt is on the Colorado, near Eagle Lake. We called Mrs. Sutherland "Aunt Fannie"—her eldest son William, a young man of nineteen [sic], just home from school, went to San Antonio to learn Spanish, and was killed with Travis at the "Fall of the Alamo." I learned from her and the other ladies many thrilling tales of the runaway times of '36—when women and children fled in terror

*before the advancing forces under Santa Ana—savages who burnt and plun-
dered and committed all kinds of outrages. They told me it rained almost every
day for six weeks of that dreadful time.*[18]

In 1838, only two years after the war with Mexico, the battle of San Jacinto
was already being celebrated with a "San Jacinto ball" to commemorate Texas'
independence. Mary Maverick also noted that, when March 6 came around,
Fanny Sutherland stayed in her room alone the entire day, grieving for her
son William. Stories of the Alamo and San Jacinto were passed on not only to
relatives but also to new settlers like Samuel and Mary Maverick, who came
to Texas after its independence. These were the local versions of the larger
myth, and they solidified the Texas identity both in their descendants and in
those who arrived later and took up that identity as their own.

CHAPTER 12

The Texas Revolution as Myth
and Identity Ritual

he Texas Revolution was clearly a life-changing experience for those who lived through it. George Sutherland, John Sutherland Menefee, Francis White, Thomas Shelton Sutherland, and Frances Menefee Sutherland never forgot their ordeals and losses. In their stories of the rebellion, a strong sense of Texas as a place and a strong loyalty to the idea of Texas as a sovereignty is evident. Whatever identity these men and women nurtured before the war soon became a Texas identity, one they conveyed to future generations. The tales told right after the conflict generated feelings and a spirit of the Lone Star State that is still alive and well. People who move to Texas today or spend much time in the state, even those who have not been privy to those accounts, sense that feeling. The Texas War of Independence is not just a historical event; it is also a meaningful part of local culture.

Why then did the Texas Revolution seize the participants' imagination so completely? Why is the historical memory of that event so deeply felt that today it still defines Texas identity? How did it become such an entrenched part of local culture? To answer these questions, I suggest that we look at the short six-week period of that campaign, from March 6 (the fall of the Alamo) to April 21 (the battle of San Jacinto), as a rite of passage.

The analysis of rites of passage is almost as old as anthropology itself, originating with Arnold van Gennep, nephew of the founder of sociology, Émile Durkheim.[1] Anthropologists are very familiar with van Gennep's simple but brilliant analysis of the rituals that mark one's transition from one state of being to another. These include the ceremonies associated with birth, initiation, marriage, and death as well as membership in a group or acquisition of group identity. It has long been established that such rites all take on a similar form.

A rite of passage has three stages. First, the initiates are separated from the group and symbolically removed from the state of being they had occupied. Then they pass through a liminal period, a kind of nonstate during which their behavior is topsy-turvy and a condition of antistructure, or liminality, exists. Anthropologist Victor Turner defines *liminality* as a betwixt-and-between condition in which people become "structurally" invisible, that is, they have no clear status in society, are stripped of position and property, and live in a state of structural chaos.[2] In short, their relationship to society and to their own state of mind is the opposite of a "normal" state of being. Finally, the initiate is brought back into society with a new status, having moved from child to adult or unmarried to married. This tripartite structure of a rite of passage is found in almost all societies. I suggest that the meaning that participants in the Texas Revolution derived from their experiences is analogous to the emotional and structural experience of a rite of passage.

The best-known tale that Texans tell about themselves is the Alamo story. Not surprisingly, all Texas schoolchildren know this story by the time they study Texas history in school, if not before. What is remarkable, though, is that most children and adults in the United States also know it. Movies such as *The Last Command,* John Wayne's *The Alamo,* and the immensely popular television series *Davy Crockett, King of the Wild Frontier,* as well as popular books on the Alamo such as Lon Tinkle's *Thirteen Days to Glory,* James Michener's *Texas,* and *A Line in the Sand* by Randy Roberts and James Olson all attest to the attraction in American popular culture of the idea of dying for a cause.[3] For years I asked my students in Minnesota whether they knew the reason the United States had fought a war in Vietnam. Most of them did not. But when I asked them why the Alamo battle took place, they recited the tale enthusiastically. The powerful story of the Alamo resonates far beyond the boundaries of Texas, not only to the rest of the United States but also in the global imagination. The cause was Texas, but in the popular imagination, it was simply freedom.

The Alamo is presented to Texans as a sacred place, etched in our memories through the many books and movies about that fatal day. No battle in U.S. history has received more attention, and the message is always the same: The Alamo signifies supreme sacrifice, the glorious fight for freedom from tyranny. William Travis, James Bowie, and Davy Crockett are men-gods who engaged in the most heroic of acts, giving their lives so that others could enjoy liberty. The ultimate sacrifice usually ends with William Barrett Travis's symbolic words in his last letter written from the Alamo before its fall, "God and Texas—Victory or Death" (March 3, 1836). These same words were read to the American public by George Walker Bush when he was sworn in as the forty-third president. It is almost impossible to overstate the emotive content of the incidents at the Alamo.

Less well known outside of Texas is the account of the battle of San Jacinto. Even in Texas it is the unaccented story, although ironically this conflict marks the beginning of Texas as a nation. Another important event during the short war of Texas independence was the execution (on Santa Anna's orders) of Texas prisoners of war at Goliad, which even the Mexican officers found shameful.[4] This incident certainly affected the Texas army since it made surrender synonymous with death, but curiously it has captured neither the national nor the local imagination. Even most Texans would be hard put to describe what happened at Goliad and why.

What is noteworthy to me is that the battle at the Alamo (the slaughter of Americans) and the victory at San Jacinto (the slaughter of Mexicans) are a paired set in terms of Texas history; that is, the one takes on meaning only in the presence of the other. When considered in this way, it is clear that these events constituted a rite of passage. As such, these two battles have come to be regarded in the Texas imagination as a passage from one identity to another, a structural change from being a part of Mexico to becoming an independent Texas nation. What is extraordinary is that this way of telling the story, as a paired set and an identity rite, developed in just a few years after the events. Early histories of Texas, written less than ten years after the war, immediately focused on the heroism at the Alamo and the sacredness of the funeral pyre, leading to the ultimate, surprising triumph of the exhausted Texans at San Jacinto, who were invigorated by the cry "Remember the Alamo!" The telling and the retelling of the stories so soon after the events created a ritual testament for future generations. In *Inherit the Alamo: Myth and Ritual at an American Shrine,* Holly Brear notes that during annual performances held at the Alamo on March 6, the battle is described as the symbolic birth of Texas, with April 21 as Texas' epiphany and the time in between as the gestational period.[5] While I agree with her that the events of March 6 through April 21 are a unified narrative of the Texas creation myth, I propose a different interpretation.

I see the story of the fall of the Alamo as an episode that marks the symbolic death not just of the men inside the fort but also of Mexican Texas. Historians like to point to the declaration of independence by my cousin George Childress as the moment of separation from Mexico, but this statement was just a lawyer's document, written in haste in one day, as the provisional "government" of Texas met and then fled from Santa Anna's forces. The point of separation between Texas and Mexico was not this declaration or even the several skirmishes leading up to the Alamo conflict. These clashes were preparations for the main event—the dramatic confrontation between an organized, well-equipped, conscripted Mexican army that found itself face to face with a ragtag group of iconoclastic, generally undisciplined volunteer adventurers. In this fight Santa Anna is portrayed as supremely masculine, powerful, and ruthless, crushing the men at the Alamo with a breathtaking finality.

Less known among the general public is the fact that most of the men at
the Alamo, that is, the main "actors" in this ritual of separation, were not Texans.[6] Most of them had come from the United States and were adventurers,
storytellers, fighters, and rascals, but few of them had settled in Texas or had
a personal stake in the outcome of the war. Although some of the men at the
Alamo were from Gonzales and other Texas communities, the names that are
famous today are mostly those of men who had no roots in Texas; they had no
family ties to the place.

Davy Crockett, the consummate yarn spinner and adventurer, arrived in
Texas from Tennessee with a coterie of adventurous men only a few days before the Alamo battle. He had left Tennessee after losing his seat in Congress but not before delivering a concession speech, in which he told his constituents to "go to hell" and that he would "go to Texas!"

James Bowie and William Travis had been in Texas for a while. Bowie
had killed many men in hand-to-hand combat on his way to Texas, but then
he married the daughter of the governor of Coahuila and Texas and lived for
the most part in the area around Monclova. Only when his wife and children died in the cholera epidemic of 1833 did Bowie become involved in the
Texas politics of separation. Travis was an army regular who had been kicked
out of military training in South Carolina for starting a rebellion against the
school. He abandoned his wife, who was pregnant with their second child,
and lit out for Texas.

These men, so the story goes, gave their lives for Texas and then were refused a Christian burial. Instead, their bodies were piled high outside the Alamo mission and burned in a heap. There is no doubt that the funeral pyre
forever fixed the men as heroes and the Alamo as the "Shrine of Texas Liberty" in the minds of generations of Texans. The Alamo sacrifice irrevocably
dissolved Anglo-Texan ties with Mexico, although the outcome of that sev-
erance was still very uncertain. Texas then moved into a period of instability.

The liminal phase of the rite of passage (between separation from Mexico
and emergence as an independent nation) lasted for six weeks. This time
constituted an intermediate state of being during which the people of Texas
were thrown into upheaval. When they were forced to flee the advancing
Mexican army, their homes were burned behind them, their animals killed,
and their possessions confiscated. Hundreds of families, laden with whatever they could carry, laboriously made their way toward the border with the
United States, the Sabine River. Theirs was an unsteady, emotional journey,
undertaken in fits and starts. Never sure of the whereabouts or fate of the
Texas army, fearful of capture by the Mexican army close on their heels, and
threatened with attack by the Indians who were taking advantage of the

chaos, they were driven forward toward the Sabine for six miserable rain-sodden weeks.

The women and children in the Runaway Scrape faced more than political and social turmoil and danger from the Mexican army and the Indians. They were also subjected to extreme physical suffering. Torrential rains, the worst in Texas' history, according to accounts from the time, hampered their progress. Crossing swollen rivers and exposed to the wet and cold from sleeping out in the open, they were even unable to light a fire in the rain to cook food. Many lived on raw deer meat and came down with intestinal parasites and diarrhea. Babies and the elderly in particular sickened along the way. Those who died were buried en route. Their emotional state during this time was a combination of fear of attack, confusion about what might happen next, despair upon hearing the bad news of the Alamo, anxiety over the safety of their husbands, fathers, and sons, and their own hunger, exhaustion, and exposure. The main social actors in the Runaway Scrape were women and children. Frances Menefee Sutherland, my great-great-great-grandmother, a tough woman both physically and emotionally, never forgot the trauma of that flight. Afterward she told gripping stories about it to everyone she met.

The liminal phase of the rite of passage ended when Sam Houston halted the retreat of the Texas army and prepared at last to face Santa Anna's forces. The ethos turned from despair and confusion to anger and revenge—for the Alamo, Goliad, and the deprivations their families were enduring. In this phase the main social actors were the male Texans, for at this point in the war with Mexico, most of the soldiers in the Texas army were Texans, troops who had a stake in the place and who called Texas their home.[7] The Texas army swelled to approximately fourteen hundred men as it passed through the settled areas where the women and children were fleeing, and although volunteers from the United States, such as the Louisiana Greys, were there—and much appreciated by the Texas army—this was the Texans' moment. At San Jacinto, the Texas identity became firmly established.

Santa Anna, even at the time a mythological figure portrayed in the history books as a cruel autocrat at the Alamo and Goliad, is reinvented in the battle of San Jacinto as an ineffectual leader. Only six weeks after the Alamo, he is portrayed as a disorganized individual, weakened from having sex in the afternoon with an octoroon (who is later made famous in song as the allegedly "Yellow Rose of Texas"). Like Samson, Santa Anna is sapped of his full strength and masculinity by a woman and must run from the Texans and hide. By putting on the clothes of an ordinary soldier, he conceals not only his status but also his physical body, crouching in the bushes like a scared boy. He is demasculinized, degraded (both literally and figuratively), captured, and humiliated. The Texans, on the other hand, after weeks of miserable retreat, emerge as determined, angry fighters. The battle is a slaughter, with the Texans chasing the Mexicans into the bayou, stabbing them ferociously, turning the murky brown water to blood red.

FROM THE LARGER MYTH TO LOCAL IDENTITY

This is the mythological history, experienced by people at the time as a rite of passage. It is the story told in Texas history to schoolchildren, the one reenacted on March 6 at the Alamo and April 21 at the San Jacinto Monument, and the tale written up in the many books about the war.[8] Along with it are other, more localized, accounts that are told among families. It is my sense that these local stories give foundation to the larger myth and have solidified it in the minds of millions of Texans from 1836 to the present. Many families, both Anglo-American and Texas Mexican families who joined the revolution, have their own variations. These local stories are renditions of the larger myth, constantly solidifying its enduring symbolic truth to present-day Texans. My family's experiences of the insurrection are only one version of the myth.

CHAPTER 13

Aftermath of the War: Tragedy and Humor

eace in Texas after the battle of San Jacinto was not a certainty. As the huge Mexican army retreated during the hot summer under orders from the captured Santa Anna, Gen. Thomas Jefferson Rusk, who later became secretary of war for the republic, followed the troops to Victoria. There was concern that they might decide to ignore their orders, then turn and fight. To the disgust of José Enrique de la Peña, the Mexican army did not turn back and fight but made a disorderly retreat, frantically discarding supplies and ammunition along the way.[1]

The Texans, of course, were not at all sure the war was over until the soldiers were out of Texas, and they followed the Mexican army's retreat from a distance. Also, to guard against a new invasion from Mexico by sea, they set up Camp Lavaca near Garcitas Creek (the site of La Salle's ill-fated fort) and another camp at Dimitt's Landing, where the Lavaca and Navidad rivers join. George Sutherland was elected captain of a company and sent to Victoria. Samuel Rogers, who was in Major Sutherland's company, gave a heartrending account of this moment. Rather than dwelling on their fear of the Mexican army's return, his narrative focuses on the tragic aftermath of the war, his family's suffering, and his witnessing of the dying:

> Yes, we were at home again, but only for a few days. The report that a Mexican army was again about to invade the country caused General Rusk, then our commander at Victoria to issue the order that our families should be taken east of the Colorado River immediately and the men to join the army.
>
> Well, if there ever was a time that caused me to almost wish that I had never been born it was then. Had nothing for my family to eat—not even bread. You that may read this having never been in that condition can but poorly imagine my feelings.
>
> We organized a company and elected Major George Sutherland our captain, and presented ourselves to General Rusk for duty, and reader, what do you think was our duty? Went to Victoria to nurse the sick and bury the dead, which we did by putting from six to ten nearly every morning wrapped in their blankets a few inches below the surface of the ground. The mortality was greatest among

the volunteers from the United States, unacclimated as they were with nothing to nourish them, death soon did its work. The government was so poor that our rations were every morning a pint of half rotten beans. . . . There was so much sickness and death that had the army stayed there the entire summer of '36 there would have half of the men died.

The army moved from Victoria to Colett west of the Guadalupe River where the health of the army was much better. . . . The next place our company was assigned to was where Port Lavaca now stands. . . . There were some twenty-five or thirty patients there, some four or five died the night after we got there. They were mostly young or middle aged men. I do not remember of seeing a grey-headed man among them but what mostly impressed me was the language of the dying. Some were praying, some cursing, some talking to a loved absent wife or child and one requested his wife to give him a drink of water; her name was Martha, but she was not there. Do you think I did wrong in taking the place of a loved wife and giving him a drink of water, or do you think that was evidence of my extreme weakness that I should weep like a child when he handed back the cup and said, "Thank you, dear." [2]

The company that George Sutherland organized in April 1836 to protect the Texas coast from invasion by the Mexican army included his wife's brother and his sister's husband, William Menefee (age 45), and many of his young nephews, including 1st Lt. James G. White (sister's son, age 26), F. M. White (sister's son, 25), James Dever (wife's sister's son, 23), Ben White (sister's son, 19), D. N. White (sister's son, 19), George Menefee (sister's son and wife's brother's son, 22), Samuel Rogers (sister's daughter's husband, 26), Thomas Read (26), and many others.[3]

Stationed at Camp Independence near Port Lavaca, they tended to the dying and the dead. Finally, provisions from the United States arrived. Samuel Rogers describes the arrival of the supply ship: "The Durango, a vessel commanded by Captain Chase, had come into the Lavaca Bay, but could not come nearer the shore than a mile and a half or two miles, so the cargo had to be taken off by small boats and that duty was assigned to Captain Sutherland's company. In taking the corn from the vessel, Captain Wildy, one of our company, came upon a sack of coffee."[4] Here Rogers paused in his memoirs to describe the level of the temptation facing the men. They had not tasted coffee for three or four months. They had suffered in the war, been deprived of food and drink, and thought perhaps this was fortune's way of compensating them for their trials. Rogers remembered a saying that he maintained was based on divine truth: "Ill gotten gain confers no happiness," and another, which he put bluntly, "don't steal," but then he added,

[B]ut when a company of soldiers in Texas wants coffee bad, they forget all those wise and good precepts. When Captain Wildy brought the sack of coffee from the boat he did not put it with the corn sacks but carried it to a little thicket of bushes that was about 75 yards from the place we had stacked the corn. Then Wildy, acting as commissary, issued out the coffee, a pint to each man. . . . A short time after the coffee was issued, every fellow was anticipating the pleasure he would enjoy in a short while in drinking a cupful of delicious coffee. In fact my mess mate Frank, now the Hon. F. M. [Francis Menefee] White of Edna [related to Rogers's wife], had found a piece of old skillet in which I was trying to parch some when we saw a small boat land near the tent of our captain. We saw that it was Captain Chase and the mate from the vessel. Approaching the Capt. he said, "Capt Sutherland, some of your men have taken some of the ship's stores, a sack of coffee." Our Captain being perfectly ignorant of the affair told him that he must be mistaken.[5]

By this time a great crowd had gathered around the captain's tent. Captain Wildy was there and, when told of the cause of Captain Chase's visit, had this to say:

"What," says he, "a sack of coffee stolen by Captain Sutherland's company. That can not be. I would have you understand, sir, that this company is composed of honorable, honest men."

Chase replied, wisely, "I am not going to dispute with you about that, but the coffee is gone. It might have been taken by mistake."

Wildy said, "Yes, sir, if it has been taken at all that is the way—by mistake, for they are all honest men."

From Wildy's impassioned speech, Sutherland obviously knew something was amiss because he told Chase to wait a few minutes and said that if the coffee had been taken by his men, it would be restored. He immediately went to Samuel Rogers. Unlike Rogers, Sutherland was not exactly a loquacious man, so he asked Rogers,

"Did you get any?"
"Yes, sir."
"Where is it?"
"At my camp."
"Go and get it."[6]

Rogers did just that, carrying his small portion in a handkerchief. All of the coffee was restored, but the men were angry about their loss, and one of them,

the most devilish fellow I ever saw in my life, said he knew how to get some
powder which he put in the cannon, "Sam, let's fire at old Chase's vessel for
taking that coffee from us." He put a ball in it and fired away at the vessel.
He must have put a lot of powder because the ball landed only fifty yards from
the boat. This caused Capt. Chase to make another complaint against Capt.
Sutherland's company and was the cause of our being ordered from that place.
We stayed there [only] long enough to bury nearly all our volunteer friends what
we had been nursing [these were volunteers from the United States who came to
Texas to fight Mexico]. These were a noble set of men and I hope that their tents
have ever since been on the bank of the Crystal stream that flows from beneath
the throne of God. Of course we had to report to General Rush of the firing of
that cannon.[7]

Obviously Rusk was glad to get rid of Sutherland's company because, when reports came in that the Karankawa were killing the livestock that the Jackson County settlers had recovered after the battle of San Jacinto, he let Sutherland take the men home to deal with the threat.

By October 1836 the men in Sutherland's company had received honorable discharges from the Texas army. Sam Rogers was aware that his wife and children were still weak and sick from the ordeal of the Runaway Scrape. Since he knew they were living with his Aunt Mina (Jemima Heard) in Egypt on the Colorado River, he immediately set out to find them. Exhausted from the war and worried about his family, Rogers described not only his despair and delirium but also his faith in God and sense of hope as he talked to his mare, Sally, in the manner of so many cowboy songs:

I felt that night that I wanted to be alone with [God], the cup from which I was
then drinking was very bitter and I knew that He was the only one that could
sweeten it. A little more than half the distance past from Mustang Creek to the
Colorado and I think my little mare is failing.

"Hold up, Sally, a little longer, to the Colorado. The sun is just arising. Please
put me across as soon as you can."

"I will," she answers. "They say your wife is very sick. Doctor Williams and
Mrs. Heard are attending her."[8]

It was not until the end of October that his wife recovered enough to travel home to the Navidad.

As Sam Rogers tells it, the aftermath of the Texas War of Independence was a miserable period of death, illness, hunger, and struggle to survive. But it was not a misery without humor. Rogers shows an ability to laugh at the foibles of men desperate for the taste of coffee, normally honorable men who are not above prankish revenge. This mixture of humor and tragedy, irony and despair, bitterness and hope that formed in the minds of those who experienced the times quickly became part of the Texas persona.

❖

CHAPTER 14

Getting Rid of Wildness

he years of the Texas Republic (1836–1845) were the years that transformed people into Texans. They wrote their origin myths, established their government, schools, and religion, and increased their families. But before they could establish "civilization" in Texas, there was another battle they had to fight. It was not enough to create the foundations of civilization; they also had to rid Texas of the vestiges of "wildness," the reminders of savagery, the last threat to their security. For them this meant getting rid of the Indians.

SAMUEL ROGERS

One of the best descriptions of these years, full of irony and without the self-righteousness of John Henry Brown, comes from the memoirs of my great-great-grandfather Samuel Rogers. Sam Rogers was born June 18, 1810. At nineteen, he married fifteen-year-old Mary White, daughter of Jesse White, one of the original leaders of the Alabama Settlement. The next year Sam and his wife were part of the huge migration to the Alabama Settlement, but the hardship of the wilderness and the fevers of the Texas coast were too much for Mary, who died in 1833, when she was only nineteen, leaving two children in the care of her relatives. Sam Rogers was grief stricken: "Death came and took from me the one that made even the wilderness of Texas with all its privations and hardships a paradise. I did not want to record this, yet all is uncertain and how fleeting were all earthly enjoyments. Give me submission and let me confidently believe that the hand that wounds will make alive. After the death of my wife, I gave up housekeeping. My two children were taken by their grandmother [Mary White]. Catherine, my oldest, was nearly four years old; William, my son, was about two. My home then for some time was at Cox's Point on the bay where I was in the employ of Major George Sutherland."[1]

During the war with Mexico, Rogers married his second wife, Lucinda Hardy. Like other women in the Runaway Scrape, her health suffered from the experience, and in 1850 she died at a young age. The next year, when Sam turned forty, he married fifteen-year-old Mary Evans. Mary was born in Alabama the year before Texas independence. She and Sam went on to have nine children. Two of them died at age sixteen, but all of the others lived. The three youngest were daughters, and it was they who looked after their father and mother until their parents' deaths. These daughters married the three Sutherland brothers, grandsons to George Sutherland.

In 1929 Lizzie Laura Rogers Sutherland described her father in the following way:

> *My father had a wonderful collection of books. His education being limited, he would sit for hours reading to improve it and was ordained a Methodist preacher. He was not a member of the conference but went as often as he could to preach in nearby churches and schools and to help with Camp Meetings. There is still a school house standing [the Rogers Chapel] with its seats made of split logs in or near by his community.*
>
> *In those days there was only a few doctors and unless a person was seriously ill my father was called upon to visit the sick. His homemade pills would generally have a good effect. I have been told he was sent for and rode a mile in a terrible hurry as a child was choking to death. He found the child had a sweet potato peel in the roof of his mouth.*
>
> *If my father had enemies he did not know of it but could number his friends by the hundreds. Having a bunch of cattle he would kill a beef and go to each neighbor in his little buggy taking all some of this meat. I can remember at one home of a little boy whose mother had passed away, the father was having a hard time making a living for his three children. He came to my father's house and asked him to give [the little boy] a home which my father did for several years until the boy was older and could find work. In the later part of his life my father lost his hearing and had to use a trumpet to be able to carry on a conversation.*[2]

Samuel Rogers's autobiography, written down by his youngest daughters when he was already stone deaf and "much afflicted," as he said, vividly describes Texas during the republic years. According to him, "during the years 1836 to 1840, we did very well. We whipped the Carancua [Karankawa] Indians and they gave us no more trouble."[3] To deal with the only remaining problem—the Comanche—on March 19, 1840, peace talks were set up between the main Comanche chiefs (accompanied by a band of sixty-five men, women, and children) and the Texans. The major topic of negotiation was the highly emotional issue of the return of white captives, mostly women. The Comanche came to the council house in San Antonio to talk, but they kept the prisoners outside town and refused to release them immediately. Even then they produced only one captive. Emotions among the Texans flared, and a fierce fight exploded into a bloodbath. Thirty-five Comanche were killed, mostly chiefs, but also three women and two children. Seven Texans were killed, and eight wounded.

To retaliate for the betrayal and murder of their chiefs, the Comanche began a series of raids on the settlements. The most devastating attack took place at Dimiville (or Linnville) on August, 8, 1840. The town was destroyed, many of the inhabitants were killed, and the remaining women were taken as prisoners. Men from all over Texas were called to arms. In a desperate attempt to recover the women, they met the Comanche at Plum Creek near Lockhart a few days later for a showdown.

Many men from the Alabama Settlement took part in the Plum Creek battle, including Samuel Rogers, his grandson Russell Ward, Sam's brothers Franklin and John, Samuel A. White, Patrick Usher, and historian John Henry Brown, who at this time was living with his uncle, James Kerr. Samuel Rogers, who took part in the attempt to find the women, described this time in a chillingly matter-of-fact tone: "They had killed Major Watts and took his wife. We rescued Mrs. Watts at the Battle of Plum Creek. The other lady was a Mrs. Crosby of Victoria. The Indians killed her when we charged them at Plum Creek. They also shot Mrs. Watts but not fatally. After the battle we took Mrs. Watts on a litter made of two piles placed horizontally and a blanket stretched over them, to the house of Mr. Wood about seven miles from where the battle was fought. It was after night when we started with her and the road was very rough but about two o'clock in the morning we arrived at the house where Mrs. Watts remained until she recovered."[4]

In contrast to his flat tone on the rescue of Mrs. Watts, Rogers described his own part in the campaign against the Comanche with deep emotion. It was for him a period of great suffering. He lost his hat in the early part of the fight and in the Texas sun became very thirsty, unable to find water until they finally reached the river:

> I don't think that I ever came so near dying for water as I did then. There were some 15 or 20 of us that had a running fight with the Indians for at least twenty miles. We had to go to the San Marcus River for water. I was so exhausted I stayed at the river longer than the rest did. I was left alone but that gave me no uneasiness as I know [sic] I could find my way back to camp. On my return to the ground where we had run the Indians I came upon 12 or 15 Indian ponies all with saddle on them. The Indians in their flight had deserted them and concealed them in the brush of chaparral. I collected the ponies and tried to drive

them to camp but my horse was so completely broken down I could do nothing with them and had to leave them. I had to travel very slow, and when in about eight miles of camp, I came upon an Indian lying on the ground with a carpet sack by his side. The carpet sack had attracted my attention. Thinking that I would find something in it of importance to me, I dismounted and took a seat by the Indian and commenced an examination. Here I found a plug of tobacco, a shaving box, a book and some ribbon.[5]

Rogers had been sitting next to the Indian for about fifteen minutes when a stranger rode up and said, "'Son, why don't you kill that Indian?'

I replied that the Indian was dead.

'Dead, the devil, feel his pulse.'"

Rogers put his hand on the man's heart and found it was beating perfectly. On examination, they found that the Comanche's collarbone was broken on the right side by a rifle ball, leaving his right arm useless.

The stranger asked Rogers, "'How long have you been sitting here?'"

Sam told him.

"'You may thank your God that Comanche is right-handed. Let me have your knife.'"

However, Rogers knew what the man was planning to do and said, untruthfully, that he did not have one. The old man pulled out his own knife and began sharpening it on his shoe. Rogers protested, suggesting that they shoot the Comanche and put him out of his misery. But the man refused and tried to cut the Comanche to the heart. The knife would not go in that far, so he cut the skin and held the knife with one hand while using the other to hammer it into the heart.

Rogers cringed: "Never shall I forget that scene. The Indian digging his heels in the dirt with an unearthly yell, raised the body entirely from the ground and then became still in death. I could not help saying to him, 'You are a cruel man.'"

The stranger answered with perfect coolness, "'Perhaps I am but I must scalp this Indian.'"

And he proceeded to do so, saying that he had scalped several that day and would get two dollars apiece for the scalps. Then he turned to Rogers and said, "'Young man, I have something to say to you. A little while ago you said I was a cruel man. Did you ever leave your wife and children at home and go in pursuit of something to eat and return to find your wife and children murdered?'"

Rogers choked, "'No.'"

"'Then you know nothing of my feelings.' I saw tears come into the old man's eyes, and my own eyes became watery as he bade me good-bye. His name was Greyland. I was told that the Indians killed him not far from the place we met." Rogers continued, "It was late at night when I reached camp. They thought I was either lost or the Indians had killed me. Then, Mr. Crosby, the husband of the lady taken prisoner and killed, arrived in the camp and went to see his wife's body where she had crawled into a thicket of bushes when she was shot. She was a very beautiful woman. Her husband stood looking at his wife saying nothing, weeping no tears."[6]

After the fight at Plum Creek, Felix Houston, their officer, divided the plunder taken from the Indians and gave each man who was in the fight his share. Rogers got a mule, an Indian pony, a few yards of calico, some ribbon, and a lady's silk dress, which was "rather worse for the wear of the Indians. I had no use for it myself and my wife was not accustomed to wearing silk dresses those days, so I left it on the battlefield. Though I believe if Minnie [his daughter] had been in existence then and grown as she is today, I would have brought it home, for she likes finery as well as a Comanche Indian."[7]

This story, told by octogenarian Sam Rogers to his daughter Lizzie, my great-grandmother, is one he had told many times throughout his life. The somewhat dry narrative style, in combination with the horror of the events, gives it its punch. Never failing to inject humor into what was otherwise a grotesque event, he follows his own role in the battle of Plum Creek with the lurid killing of an injured Indian and ends with a discussion of what to do with a silk dress plundered from the Comanche. He juxtaposes the savagery of Mrs. Crosby's death and the killing of the Comanche by Greyland with the Comanche penchant for finery, a trait he considered frivolous and unsuitable even for his own wife.

RAIDS IN THE ROBERTSON COLONY

Throughout the 1840s and 1850s, Indian raids plagued the Texas settlements. Most of the attacks were for stealing horses or anything else that might be of use to the Indians, but when a raid took people's lives, it was always a traumatic event.

One of the most memorable was an incursion in Bell County in 1859, in which John Riggs and his wife, Jane, were killed while trying to save their children. The mother, who was fleeing with the youngsters, was left dead with her two young sons nearby. When the parents' bodies were found, the nine-month-old son was nursing at his dead mother's bloody breast, and the father's mangled body lay not far away. The two little girls, nine and five, were taken away on horseback by the Indians. One Indian, while riding at full gallop and trying to pass one girl to another man on horseback, dropped her to the ground and left. Her sister, seeing this, struggled and pitched until she was finally dropped as well. The two sisters, barefooted and with their clothes nearly ripped off, followed a path back to an unoccupied house, where they were found, nearly starving.[8]

In 1858 and 1859 Indian attacks were so frequent that many settlers abandoned their homes and moved into more secure areas that had been established earlier.[9] In 1859 and 1860 the Texas Rangers made a concerted effort to search for the Indian raiders and rescue the captured white women and girls. These volunteer companies, who received no pay and were not authorized by the government, elected their commanders and brought their own equipment, including horses. After the massacre of the Riggs family, squads of Rangers scouted the area regularly, looking for Indians. Historian John Henry Brown was a leader of one group called the "Independent Blues." They hunted for "reserve Indians" (Indians removed from the Brazos to Fort Cobb in 1859) as far north as the Red River to see that they left Texas, even though there was no evidence that the reserve Indians were responsible for the raids.[10] Another group of rangers, with the romantic name of the Bell County Rovers, scouted from October 1859 to January 1860.[11]

The search-and-destroy missions against the Indians into the 1860s was partly an attempt to ensure the colonists' safety. When Indians and Texans killed and scalped each other, it was part of the struggle for domination of Texas, but when the Comanche carried off settler women, another set of emotions came into play. These feelings carried moral and racial implications and were fixated on the outrage over sexual relations between "savage" Indian men and "civilized" white women. The deepest horror of the "wild" was directed at the Comanche practice of capturing women and children and turning them into Comanche.

CHAPTER 15

The Wild Woman of the Navidad

n the settlers' rush to stamp out wildness, another group of stories about sightings of mysterious, naked wild people burst into the imaginations of the colonists living in the Lavaca-Navidad area. Sightings of the wild man or woman of the Navidad captured the fantasies not just of Texans in the republic. Newspapers all over the United States picked up the thrilling story, and its progress was regularly reported along the East Coast.

According to the *Cavalcade of Jackson County,* the periodic appearance of the wild woman of the Navidad between 1840 and 1850 "was a standing subject of speculation and supplied the headlines of newspapers throughout the United States. The creature, without a name and culture, was one of the most discussed characters in the early history of Jackson County and Texas. People lived in fear of their lives, and their property was never secure from the greed or curiosity of this wild individual."[1]

The story of the feral woman was immortalized when the icon of Texas folklore, J. Frank Dobie, published the story as told by Sam Rogers. Dobie and my father were in the habit of sitting on the veranda at the home of my grandmother Mary E. Robertson Sutherland, at 1611 West Avenue in Austin, telling tales from old-time Texas, a phrase that Dobie used for the book in which he published "The Wild Woman of Navidad."[2] When the book came out, my father's sister Alice wrote to Dobie to tell him of the living children of Samuel Rogers, and he replied that he was "surprised to learn that Sammy Rogers still has living children. I hope they inherited his sense of humor."[3] Great-aunt Mabel, who kept a copy of this letter, scratched out "Sammy" and wrote "Samuel," obviously piqued that Dobie, in an attempt to claim familiarity with Sam Rogers, used a nickname no one in the family ever did.

A number of theories circulated about these wild people and their origins. Some hinted that the Wild Woman of the Navidad might be an "Indian squaw" traveling in the company of a runaway slave. In May 1834, before the Texas Revolution, Mrs. Dilue Harris wrote the following: "We had quite an excitement and considerable fright in this month. Father and brother were in Harrisburg having work done by the blacksmith; there came a man with a letter from Mr. Smith notifying father and the men in our neighborhood that one of his Africans had run away. He had a large knife he had stolen, also a flint and steel for striking fire. The runaway Negro stayed in our neighborhood for several months. The men tried to capture him but did not succeed. Mr. Battle caught him and tied him, but the Negro cut Mr. Battle severely. He then left our neighborhood, crossed the Brazos and Colorado rivers and made his way to the Navidad bottom. It was said there was a Negro woman with him, but some said it was an Indian squaw. He was often seen by travelers, and was called the 'Wild Man of the Navidad.'"[4]

Around the Navidad area, people began to notice the tracks of three human beings who had walked through the fields, the size of the tracks indicating a man, a woman, and a child. These "wild" people took yams and roasting ears of corn but otherwise caused no problem and were never actually seen. Settlers speculated that they were runaway Negroes or a stray remnant of the Karankawa, who had been run out of the region earlier. Some people thought the tracks might belong to children lost during the Runaway Scrape, who, now having "gone wild," were too frightened to approach human society. Fear of reversion to wildness still beat in people's breasts.

Then, one spring morning in 1845, Sam Rogers went out to his fields, as he always did, and noticed the tracks of three people who had passed by during the night. He knew immediately that it had to be the "wild people." Word of their presence in the area electrified the Alabama Settlement. Rogers carefully described what he had seen: "There were three different sets of tracks, one was quite a small track. It was not a shoe track but I think it could have worn a number four shoe. Others and myself thought it might be the track of a female while the other track was larger and it always had a shoe on one foot. The third track, quite a large track, could not have worn a shoe less than number nine or ten."[5] The discovery of the footprints was exciting, but since no one had ever caught a glimpse of any people, they decided the prints must have been made by mysterious creatures. The newspapers reported the story of this latest finding of tracks, thrilling readers much as stories of UFO sightings do today.

Unaware of the stir they were causing, the "wild people" continued their nightly visits to fields and houses. At first they seemed to do no harm and appeared only to be looking around the area, poking into things and walking around in the darkness, but each time the same set of three tracks appeared. Suddenly the largest set of tracks disappeared, and later a man's skeleton was found near the river bottom. Stories circulated around the community that one of the three mysterious beings had died. Later the smallest of the tracks disappeared, too, leaving only the remaining medium-sized tracks. Every morning

in the field Sam Rogers could see where small hands had dug up sweet potatoes. At times someone had come into the yard to collect roasting ears of corn.
Everyone concluded it must be a woman.

Excited by the idea of a lone woman running wild, the young men of the
Navidad bottom decided to catch her. After several nights of watching for
her in the yam fields, sure enough, one day they spied the slim figure of a naked human form, long hair flowing behind her. It was just a fleeting shadow,
but it was the first real sighting. The Negroes of the area called the figure "it"
and "the thing that comes in the night." Now that they knew it was real, everyone was a bit afraid of it. However, the young men's attempts to capture
her apparently scared the wild woman, and she left the area for some time.
The men eventually gave up their nightly vigils.

Soon after, the wild woman appeared again, but this time she began going
into people's houses. As in the rest of Texas, houses in Jackson County had
open doors generally guarded by dogs, who alerted the sleeping residents
when anything, animal or human, approached. But when the wild woman
came, she stepped over the sleeping dogs, opened cupboards in the cook room,
and took half of any meat, butter, and bread there. Then she departed like a
ghost. No dog ever woke up during her visits. Soon the wild woman was entering every house in the vicinity, bypassing even the most vicious dogs. The
"thing that comes in the night" was driving everyone wild with curiosity. Because they never saw her and the dogs never barked during her visits, people
feared she might be an apparition. But since the wild woman took only food,
most of the settlers agreed that she must be harmless.

Suddenly the pattern of her visits changed again. In addition to taking
scraps of food from the cupboard or corn from a crib, the wild thing began
to pilfer valuable tools, chains, and other household items. When she took
tools such as blades or a saw, she often returned them polished and clean to
the exact place where she had found them.

Then came the theft of the seine. Samuel Rogers's wife, Lucinda, had
made a huge seine for the Rogers men to catch fish in the creek. In return
for her extra effort in spinning the heavy thread, her male relatives promised
to buy her calico material so she could sew herself a new dress. Making the
seine was a huge task. After the day's chores, the men carded the rolls of cotton while the others worked the spinning wheel. When the net was finished,
Sam killed one of his four-year-old "beeves" and sold the hide to collect one
dollar to buy lead sinkers. The seine was put across the creek at night. In the
morning they hauled out enough fish to feed the whole family. One morning they went to collect the fish and found the seine cut in half, with one
half bobbing uselessly in the water and the other half gone. This was the last

straw. Now quite angry, the Rogers men decided to set up a watch for the wild thing. In spite of their night vigils, however, the nocturnal visits continued undetected.

A few weeks later, Lafayette Ward, Sam Rogers's grandson, was walking in the canebrakes by the river and suddenly found himself face to face with the mysterious being. The creature was carrying a handcrafted trunk made of woven grass, but in a split second it dropped the trunk and fled. Lafayette got only a quick glimpse of the naked person with the long hair, but he took the trunk back to his grandfather. In it they found many things that had gone missing, including a saw and one of Sam Rogers's shirts. The shirt was frayed, but it had been painstakingly and beautifully mended.

Rogers reported the following in a letter: "I am sorry that trunk was destroyed as it certainly was a great piece of workmanship and manifested considerable ingenuity in its construction. In it were a great many things that he had taken from the houses, in fact nearly everything that one had ever missed. . . . There was a Bible and a novel and many things of his own make. The shirt of mine that had been taken from the clothes line had been ripped in the back and sewed. It was so well done that my wife and several other ladies said it was as well done as the most skillful seamstress would have done. The thread that had been spun without cards or wheel was of as fine quality as some bought from stores. How the needles were made was a puzzle to all that saw them."[6]

The men, determined to catch the wild woman, stepped up their efforts to find her. They combed the river bottom of the Navidad and found several places where she had made her home, including two trees that she used for shelter during high water. They found a workshop with baskets, a snare for small animals, and cups, spoons, knives, and forks from people's homes. Leaves and Spanish moss had been arranged to make a bed, and a big collection of books had carefully been kept dry. One was a Bible with the relatives' names of one of the families in the area.[7] Finding the books led people to presume that the wild woman could read. What if, they speculated, she was not a savage but a civilized person?

This prospect imparted a new urgency to the search. The possibility that she was a lost civilized person made them more sympathetic to her. They left notes for her, offering her a home if she would come in from the wild. She did not respond. Finally, a huge hunt was organized. Lines of riders slowly combed the woods, their lassos ready should she dart out of the brush. Men on foot waited with leashed hounds to chase her. Soon she was flushed out and spied running across an open space as fast as a frightened deer. She had on no clothing, but her long hair covered her body, almost reaching her feet.

Swinging a club and dodging the lassos thrown at her, she disappeared into the dark forest. For months her tracks did not reappear. Not until the severe winter of 1850 were tracks in the snow found. The men immediately organized another hunt on horseback with lassos. This time, when they flushed her out, the dogs were able to tree her.

The wild woman of the Navidad turned out not to be anything that people had imagined—not a wild creature at all, not even a woman. He was a Negro man with long hair, completely naked, small and lithe, with small hands and feet, trembling with fear, talking in a language no one understood. The settlers were disappointed that he was only a runaway Negro and not an ape or a woman or a child lost in the Runaway Scrape as they had imagined for so long. Because he was not as wild as they had pictured him, interest in him waned.

Nevertheless, at bedtime, when my father told my sisters and me about the "wild woman of the Navidad," I wanted to know what happened to the runaway slave. I wanted to know what became of this mysterious being who turned out to be not wild, but also not fully part of civilization. My father said that his story unfolded slowly. A sailor who had spent some time in a Portuguese colony in Africa figured out that the "wild man" spoke some Portuguese. The wild man told the sailor that his parents had sold him to slave traders but that he had escaped from the slave ship with another man and had crossed river after river until ending up on the Navidad, where he stayed. He had been in the wilderness since some time between 1820 and 1830. He had watched the entire settlement of Texas, the massive increase in population, the war of independence from Mexico, and the march of the Mexican troops across Texas. He had watched the families in the Runaway Scrape fleeing and abandoning their possessions and had seen the Indians driven off the land.

Soon after, the settlers named him "Old Jimbo" and sold him at a public auction. After the Civil War, he received his freedom and moved to the ranch of a man named Tijerina on the San Antonio River, where he lived until he died in 1884.[8] The priceless history he had witnessed, the story he could have told of his survival during those years, his loneliness, his fears, and his flight from the young men of the Navidad, who thought him a desirable woman—all of this knowledge died with him. But the settlers were glad that he was no longer wild and that Texas had become civilized—like "Old Jimbo."

CHAPTER 16

The Civilizing Elites:
Elijah Sterling Clack Robertson

I n the fifteen years after Texas gave up its independence and joined the United States—but before seceding from the Union—people were still constructing Texas in their imaginations. The Alabama Settlement's imagined community—a hard-working, agricultural Methodist congregation with large, tight-knit, intermarried families, loyal to each other and to Texas—was very different from that of the Robertson family. The Robertsons saw themselves as the elites—educated, refined, and destined to be affluent. They were building their society around a slave plantation culture, one in which they would be the leaders, the political movers and shakers in the state.

The Robertson vision of life in Texas is perfectly manifested in the house that Elijah Sterling Clack Robertson, son of the empresario Robertson, built at Salado just before the Civil War. It is an imposing plantation house that sits on a rise overlooking Salado Creek. Here, generations of Robertsons have been born and raised, beginning with Sterling's own twelve children, as well as his many grandchildren and great-grandchildren. Robertsons have lived in the house since it was first built in 1859 and still live there today. Cile Robertson Ambrose, one of Sterling's great-granddaughters, now calls it home. My father spent his childhood running around the house and swimming in the "Salao" (as Salado Creek was affectionately called). Although my older sisters have memories of the homestead, I myself went there only recently. Cile Ambrose led me, my aunt Liz Carpenter, and my sister Gayle through the structure, graciously regaling us with the history of the rooms, the portraits, and the furniture, much of which my aunt Liz remembered from her childhood. We saw the oil portraits of Sterling and his wife, Mary Dickey Robertson, and the heavy oak chairs with growling lions' heads on the arms. As I stood in the office Sterling built to hold his father's papers on the Robertson colony and his own documents on running the plantation, I looked out at the blue Texas sky across a wide expanse of land and was struck by the history contained in that one room. Perhaps sensing my feeling, my aunt Liz explained, "In this room my mother, Mary Elizabeth Robertson Sutherland, used to say to me, 'remember who you are.'"

Later that day we drove down to Salado Creek, where the Robertson cemetery rests in a copse of oak trees. There, Sterling, his wife, and his mother-in-law are buried side by side. I read the inscriptions on my great-grandfather Maclin Robertson's grave: "He was a man loyal to his God, his traditions, his friends and his family."

Maclin's wife, Alice Josephine Woods, lived for ten years after her husband's death, and her children's warmth toward her is apparent. They wrote on her headstone, "We cannot see her but she is with us still. A mother like ours is more than a memory. She is a living presence." My sister Gayle looked up at the Robertson house on the hill above the cemetery and then turned and looked down at Salado Creek, below the trees. "Since I can remember," she uttered in her quiet voice, "I have had a recurring dream that takes place in this spot, but until now I did not know where it takes place. This is the view in my dream." Memory plays tricks with the mind but usually holds some form of larger truth. "Remember who you are," my grandmother said.

ELIJAH STERLING CLACK ROBERTSON

Sterling Clack Robertson, in his zeal to one-up Stephen Austin in the empresario game, realized early on that one of his biggest handicaps was his lack of a working knowledge of Spanish. Austin was accomplished in speaking and writing Spanish in the gracious, somewhat formal style of the times. He could elegantly present his case to the Mexican government and translate the land documents and communications with ease. His language abilities positioned him as a mediator between the colonists and the Mexican government and gave him a political edge over other land agents. Recognizing that it was unrealistic or perhaps just too late for him to acquire a facility in Spanish, Robertson brought back from Tennessee his twelve-year-old son by Frances King and delivered him to the Spanish mission in San Antonio with instructions to learn Spanish. There, in the Mission School of St. Mary in 1832, Sterling Clack Robertson, the son, was given his grandfather's Christian name, Elijah, since the Catholic fathers deemed the Scottish names Sterling and Clack to be heathen. He was never called Elijah but was known as Sterling, just as his father was.

Sterling was born on August 23, 1820, in Giles County, Tennessee. He went to school from age six to eight and then again for a short time when he was ten, and that was all the schooling he had until he was sent to the mission in San Antonio. He boarded in the house of John W. Smith, the man who carried the last dispatch from the Alamo before it was attacked. Smith's boardinghouse was a well-known stopping place where men such as Jim Bowie and Samuel Maverick stayed.[1] By all accounts Sterling was more interested in high jinks and flirting with the girls than his studies, but out of necessity he managed to learn Spanish. When Sterling was fourteen, his father decided his education was complete, and, besides, he was getting into trouble in San Antonio. In a letter addressed to Maj. Sterling C. Robertson of Austin's Colony, John Smith summed up the situation:

> *San Antonio, 17 August, 1833.*
> *Dear Sir,*
> *I have just time to drop you a few lines to inform you that Sterling is well and also to inform you that you had better send for him as soon as you can. Perhaps board him in other places closer than here. He has quit his school and is now doing nothing and this isn't a very good place for boys. You may act as you think best. In great haste, I remain yours truly, John W. Smith.[2]*

Acting quickly, Robertson sent David Wright, a trusted friend, to collect his errant son. At this time, there was no road between San Antonio and Robertson's colony. Because of the danger of Indian attack, Wright and the young Sterling traveled by moonlight and slept in a thicket during the day. Wright was one of those men who seldom spoke. At one point in the journey they heard the screech of an owl, and Wright, without uttering a word, spurred his horse and shot out at a full gallop. Sterling followed close behind as he knew this meant the sound came from an Indian.

Sterling had been home only a few days when his father had him saddle up again to take a dispatch to San Felipe, the capital of Austin's colony. This was a risky eighty-mile journey with barely a bridle path for directions and Indians all along the way. His father put him on his swiftest horse with the following instructions: "Be back before sunset the fourth day, travel by moonlight and hide in a thicket by day, keep a sharp lookout for Indians, if they pursue you, ride not too far ahead of them, lest you distress your horse, do not allow them to head you off however and fear not, for no Indian is mounted on a horse that can catch you."[3] Nevertheless, the elder Robertson was pacing up and down in front of the cabin when his son rode up. Needless to say, he was relieved to see that Sterling was safe.

With a knowledge of Spanish now under his belt, Sterling was taken to the Robertson colony land office at the falls of the Brazos, where his father put him to work translating and copying land grants into Spanish. For this work, he was granted 1,107 acres of Texas land.

At this time the Comanche and Kiowa were regularly raiding the Robertson colony area. To drive away the Indians, Robertson formed a ranger company around the end of 1835, and Sterling enlisted. He was only fifteen years old, but he became a ranger and confronted the Indians in battle. In one fight, he set out in pursuit of Indians who had stolen horses from the settlement and came upon the cool water of the Salado Springs, where he and the other rangers rested. Impressed with the beauty of the area—the watercress-laden creeks and the groves of pecan trees—he decided that some day he would settle on the banks of Salado Creek.

When war broke out in the spring of 1836, empresario Robertson, fearful of losing the colony's precious land documents, which represented the only records of his efforts to colonize Texas, put the archives in an oxcart and gave his son the awesome responsibility of hauling the papers to safety in the United States. This experience of putting his life on the line, of urging an oxcart over the muddy paths and engorged rivers during the torrential rains of the Runaway Scrape, forever seared in young Robertson's mind the importance of those records. They became a sacred responsibility he passed down to his many children and grandchildren, until many of the papers came to rest with my father.

The war with Mexico changed everything in the country and ended the empresario system. During this period of instability, land agent Robertson, in perhaps his first nurturing moment as a parent, sent his son to Jackson College in Columbia, Tennessee, for two years (April 1837 to May 1839). In Tennessee, Sterling lived with Col. Hugh Porter, who was probably a relative of his mother, Frances King. His mother seems to have migrated to Texas at this time and was living with the John T. Porter family. Then, on December 18, 1837, Sterling Clack Robertson, now a senator in the congress of the Republic of Texas, had an act passed declaring that Sterling, son of Sterling Clack Robertson and Frances King, and James Maclin Robertson, son of Sterling Clack Robertson and Rachel Smith, were his "legitimate children and capable in law of inheriting their parents' property, in the same manner as if they had been born in lawful wedlock."[4] The act was signed by Sam Houston, president of the republic, and was published in the *Telegraph and Texas Register* and the "Laws of Texas."[5]

Although Malcolm D. McLean, Robertson's biographer, believes that the empresario must have married Frances King in Tennessee and married Rachel Smith in a Protestant ceremony that would not have been recorded in Catholic Texas under Mexico, there is no record of either marriage or of the empresario's ever making a home with either one of these women. Robertson family members, in particular my grandmother Mary Elizabeth

Robertson Sutherland, who discussed this subject with McLean, viewed any mention of the illegitimacy of their ancestor Sterling as a disloyalty to the family and a taint on the family name. In fact, some Robertson family members held that Frances King died soon after Sterling was born, which would have been convenient for family honor if it had been true.[6] But young Sterling's reaction to the legal publication of his out-of-wedlock birth showed that he knew it to be true.

In 1839, when Sterling returned from Jackson College to Galveston, Texas, he was clearly worried that the public announcement of his illegitimate birth would adversely affect his standing in the community and that his friends and acquaintances might shun him. Anxious, he walked stiffly down the streets of Houston, not daring to greet anyone. Soon an old friend hailed him and spoke to him affably. Shortly after this, he received a message asking him to stop in to see the postmaster general, Major Robert Barr. To his amazement, Barr offered him an appointment as assistant clerk in the post office for twelve hundred dollars a year. Stunned by the gesture, Sterling asked the major whether he would like any recommendations of character, to which Barr replied, " 'No,' says he, 'I know you. That is sufficient for me.' "[7]

Elated with the outcome of his return to Texas, Sterling wrote to Colonel Hugh B. Porter, his benefactor and most likely a relative of his mother, back in Tennessee: "To cut a long story about nothing short, I have been received with open arms by all who knew me before I went away, and in conversing with one of my particular old friends, he told me that I had not lost a friend or gained an enemy since I left. He also spoke freely to me in relation to my troubles. He informed me that those acts [the legal act regarding his birth] had gained for me friends without number, that all of those that had ever spoke[n] to him upon the subject, said that they lamented and pitied me and all they feared was, that on my return I would give way to it."[8]

Then, on June 28, he wrote his teacher another letter: "I find I am not forlorn, and deserted being whom I thought myself at our last interview. Instead of being spurned as I imagined myself to be, I find them ready to assist me in any way I may have occasion for—and when I mention my intention of returning to the U.S., they one and all (that is my friends) endeavor to use their influence to persuade me from it."[9] Sterling's fellow Texans seemed to have no problem welcoming someone with a stain on his past (it is even today their most endearing quality), and so Sterling became the second-generation Robertson to discover that people in Texas are more interested in other people's character and grit than in their checkered past. This personal experience cemented for Sterling his determination to make his life in Texas, just as his father had.

Sterling soon became chief clerk in the post office of the Republic of Texas, and, because of the shortage of educated men, he even served for a few months as acting postmaster general at the age of nineteen. In 1840 he left his job and, while living with his cousin Henry Villars Robertson, he ran for sheriff of Washington County, losing by only thirteen votes to Capt. Joseph P. Lynch, a man he met only once more, much later, when he shot Lynch dead in the streets of Belton.[10] After losing the election, Sterling was adrift for a while, riding around the country and getting to know it. In Austin he worked briefly in the Senate, but most of the time he just drifted around. Having now grown into a man of fine physique, he was genial and sympathetic, courteous and up-beat, with great determination like his father but with a softer, less pugnacious manner.[11] Although still without a direction in life, he, like most young men in Texas, was willing, at a moment's notice, to fight any threat from Mexico.

When San Antonio was invaded by the Mexican army in March 1842, Sterling immediately rode there, where he joined a group of men heading for the Rio Grande in hot pursuit of the retreating Mexican army.[12] This was his first visit to San Antonio since his school days at the mission before the Texas Revolution. Walking the grounds of the Alamo mission was a moving experience. The mythology surrounding the Alamo and the emotions it invoked were already well set in his thoughts:

> The Alamo, once the strongest fortress in Texas, now one confused and irregular mass of stone and mortar. The roof fallen in, and the walls of the outer enclosures entirely demolished. The room where Bowie fell, is now half filled with rock and dirt. Crockett's citadel and last retreat is only marked by a high mound of earth, the rock of the wall having been removed after the revolution, by citizens of the town to repair their dwellings. I saw the place where Travis fell, surrounded by his brave companions. They are gone, the martyrs of Liberty and Freedom.
>
> Oh! Could I speak my thoughts, or had the language of an Irving or a Stephens to write. Eight years since I stood on the very spot, a boy in all the bloom and freshness of youth, viewing with pleasure and wonder the Mexican soldiery drill and perform various evolutions, strange and new to me then, but not now. Little did I dream of the miseries and troubles then in store for me. I thought of the great and important change in everything since—of our throwing off the Mexican yoke of oppression and maintaining almost miraculously our Independence up to this present period—of the many dear friends, gone to the cold and silent grave—of my situation then, and of my present prospects. In fact nothing was left unthought of, which has occurred since the time I left San Antonio, a wild white headed boy of fourteen, down to the dark haired youth of twenty-two.[13]

On the way to the border to push back the Mexican advance into Texas, he received the news that his father had suddenly died of pneumonia. Devastated, he returned home and wrote in his diary, "I felt lonely indeed. The last link is broken almost between me & the world. Alone and unaided I must make my way through the world."[14] From this statement it seems that his mother had already died.

By October 1842 Sterling had become a captain in the militia of the Republic of Texas. Along with sixty-eight of his fellow soldiers he marched to the Rio Grande, captured Laredo, and returned home by Christmas. By 1844 he had become a colonel in the Texas militia and a grand master in the Masons of the republic. He was now twenty-four years old, a dashing cavalry man with a narrow face, a wiry body, and piercing eyes, perfectly comfortable on a horse in the company of other men riding to defend Texas. And he was a straight shot. Texas was in his blood.

By the time he was twenty-five, he realized he needed a livelihood so that he would not be forced to sell the land he had inherited from his father. In the spring of 1845 he went to a small town in Walker County, Texas (part of Robertson's colony), to work as a clerk in a country story. He wrote the following in his diary: "Today I am regularly a Counter Hopper, for the first time in life; the business is not objectionable to me at all, if I can make money by it."[15]

Far removed from any news of the outside world, the town had only about twenty families. Social occasions such as weddings were infrequent, but there were eligible women. He had his eye on a beautiful young lady with "pearly teeth" and seemed happy enough. Still, he was bored and commented, "I fear this life will not suit me, as I have lost twenty pounds in as many days, without any sickness, or indisposition—I feel debilitated, but well."[16]

To fill up his spare time he began reading a copy of Blackstone's *Commentaries*, which he had brought in his saddlebags. Finally, after ten months of trying to be a merchant and making a total of $85.50, he went on the road again. His friends urged him to apply for a license to practice law in the district court of Milam County (also in his father's colony). He was "admitted a member of the honest fraternity of Lawyers, and Swore to do my Clients Justice—but I felt myself as incompetent to practice Law as if I never had looked into a book—I had read some of the Statutes of the Country and Blackstone's Commentaries nearly through, and that too, when everyone else was fast asleep."[17]

Now able to practice law, Sterling fell in love with a cousin, Eliza Hamar Robertson. Her father, James Randolph (Randol) Robertson, and the empresario Robertson were first cousins. Randol had come to Texas with the empresario and settled in Robertson County. Madly in love, Sterling and Eliza married in her father's home on July 29, 1846.

To support his wife, now pregnant with their first child, Sterling went to work at the capitol in Austin. While he was away, he and Eliza wrote each other passionate letters. Their first child, a son they named Sterling Clack Robertson, died within nineteen days of birth. The second son Eliza also named Sterling Clack Robertson. He survived to adulthood, but Eliza herself died three months after giving birth to her third child, a daughter, who lived for only eight years.

Eliza's letters show her to be a complaining, weak, overly sentimental, unsympathetic person who was shockingly callous toward the slaves her father and mother owned. Her father had become a "planter" and owned twenty-four slaves, a large number in Texas in those days. Both Henry and Randol Robertson's plantations were known to carry out beatings of the slaves.[18] Eliza was raised in this harsh atmosphere and was unmoved when a slave was beaten nearly to death:

Sept. 11, 1847

My Dear Husband,

I dream of you and my poor babe [the first boy who died] every night. I can think of nothing but you and how hard you have to work and away down there and have to sleep by yourself these cold nights. I cannot stay here, that is certain. I have got a very bad sty in my left eye that hurts me very much. It makes my head ache. I am sorry to hear that you and Wash [Sterling's slave] had such a fight. I hope Wash is not guilty of killing that child. I cannot believe it.

Speaking of fights I think we had one here last Thursday that will last yours. Mother went down to Masia's [her parent's slave] house to make Anderson hush crying and to make him come out of the house where Ry [a slave woman; Anderson is her son] was spinning. When she got there Ry would not let him come until mother threatened to hit her. She [Ry] told mother that nobody should whip her that morning but Father. Mother picked up a switch to whip her with and Ry ran at Mother and took the switch away and was going to fight when Mother made Musor [another slave] and Masia hold her and then it took Mother and Medosa [another slave] both to whip her and I whipped Anderson. So between four of us we gave them a severe beating. Father, Mr. Fogarty, Mr. Danson and Hage [another slave] had gone hunting. Mother has not told Father about it yet for she was afraid he would whip her again while those gentlemen were here. When she does tell him I expect he will seriously beat her to death. I don't care much if he quite kills her, for if you trade for her she might fight me some time when you are gone from home.

I am glad that Wash was thoughtful enough to make me a coop, for I intend to raise chickens and ducks and turkeys when I get home. I have been helping mother to pick her chicks today. I never picked any before. I do not like to do it at all, but I will raise and pick them too rather than do without or give a dollar for feathers. My little turkeys that were hatched while you were here, come up three times a day for me to feed them. They are the only pets I have now you are gone. Medosa's knife was so dull and my hands tremble so that I can not make a pen [a quill pen made from a turkey feather] that will write worth a cent. My eye and head hurt me so I cannot write any more this time. . . .

Yours from, Eliza Hamar Robertson[19]

Eliza's hard-hearted attitude toward the slaves, the constant complaints about her health (which was poor), and her sentimentality toward her husband and the turkey chicks, who are her "pets," are, to say the least, jarring. In his letters, Sterling described events in Austin of which he was contemptuous and gave his views on who was a "common" man and who was a person of "quality." His preoccupation with status and position, perhaps exacerbated by his own illegitimate status, was more important to him than any problems with "unruly" slaves:

City of Austin, December 22, 1847
My Dear Wife,
I will now proceed to give you the news of yesterday and today—Yesterday the new Governor, George L. Wood, and Jno. A. Green, Lt. Governor, were installed into office for the succeeding two years—Henderson, the ex governor delivered a very good valedictory, the Lt. Governor's address to the senate was a poor thing. Gov. Wood then delivered his inaugural which was anything but fine, good or interesting. He is very common in point of talking—brave and a good soldier, none will deny him to be, but there the story ends. . . . Upon the whole, we have a very common set, for the officers of our state. You would be surprised, were you here, to find such common men occupying so many distinguished situations in the state.[20]

Robertson's letters illustrate how he judged his fellow man—common or superior—a way of thinking that he passed on to his children. Unforgiving of people he considered "common," Sterling saw his own family as "superior" in quality. From Austin he wrote the following to his wife:

I am tired of men. I have them on all corners and for bad fellows. Oh, my dear, if I can possibly help it, this is the last time you and I will be separated again. . . .

*I saw Mrs. Robertson and Alicia yesterday across the Representative Hall
at the inauguration for the first time since their arrival. Felix [Robertson, a
cousin] I see every day. He says he has been trying to get a fight out of the Austin
boys ever since he has been up here, but that they are all cowards and won't fight
him. I believe he is the only one of the boys — you know Felix can get along anywhere — he comes up to the Representative Hall every few days and makes himself very agreeable among the members — you know he is smart anyhow, and
it would amuse you to hear some of his original remarks about men and things
around him.*

Yours Sterling [21]

In 1848 Sterling was appointed translator of Spanish deeds in the General Land Office in Austin, an office that subsequent Robertsons have held
(including my father). After Eliza died, in 1852 he married Mary Elizabeth
Dickey, a much healthier woman, both physically and mentally. She bore him
twelve children, all of whom lived to adulthood. In 1853 they moved from
Austin to the Salado Springs, where, during his Indian-fighting days, Sterling had first seen the land he chose for his home. Poised on the edge of the
Balcones Fault, this area of Texas resembles western Tennessee, with its rolling hills covered in stately oak trees. Cutting through the land was the spring-
fed Salado Creek, beautiful with its cool swimming holes, eddies in the po-
rous limestone rock, and crisp watercress on the edges and banked by huge
pecan and oak trees.

In 1854 Sterling began constructing the Robertson home in Salado. Con-
sistent with his concern for status, he chose to build a classic Southern plantation house adapted for Texas. This house stands intact today mostly in its
original condition. It has twenty-two rooms with high ceilings, eleven fireplaces, two stairways, two halls, and four porches.[22] The front porch opens
into a wide hall with an impressive carved staircase. On each side of the hall
are two large rooms. On one side is the front parlor with a traditional fireplace mantle and a back parlor that was used as the family room and library.
In this room portraits of the family are hung, and on the mantle is a marble
bust of Sterling made by Elisabet Ney, an early Texas sculptor. In the back
parlor the ladies met for tea and held their literary society meetings.

The other side of the main hall holds the master bedroom in front and, behind it, Sophia Dickey Lynch's room. Mrs. Lynch, mother of Mary Dickey
Robertson, lived with the Robertsons for a long time. It was her role to man-
age the plantation and the house and keep the keys to the storeroom. On
each side of the front porch at the two corners of the house there is a small

room. One was a "stranger's" room for the use of any passersby who needed a place to sleep. It is entered from the front porch and does not lead into the rest of the house so that a guest may arrive and leave without disturbing the Robertsons. Visits by "strangers," people passing through the area, were always welcome because they brought news from afar and provided social contact beyond family and close friends. The corner room on the other front side of the house was Sterling's office. There he kept the Robertson colony papers and his own records and diaries. A large number of "service rooms" are located behind a passageway in the back of the house, beginning with the family dining room, followed by the kitchen, the servants' dining room and kitchen, and the laundry room. The last room, leading to the outside, is the dirt-floored smokehouse, where meat was hung from the rafters and smoked in order to preserve it. The service rooms and fireplaces are made of common Texas limestone, but the front of the house is framed in the more prestigious wood clapboards. Behind the house is a row of limestone slave quarters and the stables where Sterling raised thoroughbred Tennessee horses, as had his father. This house today has been described as the most complete surviving example of a plantation complex in Texas.[23]

At the plantation, Sterling, his wife, and slaves raised horses, cattle, hogs, poultry, and goats. They hunted deer and rabbits and grew corn, sugarcane, and cotton. Bees were kept for honey. Much of their produce they sold or bartered to friends and acquaintances living in the town of Salado. Annie Lingham, a friend of Mary Dickey Robertson, wrote her on July 9, 1857, from town to ask for honey and to give news of Sam Houston's visit:

Mrs. Robertson, If you have not disposed of all your honey, Sister Mary would be glad if you would reserve eight gallons for her and she will send a cart out the first opportunity. We have had a good deal of sickness in the family since my return. The baby was quite ill for a week. She is now improving slowly.

I have been looking for Mrs. Lynch all this week but she has not yet arrived. I presume you or your Man will be in the 14ᵗʰ to hear Gen'l Houston. They do not intend having a "barbeque" as eatables are too scarce. I attended a party the evening of the 4ᵗʰ, the most pleasant we have ever had, quite a number of strangers were there.

The books which I brought home with me and the handkerchiefs I will send out by the earliest opportunity. The children are almost well of the whooping cough so I hope it will not be long before you come in to make us that visit, but tell Mrs. Lynch that need not keep her away. Love to Mrs. Lynch and the children, Yours in haste, Annie Lingham.[24]

STERLING ROBERTSON'S RECORDS

Like his father, Sterling had a high regard for documentation. For twenty years he kept diaries recording his plantation activities, the weather, his family life, and the events of the times. These journals show him to be constantly busy—planting and harvesting, making trips to Austin to sell his produce, tending to the sick around him, breeding and raising horses, and establishing the town of Salado. In 1858 he was elected chief justice of Bell County.

In 1859, the same year he finished building his plantation house, he founded the town of Salado with a donation of one hundred acres of land, which he put into a joint stock company. The land was surveyed into blocks, lots, and streets that were sold to people, who immediately began moving into the community. A strict teetotaler, he imposed the following rule on everyone who bought lots in the town: "No retailing of intoxicating drinks is suffered in or near the town. A violation of this rule would forfeit the title in town property in addition to the usual penalties for such offences."[25]

A great believer in education, Sterling established Salado College on the land he had donated so that his twelve children and the settlers in the area would have access to higher education. He was confident that a college would attract a better class of settlers to Salado. The profits from the sale of the town lots were used to finance the school buildings. Sterling's daughter Luella graduated from Salado College, the first woman to earn a degree in higher education in the state of Texas.

Sterling designed the college so that it would be worthy of educating his children, whom he viewed as superior to the general population. Because he wanted the college to be strictly nonsectarian, he put the following in the charter: "[W]hilst the Bible is to be taught and its authority regarded as paramount in all cases, no sectarian or denominational peculiarities will be introduced."[26] Although Sterling was a religious man, unlike his father before him, he never went to church and was not particularly friendly to any established churches.

Robertson also set up Salado College under strict nineteenth-century rules requiring "boys and girls to be separated from each other and to observe the proper comportment of gentlemen and ladies." Among the rules for students were "punctual attendance, no whispering, talking, changing of seats or idleness in school hours, which went from 8 AM to 5 PM. Nothing to be said or done calculated to hinder progress, wound feelings or hinder the prosperity of the school, no longings of an indecent or immoral character, boys and girls to accept different playgrounds, neatness in person and attire at all times and true courtesy in manners and general deportment as becomes those who would be gentlemen and ladies, no visiting or bathing in the Salado [Creek] on school days without special leave." He also required that students produce "perfect lessons."[27]

With a curriculum based mainly on mathematics, Latin, and literature, the college was one of the earliest institutions of higher education in the region. It fulfilled a great need at the time and helped turn Salado into a desirable place to live. For a while it was one of the best schools in the state. Although Sterling gave land and money to set up the college, the school never received a dollar of endowment and existed solely on tuition fees. Thus, its finances were always uncertain. In 1868, when various Presbyterian synods wanted to locate a university in Salado, they proposed that the college donate its grounds to the new university in return for financial support from the synod. The school desperately needed the monetary backing that a church synod could bring to it. Nevertheless, Sterling, in a heated debate with the other trustees, vigorously opposed the proposal on the grounds that it would go against the nonsectarian charter of the college. The petition was killed. By the 1880s, colleges founded by churches were springing up all over Texas, and in 1883 the University of Texas was established, triggering the decline of Salado College.

The Robertson women were very active in town and college matters as befitted their class status. In 1868 Mary Dickey Robertson and three teachers at Salado College organized a ladies' literary society that met in their homes. The society was given the somewhat pretentious name Amasavourian (from the Latin *amo* and the French *savoir*, meaning "love of knowing"). To buy the books they would read, they organized a fair to raise money. Eventually they created a circulating library, the first one under the management of women in Texas.[28] Both Mary Robertson and her daughter Luella were regulars at the live readings and volunteers at fairs to raise money for the purchase of more books. Charles Dickens was a favorite. One of the first books read at the meetings was *David Copperfield*, and the last play presented was Dickens's "A Christmas Carol" in 1876.

The Robertsons settled into Central Texas as members of the civilizing elites. They encouraged education and followed a lifestyle of Southern plantation owners—with a Texas twist. Sterling was a leader in the political and judicial life of the area, a philanthropist, and one of the landed elite. His wife and daughters were refined ladies and literary members of high society. Although they considered themselves superior to common people, they fully embraced their class duty to serve and protect the community. Only the onset of the Civil War could unravel the "civilized" life they had built for themselves in Texas.

CHAPTER 17

The End of Slavery

A t the same time that Robertson was managing his plantation and establishing the town of Salado and Salado College, state's rights and slavery were the burning political issues of the day. In Belton, Gen. Sam Houston delivered a speech in 1857, when he was a candidate for governor of Texas. Houston was opposed to secession from the United States. After all, he had worked quite hard to get Texas admitted to the Union. However, he was defeated in the governor's race by Hardin Runnels, a Democrat nominated by the Southern wing of the party to oppose Houston.

By 1859 the friction between those in favor of slavery and those against it had grown extremely bitter. In the gubernatorial election that year, Houston ran against historian John Henry Brown, editor of the *Belton Democrat*, a newspaper that was started explicitly to oppose Houston and advocate states' rights and secession. Houston won the election and became governor of Texas, but Brown had found an ally in Sterling Robertson. Fellow Masons and coconspirators, they wrote each other cryptic messages such as the following:

> Dear SCR,
> I would not cross an i nor dot a t in response, as meets this issue like a bold man and will endear you to a large majority of Bell [County], many of whom have heretofore differed with you.
>   Ross and 25 dragoons have killed 13 Comanches—took a woman, child, and boy prisoner. A man and woman were wounded in Palo Pinto—1 man killed and 1 wounded high up Leon, all by Indians. Truly, Jno. Henry Brown[1]

In November 1860 Abraham Lincoln was elected president. John Henry Brown and Elijah Sterling Clack Robertson were elected delegates from Bell County to the Texas secession convention earlier that year.[2] From the convention he wrote his wife:

> Austin, January 31, 1860
>   The Convention met on 28*th* inst. . . . [T]he sense of the convention was taken yesterday on the question of the secession of the state from the Federal Union and

the vote stood 154 for it and six against it. The ordinance of secession was intro-
duced today and will probably pass in a few days and will be referred back to the
people.... We have 170 delegates and a very fine looking body of men and prob-
ably as able as any men in the state. It is Time to tell whether they will act wisely
or not—the Legislatures are cooperating fully with the convention. The execu-
tive office of the state [i.e., Governor Houston] has manifested a slight indisposi-
tion to cooperate with the convention—tomorrow we will hear more fully—the
convention went into silent session tonight. The House boy is writing for me and
it is now 12 o'clock at night and I must close. Yours, Sterling
Genl Houston arrived today.[3]

Both Sterling and John Henry Brown voted for secession, but the ordinance had to be ratified in February, and Governor Houston came to Salado
to make an impassioned speech against ratification. Foreseeing war for Texas
if the law were ratified, he advocated a peaceful settlement of the issues with
the Union. He predicted that the South would lose any conflict with the
North and that the results of hostilities would be disastrous. Although most
people listened to the great Sam Houston with respect, some on the edge of
the crowd heckled him. Ever the dramatic dresser and outrageous speaker,
Houston looked the heckler in the eye, "placed both hands on his Derrin-
ger pistol which was belted around him under a cat-skin vest and said, 'Ladies and gentlemen, keep your seats. It's nothing but a mouse barking at the
lion in his den. If he should shoot at me he couldn't hit my brisket, if it was
as wide as a barn door,' at the same moment rearing back and spreading his
arms."[4] The crowd roared with approval. Nevertheless, the secession ordinance was formally approved. Refusing to swear an oath of allegiance to the
Confederacy, Governor Houston retired to private life.

The long dreary Civil War had begun. During the conflict, the development of Texas ground to a halt. The men were away fighting, and the women
and the elderly were busy with subsistence activities. There was no money in
circulation and little to buy anyway. With the Union blockade of the Gulf
ports of Galveston and Matagorda Bay, merchants had nothing to sell and
closed up shop. People lived on what was grown locally: barley for coffee (but
no sugar), molasses from the cane-producing areas, honey, preserves made
from peaches and wild plums, wild game or beef, cotton cloth spun and woven at home, leather that was tanned and made into boots, caps made of
coonskins, ropes made of rawhide or horsehair, blankets knit by the women,
and buttons made from cow horns.

In the early years of the war, plenty of Texas cattle remained, and meat production for the Confederate army became an important business. Bell County

alone supplied masses of cured or dried beef for the troops. Cattle production also created work for Texans in tanneries, shoemakers' shops, saddle shops, and blacksmiths.[5] Removed from the central battlefront, Texas set out to survive the war with its own resources.

As serious as the problems of physical survival was the lawlessness the war spawned. The social institutions that had been created in Texas were too weak to withstand the onslaught of prolonged conflict. The times called for tough men and women. Sterling Robertson, normally a soft-spoken, peaceful man in contrast to his father, who had been hotheaded and loud, had grown up in Texas when life was rough and dangerous. In spite of his early experiences, or perhaps because of them, he had always dreamed of raising his family in civilized peace and prosperity. The Civil War changed all of that.

In March 1862, standing in the middle of the town square in Belton, Sterling Robertson shot Joseph Lynch, the man who had beaten him in the sheriff's election when he was nineteen and the ex-husband of Sophia Dickey Lynch, his mother-in-law.[6] How could a peace-loving man commit such an act?

Sophia Lynch had not been lucky in love. Her first husband, Samuel Dickey, deserted her (according to their divorce decree of 1846). She then married Joseph Lynch, who apparently was no better a husband and a confirmed drinker to boot. Sophia eventually took refuge with her daughter and came to the Robertson home, where she lived until she died. By all accounts she was a kind person, beloved by her grandchildren as well as her son-in-law. During the dark days of the Civil War, Joseph Lynch came to the Robertson house to demand that Sophia return to him. To protect his mother-in-law from the unsavory, drunk ex-husband intent on harming her, Sterling walked into the town square in Belton, confronted Lynch, and shot him dead. When the case was tried in Bell County, the jury returned a verdict of "justifiable homicide."[7]

A few months later Sterling joined the Confederate army and was appointed aide-de-camp to Brig. Gen. Henry McCulloch, a position he held until the close of the war. He was a reliable and loyal assistant to McCulloch, just as he had been to his more fiery father. General McCulloch wrote this testimonial about Robertson: "He has been of great service to me in every respect, while engaged in gathering up and fitting out our Texas forces, performing much hard labors in collecting supplies from distant portions of the country, and while his labors have been arduous, his responsibilities have been great, being compelled to carry with him large sums of money for the purchase of supplies, and when his public funds have been insufficient to meet the demands of the country, he has not hesitated to advance his own and to pledge individual means for the payment of debts he was compelled to contract in purchasing articles that were indispensable to the army. He has been a faithful, efficient, industrious officer as well as an agreeable social companion."[8]

On April 9, 1865, when Gen. Robert E. Lee surrendered to Gen. U. S. Grant, the Texas Army began to straggle home. Five days later Abraham Lincoln was assassinated, and Vice Pres. Andrew Johnson became president. For a short time Texas had no authorized government at all. On June 19, the day that slaves in Texas were liberated by proclamation and Sterling's wife was about to deliver another baby, Robertson was more preoccupied with the violence racing through Texas and the flight of Confederate soldiers to Mexico than telling his slaves of the end of bondage. He wrote the following in his diary:

> *June 19, 1865*
> *Cut five acres of wheat. Went with grandmother [Mrs. Lynch] to Mrs. Peti-*
> *grews in search of a cradle. Went to Austin to get a horse, two sacks of flour.*
> *Cutting wheat again, very sorry crop. Heard of a horrible murder today on*
> *Elm Creek. A man killed a man and two women on Elm Creek. A terrible af-*
> *fair. Many rumors in circulation as to operations of people and government . . .*
> *but nothing reliable. Saw Richard Baker today he says that he has marked and*
> *brought 29 of the boy's calves. . . . Rumors today. Flournoy and Murrals [most*
> *likely Confederate officers] all reported having gone to Mexico. John S. Forst re-*
> *ported as having been killed by the Mexicans near Matamoros. All quiet in the*
> *country.*[9]

He noted his crops and the search for a cradle for an expected baby, but not the freeing of his slaves. Life was anything but quiet in the country; rumors were swirling around, and Robertson became even more rattled as the days wore on. A few days later he wrote of new rumors—that Grant and Sherman had arrested the cabinet in Washington for not complying with the terms made with Andrew Johnson and also that Lt. Gen. Wade Hampton had killed all of the Negro troops in South Carolina. His "strangers' rooms" were filling daily with soldiers who needed a place to eat and sleep on their way home to Missouri from Shelby's command in San Antonio. Mostly traveling on foot, they depended on the local population to give them food. Robertson wrote the following in his diary:

> *Thurs. June 22, 1865*
> *Great anxiety among all our people in regards to our future. . . . All seem dis-*
> *posed to accept the situation and look to an all wise providence for our future.*

All are humbled more or less. Reconciliation is ours to make and it is to be hoped that both North and South will derive important lessons from the experience of the last four years and May God, in his infinite mercy control and direct both sections for their present and future welfare.[10]

The rumors and the violence continued. The next day Robertson's diary mentions that two men had been waylaid and killed near Georgetown. That night he read chapters 31 and 32 of Isaiah at prayers.

Elijah Sterling Clack Robertson was the confidant of John Henry Brown, who also served with McCulloch as adjunct general.[11] During the war both Brown and Gen. Henry McCulloch often came to the Robertson home and stayed in the strangers' rooms. The McCulloch brothers, both Ben and Henry, were from the Gonzales area and were well-known participants in the Texas Revolution. One day Henry McCulloch arrived at the Robertson house, with the U.S. Army in hot pursuit. Given a fresh mount, he rode off immediately. Soon a detachment of Yankee soldiers arrived, and the commanding officer asked Robertson whether he had seen a man pass by on horseback. Robertson said he had not, technically telling the truth, as he had just given the man a fresh horse. Both John Henry Brown and Henry McCulloch went to Mexico for several years and returned to Texas only after Reconstruction, when the Reconstruction government was ousted.

At this time Sterling's diary reveals a general lawlessness in the land, with murders occurring frequently. When no one was reported killed, his diary often notes, "No killings today." However, Gen. Gordon Granger of the U.S. Army soon took control of Texas and dissolved the existing state government. Provisional governors were appointed to work closely with the Union military to restore Texas to the Union. On June 24, 1865, rumors circulated that federal troops had come as far as Tyler, Brenham, and Dallas. With this development, the time was approaching for Sterling to tell his slaves of their emancipation. On July 5, 1865, he wrote the following: "Told the Negroes for the 2nd time of the President's emancipation proclamation and the military orders. Hauling wheat. Anderson called on one Miss Georgia Karnes and Mr. Harris called today to get some rail timbers. Negroes all agreed to remain with me and they have doubts [about what to do] until the policy of the government is made known."[12]

Still, the crops had to be harvested and bills paid while they waited to learn what would happen to them. On Saturday, July 8, he noted the following: "No news. We are in blissful ignorance as to our future. Still if any light ahead—more light, more light is what we need. In the absence of it here, we must look about for it to Him who spoke it into existence. May God increase our faith in him daily. May we fear him and not man. May we put our trust in him and his own good pleasure with patience for our deliverance."[13]

Like all officers in the Confederate army, Robertson had to obtain a pardon after the war in order to be reinstated as a citizen with full rights. In August he traveled to Austin in the company of several Confederate officers to apply for a pardon. In mid-August he reported, "Negroes scattered, consulting and plotting. God only knows what is to become of the poor creatures."[14]

In the meantime the Robertson plantation continued its agricultural production. Robertson planted sugarcane and operated a sugar mill. He also grew staples such as corn and wheat as well as hay for his horses. But with slavery abolished, the farm began a period of major adjustment with the "Negroes." Robertson's diary makes it clear that the switch to wage labor required a radical change in his thinking, one that we see him make slowly. He did not think that "Negroes will work without coercion," and he believed them to be dishonest and untrustworthy. On the other hand, many of his former slaves stayed with him (possibly for lack of better options) and became wage laborers on the Robertson plantation. Unfortunately, we do not have a record of their thoughts. As is often the case in historical documentation, some of the people for whom this huge change in the country was most important were rendered mute by their social standing. Robertson would report concisely, "Negroes rather restive for some days back. Don't know the cause."

August was the month for harvesting sugarcane and making molasses. Robertson averaged 12–14 gallons of molasses a day. Because the federal mail service had not yet been fully restored, the delivery of letters was erratic. Noting that the "Negroes" seemed all out of sorts and that most of them were refusing to sign a contract with him for another year, Robertson felt unsettled about the future. On August 23 he celebrated his forty-fifth birthday. He gave the Negroes "candy stew." His wife had a steer killed and barbecued. Everyone gathered around to the sound of music, and the children were given cakes, pies, and peaches and cream. Rum cakes were distributed to the Negroes.

Finally, on August 26, 1865, his slaves were truly liberated. He wrote the following:

> *Hauled two loads of wood today. Killed a beef. Read Genl. Andrews order to the Negroes and gave them until Monday to determine whether they wanted to engage in my service for the new year or not. Explained to them their new position in the world and what would be required of them.*
>
> *The follow[ing] is a list of all my liberated Negroes by families.*

Elijah, husband [Uncle "Lige" was the foreman]; Clare, wife ["Aunt Clara"
was a mammy to the Robertson children]. Children: Jim, Whitney, Elisha,
Salno, Shelley (7)

Henry, husband [Henry handled the buggy and saddle horses]; Mary, wife
["Aunt Mary" was also a mammy to the Robertson children]. Children: Aaron,
Myatto, Poe, Shano, Lucy, Stacey, Frank, Martha (10)

John [John was a body servant. He and his wife were later captured by
Indians], husband; Lucinda, wife. Children: Albert, Frances, Louisa, John (6)

George, husband; Cornelia, wife. Children: Ellen, Grandison, Edmond (5)

Ann, mother. Children: Ben and Malinda (3)

Rose, mother. Manda, Welks, Anthony children (4)

Bill, man [Bill was the carriage driver]

Daniel, man

Charley, man [Charley was named after the man who brought the Tennessee
horses to Texas for Sterling Robertson]

Alex, boy

Rachel, woman

Margarita, woman

Total Number of Negroes 41

Grandmother's Negroes (Milly, mother; Pete, child—total 2)

The above Negroes cost me $24,000 in gold—not one dollar of which was
made by me by Negro labor. The children I have raised, which would have been
my only profit.

It is good to review the past for instruction and encouragement, never for a
reason for despondency. The 29 of July 1846 I was married. Had a wife and a
law practice, twenty six years old and the world before me. Today all my prop-
erty in Negroes is gone and unless I am pardoned by the President my lands are
gone from me for my life time at least. Amounting to over $20,000 or more. I am
forty six years old with a wife and 8 children. . . . But thank God my conscience
is clear, my will good and my determination strong to make the most of the situ-
ation, though my time is shorter and powers of endurance less.[15]

Robertson's thoughts focused on his future and the adjustments he would
have to make because of the abolition of slavery. The Robertsons had to rec-
oncile themselves to running a large plantation without slave labor, to the loss
of property that the slaves represented, and to the humiliation of defeat. Sterling's diary entries do not note any misgivings about slavery or, for a religious
man, any moral quandary with the institution. He worried only about how
to deal with labor that was no longer his property. He gave his ex-slave Dan
a horse to go to Belton and noted that Dan returned, "much to the surprise

of everyone on the place but myself." Nevertheless, most of the "Negroes" were anxious for a change and wanted to hire anywhere but on the Robertson plantation: "I find that Charley tried to hire to Mr. McFarland and Bill to Mr. Bearnall though both professed a great desire to remain in my service as long as I wanted them. There is no truth and but little honesty in any of them. May the lord help the poor creatures or their fate will be a hard one. None of them will work long without compulsion. We must rely on white labour." [16]

The next day he called all of the former slaves together to discuss a contract with them: "John and Lige each [asked for] $10 per month and Henry $3.00 per month and $2 for Sarah, All of whom I employed. The others asked $10 per month and I let them go. George and wife and three children, Ann and 2 child, Rose and 3 child, Dan, Bill, and 4 child. Some of them who asked me for $10 per month have gone to work for my neighbors for their victuals and clothes." [17]

On September 1, 1865, Sophia Lynch, Robertson's mother-in-law and the overseer of the household, wrote in her bookkeeping ledger the names of the household slaves who had been freed and added, with considerable bitterness, "ESC Robertson's Negroes freed by oppression of Lincoln's Proclamation and the failure of the Confederate Cause." [18]

Sterling Robertson received his full pardon and amnesty from Pres. Andrew Johnson on November 18, 1865. Although he had not attended church for most of his forty-six years, soon after the war he joined the Methodist Church. The devastation brought on by the conflict and the loss of the Confederacy finally pushed him toward the kind of institutionalized religion he had so disliked. In 1871, when he went to vote, he was forced to prove that he was a Texas citizen by showing his pardon. He wrote these words: "Bah! I was born in Giles Co. Tenn on the 20 of Aug 1820—Came to Texas in Dec 1832 and have been here ever since—Strange proceedings that at the end of fifty years, the enclosed paper is necessary to make me a citizen!!" [19]

CHAPTER 18

Remember Who You Are

Elijah Sterling Robertson's son, my great-grandfather Maclin Robertson, grew up in the Reconstruction period after the Civil War. As I myself was growing up, somehow I came to know, through the hushed tones of the adults around me, that Maclin had killed a number of men. This was not surprising since Maclin was a Texas Ranger. According to my father, Maclin was "one of those laconic Texas men of the mythical past, men who lived both by the law and the gun, without seeing any contradiction between the two. By all accounts, he did not waste a whole lot of time on talk."[1] He also was not particularly pleasant.

But a story that my father told many times about his grandfather Maclin Robertson was the one that most stuck in my mind. Maclin rode a fiery stallion named Hal, a horse no one else could handle well enough to ride. When my father was five years old, one day Maclin rode Hal up to him and said, "Want to go to the pasture?" While Hal snorted and pawed the ground, Maclin barked, "Reach up your hand," jerked my father up, and took off at a full gallop, oblivious of the terrified boy behind him. My father described how he hung on for dear life, his little fingers grasping his grandfather's shirt. Later he remarked that if he had not already ridden many times behind his own father, he would certainly have fallen off. Maclin rode hard, simply assuming that his grandson knew how to ride. Only twice did he speak to my father, once when he scolded, "Take your hands off my shirt," and again when he said, "Your grandfather killed nine men." When he was very old, my father said of this experience, "This was the nearest I came to a direct conversation with him."[2]

When my father was finally delivered back home, he slid down Hal's sweaty flank and ran to his mother for safety and comfort. "Mama," he blurted out, "Grandpapa says my grandpapa killed nine men."

As Maclin's daughter, my grandmother was not one to question her father's roughness with her son or to contradict him. She also would not lie to her son. She was silent for a minute, then pursed her lips and said, "I don't think there were that many."

Only much later did my father suspect that Maclin was referring to *his own* grandfather, empresario Sterling Robertson.[3] I have never been sure which of my two Robertson ancestors killed nine men, but I suppose it could have been either one—or perhaps both. My relatives were not proud of our ancestors' violence. On the contrary, they tried to hide it and spoke of it only in whispered voices. Still, it was accepted as a fact of our lives, like having to eat and sleep.

Sterling, the son of the empresario, lived a life that included many dangers and hardships. During the Texas Revolution he was just a boy but had been given the responsibility of saving his father's precious land papers. Over and over he had fought the Indians and survived because of his own determination and the superiority of his horse. He had followed his father's invidious legal battles with Stephen Austin. He had been humiliated by the public announcement of his illegitimacy and overcome it. He had built a plantation on land he had picked out when being chased by Indians, and he had become a successful Southern planter in an area much too wild to be true plantation country. On the losing side of the horrendous Civil War, he saw his fortune diminished. In order to reinstate his rights as a citizen and keep his lands, he had been obliged to ask for a pardon from the United States. But Sterling was not a hothead like his father, and through all of these tribulations he maintained his dignity, his values, and his feeling of preeminence. He also had a strong sense of order, decorum, and democracy. Thus, when the Ku Klux Klan formed after the Civil War and began terrorizing the Negroes in the area, Robertson became a strong opponent of the KKK even though this stance made him unpopular.

By April 1873 his farm was prospering again. He had ten children, the oldest of whom was twenty-four-year-old Sterling Clack, the only surviving child by his first wife. Huling Parker, the son who helped so much with his crops, was sixteen. His wife was pregnant with her eleventh and last child. In pain, she nevertheless delivered a healthy baby girl on April 23, 1873. Robertson was now hiring Mexicans to work for him, although he continued to use Negro labor as well. He had finally raised the money to complete the construction of Salado College. On May 5 he reported a huge fight in Georgetown the night before, which resulted in the freeing of all of the prisoners but one.

Reconstruction ended when Gov. Richard Coke and other Democratic state officials were inaugurated in Austin in January 1874. On September 6, 1875, Elijah was elected to represent Bell County at the convention in Austin that would write a new state constitution to replace the charter of Reconstruction. Not long afterward he designated the part of his lands near the Negro graveyard for a school and a church for the Negroes. He also entertained the Indians who came through his lands.[4] The Tonkawa often came to Salado Creek and camped near the springs. Robertson would always select a steer and send it to them to eat. He also invited the chief and others to eat in the family dining room. First, however, the family removed all of the furniture in the room except for two chairs placed on either side of the fireplace, one for Robertson and one for the chief. The other Indians squatted around and listened. Great bowls of stew would be brought in for everyone to eat while the Robertson women and children kept themselves cloistered upstairs.[5]

THE NEXT GENERATION

How did Elijah's children, the generation of Robertsons who grew up after the Civil War, respond to Reconstruction? At the college their father had founded for them, they all reaped the benefit of a better education than he himself had enjoyed. Luella Robertson graduated from Salado College in 1872, followed by Huling Robertson in 1876. Sterling, the eldest, went on to Tennessee University and a business school in New York. Walter went to the University of the South and then the Agricultural and Mechanical College at College Station. Randolph and Marion went to military colleges, the Virginia Military Institute and West Point, respectively. Marion and Sterling established the S. C. Robertson Dry Goods, Groceries, and General Merchandise store in San Angelo, Texas.

Luella and her sister Birdie were among the most educated and forthright women in Texas at the time.[6] In 1875 Luella made a two-hour presentation to the first reunion of Salado College on "The Mental Capabilities of Woman and a Plea for Her Higher Education," a passionate appeal for equal education for women.[7] Two years later she married Zachary Taylor Fulmore, a prominent lawyer. Birdie graduated from Salado College in 1886 and went on to Wesleyan Female College in Macon, Georgia, where she graduated summa cum laude in 1888. She married Cone Johnson, a state senator and later solicitor for the U.S. Department of State. She never had children; instead she immersed herself in political life. She was active in a dizzying number of women's clubs — the Daughters of the Republic of Texas, the United Daughters of the Confederacy, the Daughters of the American Revolution, and the Daughters of the War of 1812. She was on the board of regents of what is now Texas Woman's University and on the executive board of the Conference for Education in Texas. In 1912 she campaigned for Woodrow Wilson, moved to Washington, D.C., in 1914, when her husband was appointed to the U.S. Department of State, and by 1920 was active in the League of Women Voters. In 1920 she was elected a delegate to the Democratic National Convention, where she supported the Democrats' endorsement of the proposed women's suffrage amendment. The Texas delegation unanimously chose Birdie Johnson as the first Democratic national committeewoman from Texas.[8]

While the Reconstruction period was somewhat liberating for women, Robertson's sons, who were just coming into manhood, had a markedly different experience. They witnessed the outrage of Reconstruction. Since they belonged to a prominent family of the defeated and occupied South, their lives were threatened, and they responded to the violence with their own brand of aggression. They made it their custom to carry a .45 under their coats and use it on any man who challenged them. Maclin Robertson, my great-grandfather, was one of the fiercest and most impassioned of the Robertson boys, quick to take umbrage like his grandfather and never hesitant to fight back.

Maclin Robertson was born in the family home in Salado on July 26, 1860. The first child to be born there, he slept in a handmade walnut trundle bed until he was grown. He attended Salado College and at the age of twenty-one began raising stock and farming. Although just a young boy during the Civil War, Maclin was old enough during Reconstruction to be acutely aware of its injustices and the hard times it brought to the Texas economy. A superb horseman, he attended the Texas Military Institute west of Austin and then became a Texas Ranger at an early age, sometime in the late 1870s. According to my father, his grandfather Maclin expressed a resolute desire to rid the country of the lawless men who preyed on society, and he had plenty of opportunity to arrest those who committed crimes in the area around Salado. On one occasion, one of these men, just released from prison, arrived in Salado and announced that he was there to "kill Maclin Robertson." Word reached Maclin, who stated matter of factly that he did "not believe in keeping a man waiting," whereupon he rode his horse to the bridge, where he encountered the man galloping straight at him. They both drew guns. According to Maclin, he shot at the man's gun hand. The bullet glanced off a pair of Mexican cuff links made of heavy Mexican pesos and went straight through the man's heart. Since Maclin had quite a good aim, it is more likely that this story was one he developed later for his defense. In fact, there was a period of time in which he had to live on a remote part of the family farm because of, according to family lore, a "problem with justice."[9]

When his father, Sterling, died, Maclin inherited the Robertson home and lands and lived his entire life in the house that his father built. His specialty was breeding Tennessee horses and top-grade cattle on the 1,055-acre ranch. A stiff-necked Southern gentleman, he always wore a long, light-gray coat, stiff starched shirt and collar, a black string tie, a spotless conservative Stetson hat, and good leather boots, all kept in bandbox condition. Every day he dressed properly for the street. If he planned on going to town or leaving his property for any reason, he always carried a black .41 on a .45 frame under his long gray coat. Like his grandfather Sterling, he was resolute, steadfast, and unwilling ever to admit that he could err, and he enjoyed expressing his hatred of his enemies.[10]

My father vividly remembered how Maclin used to walk into the parlor and bellow, "Mary E.!!!" His daughter came from the dining room, her small son in tow. Maclin then lifted his arms and turned a complete circle. When she nodded approval, he marched out and rode away on Hal, a gallon jug swinging from his saddle for the mineral water he collected each day from the springs of the Salao. However, he never left home without his daughter's assurance that his gun was not showing under the coat. Although people were alarmed at the high rate of killings in Texas, Maclin considered it absurd for an ex-ranger who had plenty of enemies not to carry a gun. In any case, according to my father, "the Robertsons were of the opinion that they should not tolerate any remark that impugned their honor and being armed helped them accomplish that goal."[11]

Maclin, in particular, had a reputation for a short fuse. He had once had a disagreement with a tenant on his land, a man named McDaniel, who was a long, lanky, taciturn farmer with an aggressive manner. When the two men had words, McDaniel was sitting on his wagon seat facing Maclin on Hal. He rose in anger as if he were going to jump on Maclin but paused abruptly as he found himself face to face with the long black barrel of Maclin's .45. Robertson merely suggested, "Jump into hell."

In 1867 the Ku Klux Klan first sprang up in Bell County. According to George Tyler in his *History of Bell County,* "The Ku Klux Klan . . . was [founded] to protect society, to put the carpet-bagger and the scalawag out of business, to restore the Negro to his sober common sense and to readjust the country to normal social conditions."[12] Since they both grew up in Bell County, Tyler was well known to my father. According to him, Tyler represented the deep prejudice of the mythical Old South and was a man who, even seventy years later, had never adjusted to the changes brought by the Civil War. When my father was a young boy, the head of the Ku Klux Klan was the local doctor. In the Robertson house, the women referred to the doctor in tones of contempt, indicating they expected more of a man of that profession. The Ku Klux Klan had by then become an intimidating movement of "Jim Crowism," lynching, and racial hatred. My father remembered the terror of the Klan at this time. He said, "The Robertsons were strongly resented at the time because they were friends of the only black family, Brown and his wife Mary, who lived nearby, and had given them jobs. During the period when terror rode at night and was whispered [about] by the day, Alice Woods Robertson, Maclin's wife, sent for Mary Brown to come and stay in the house. Mary and my grandmother were close friends and Mary ate at our table, such was my grandmother's indifference to the conventions of the times. At this time a bomb was discovered under the wooden bridge that crossed the road at the Robertson gate. Maclin was incensed and declared, 'I do not care if they attack me, but when they attack my family that is different.'"[13] He remained a bitter enemy of the Ku Klux Klan for the rest of his life.

Up to my father's generation, both the Civil War and the Texas Revolution were fresh in people's memories, and he grew up on the stories of those times. The best friend of his youth was Thomas Gordon Saunders, great-grandson of the distinguished criminal lawyer Xenathon Boone Saunders, who had commanded a Confederate army company from Bell County and given the centennial address of American independence at the courthouse in Belton on July 4, 1876.[14] My father remembered the following story of a famous case that X. B. Saunders had won, one that summed up the sentiments of the times:

> It happened in Belton where a man had shot another in cold blood. These were lawless times, but the citizens were outraged especially since the dead man was a worthy citizen and the killer a one-armed worthless drunk.
>
> The killer immediately hired X. B. Saunders. The town's indignation was so great, no one would speak to Mr. Saunders, even his own family at his own dinner table. He just ate in silence and returned to the courthouse.
>
> The day of the trial arrived, and the jury was selected. A more hostile jury of local citizens could not be imagined. X. B. Saunders was perfectly calm and called his client as his first witness.
>
> Saunders: Will you state your name to the court?
>
> Nelson: "Ya suhr, don' mind if ah do. Ma name is Jacob Cain Nelson."
>
> Saunders: "Will you state where you were born, Mr. Nelson?"
>
> Nelson: "Yes, suh, I don' have nuttin' to hide 'bout that. I was born on the Little River 'bout 1842."
>
> Saunders: "Mr. Nelson, would you tell the court what you were doing and where you were on April 3, 1865?"
>
> Nelson: "Wal, I was Gin-l Lee's orderly, suh, and I was a holdin' Ol Traveler, the Gin-l's hoss."
>
> Saunders: "Tell us what happened while you were holding the horse of the peerless knight General Robert E. Lee."

Nelson: "Well, what happened was this. A Yankee cannon ball come headed straight at the Gin-1 and hit my arm and tore it off. I nearly bled to death but I tied up the arm with one of my suspenders and here I am, praise the Lord."

X. B. Saunders paused and walked to the jury box, addressing them in emotion-torn words. "Gentlemen," he said, his lips white and trembling. "You can hang this man if you wish, but you can't hang the hand that held General Robert E. Lee's horse."

The jury rose as one man, gave a Confederate yell, and voted "not guilty." [15]

It was the finest example of *argumentum ad verecundiam* (fallacy of irrelevant authority) in the legal history of Texas.

CHAPTER 19

The Macaroni Road Comes to Edna

eaving Houston with my sister Gayle and my daughter, Frankie, we hit Highway 59 going south to Jackson County. Along the highway we see Mexicans driving huge hauls of garage-sale items toward Mexico, where they make a good profit reselling the cast-offs of Houston's wealthy. Ninety miles southwest of Houston we turn south at Ganado, a small dusty town, population 1,915, located in the center of the Texas Rice Belt. Founded when the railroad was built, Ganado is now a sad and dying burg with one operational Mexican restaurant, called Estella's. Along the main street every other building is derelict. Driving through, I notice that the cross streets are all named after the families of the Alabama Settlement.

Just south of Ganado and the highway, the Navidad River and Mustang Creek, a branch of the Navidad, have been dammed to form Lake Texana, which flooded George Sutherland's 1830 land holdings, leaving only the site where his house and sugar mill existed. The latter was excavated by state archeologists, but nothing is left of the house. The cemetery, where we are headed, is intact. We turn onto a dirt county road edged with ramshackle houses and torn-up trailers so trashed out it is hard to imagine anyone lives there. Coming to the end of the road, we scramble out of the car and climb awkwardly over two rickety metal gates. A herd of Angus cows and their calves, believing we have come to feed them, start lowing and walking toward us. Frankie stops in her tracks, finding the lumbering cows somewhat menacing. Sensing their movement, the tenant farmer across the field looks up. Hoping that he will not shoot us, I wave vigorously to show that we are not trespassing. He quickly sizes me up—middle-aged female, urban but not afraid of mooing cows, probably a Sutherland come to see the cemetery. Satisfied, he waves back and goes on with his chores.

Following the fence line to the edge of the water, we come upon a copse of giant two-hundred-year-old live oak trees surrounding the cemetery. Several of them are double oaks, having sprouted long ago from side-by-side acorns. One has been topped where it was struck by lightning. All of them are gnarled, pitted with peeling bark, and graced with long branches that reach down to the ground, then rise languidly up toward the sky. The field under the trees is dotted with cow patties, compelling us to pick our way carefully toward the graves. The cemetery sits in a small fenced area, guarded by two enormous sentinel oaks. Inside we find George Sutherland's marker:

To the Memory of
Major George Sutherland,
A Soldier of the Texas Revolution and
A Participant in the victory won at San
Jacinto, April 21, 1836. Born in the state of Virginia
Jan 8, 1788. Emigrated to the Province of Texas
AD 1830. Departed this life, April 22, 1853

Next to him the graves of his wife, Frances Menefee Sutherland, their sons John Wiley Sutherland and Thomas Shelton Sutherland, Thomas's wife, Mary, and a handful of other relatives attest to the long use of the burying ground.

The Sutherland-Rogers families had none of the education or class status of the Robertsons, nor did they live the Robertsons' plantation life. Thus, they were also spared the deprivation and indignity of Reconstruction. Their goals in life, lofty by today's standards, were modest for the times—to be honest, hard-working men and women, faithful to each other and to God. When my great-grandfather Tommy Sutherland rode over to Sam Rogers's house in 1884 and asked for permission to marry Sam's fifteen-year-old daughter Lizzie, he was twenty-three years old, the same age as my other great-grandfather, Maclin Robertson. Their lives, however, were completely different.

Lizzie Rogers also did not have much in common with the politically minded, educated Robertson women, Luella and Birdie. When she married Tommy Sutherland at fifteen, she lived in relative isolation on a ranch west of San Antonio in Uvalde County. She bore fifteen children, seven boys and eight girls. Out in the ranching country her life was lonely. Work took up so much time that opportunities for visiting were rare. They were poor, often struggling to put food on the table for their large family. Lizzie and Tommy worked hard from sunup to sundown, and the only respite was church on Sunday, that is, when they could make it. It was an honest but arduous life.

As young women, Lizzie Laura and her sisters Minnie and Emma had grown up surrounded by the families of the Alabama Settlement. Lizzie was born on Christmas eve in 1868, Emma on September 1, 1871, and Minnie on April 8, 1874. As the youngest of the nine Rogers children, they spent their childhood on their parents' ranch, two miles from Ganado. Sam was fifty-eight when Lizzie was born and already hard of hearing, but the sisters admired their father and were very close to him. She and her sisters communicated with him mostly by writing. Often the sisters went fishing with him down by the Navidad and Sandies rivers, where they wrote messages to him in the sand.

They were close friends with the Sutherland boys and the girls, Belle and Frankie, and with a younger cousin, Francis L. Heard, whom they also called Frankie, which annoyed him no end. Frankie Heard remembered Uncle Sam and the Rogers girls fondly: "Mr. Sam Rogers, by the time I came along, was an old man or by the tokens of those days was old. He was hard of hearing, had a speaking [hearing] trumpet and was confined to his bed most of the time. We thought a great deal of him and we visited there quite often. The front door entered into a Hall, the back end of which was the dining room, which was the usual custom. On the east side was Mr. Sam's bedroom and library. There was a fireplace, and over the mantle there was draped a sword, and under that a long-barreled gun of some sort. In the yard, which was surrounded by a fence, the chickens kept the ground bare, not a trace of vegetation. On the bare ground there were several cannon balls, too heavy for the little lad to pick up, but they were round and would roll so they were something to play with."[1]

The schoolhouse they all attended served as a church on Sundays, that is, whenever a preacher came to town. The youngest sisters, Minnie and Emma, had no brothers at home, so early on they became adept at riding horses and rounding up the sheep on their father's ranch.[2] The ranch was about five miles from Texana, but when the railroad came through in 1880, Texana collapsed, and they moved to Edna.

The New York, Texas, and Mexican Railway was built to run from Wharton County near Houston all the way to Vera Cruz on the Gulf of Mexico. It was financed by Joseph Telfener, an Italian count who brought construction workers from his native Lombardy, and became known in Texas as the "Macaroni Road." Named after one of the count's daughters, the town of Edna was built as a railway station. Nine miles to the east of Edna, the small town of Ganado was built, named for the herds of cattle that the settlers had seen when they first arrived in the area. The train spelled the death of the first town of the region, Texana, which had thrived on the traffic in goods from Matagorda Bay. By 1881 everything came by rail. The tracks passed within a few hundred yards of the Rogers home, and Minnie and Emma made money by churning milk into buttermilk and selling it to the Italian workers for five cents a glass. Uncle Sam refused to ride the train because, he said, "it might run up against a stump." His daughters finally persuaded him to travel the eight miles from Ganado to Edna. After that, he never got on a train again.[3]

Today Ganado is a small, worn-looking, dusty town with practically no activity unless a car veers off Highway 59 in search of a Mexican restaurant, but in 1881 Ganado was a thriving community. When it was formed, the streets were named after the original families who came to Texas: Sutherland, Gayle, Devers, Menefee, Heard, and Rogers. During that era, the community was growing, and the train regularly came whizzing through. What the village needed, of course, was a telegraph office. Naturally, no one knew how use a telegraph, so a telegraphy school was set up in Ganado. According to Emma Rogers, "quite a bunch of us young folks attended just for the pleasure of having somewhere to go, as well as to get the education. I don't remember that many of us finished, but we had a good time and could write a dot-dash and a dot."[4]

In Ganado and Edna, socializing meant picnics, barbecues, and visits to each other's homes. Dances held in neighbors' homes were always exciting occasions, and one of the "old Negroes" would play a violin for the music. Weddings were big events, too. Emma remembered one wedding that took place on the other side of Sandy Creek: "My brothers Clark and Mack and my sister Lizzie and I were invited. After the wedding and a wonderful supper, the dance began and ran into the night, when it began raining. When the rain stopped and we were to go home, the creek had risen from bank to bank, and since those creeks don't run down in one day, we crossed on small boats that we paddled across, and our brother Frank met us with a wagon with quilts for covers. After sleeping in the back of the wagon on the way home, my eyes felt as big as saucers."[5]

In 1883 Emma went out west to Uvalde to live with her sister Rosa Witt, whose house was on the banks of the Nueces River. There she attended school and helped Rosa with the children. As an experienced horsewoman, she also helped her brother-in-law with the stock roundups. Difficult horses posed no problem for her. She remembered one frisky black horse that no one thought she could handle, but after a few runs around the field, she had him as tame as a lapdog. Not long after, her brother Clark came in a hack to take her to Uvalde to visit Lizzie, after which they returned by train to Ganado.

At this time, the Sutherland family in Jackson County consisted of the first Thomas Shelton Sutherland and his wife, Mary Elizabeth. They lived with his mother, Frances Menefee Sutherland, in the house that his father had built after theirs was burned to the ground by Mexican troops in 1836. They had eight children. One of the daughters, Talitha, who was born in 1849, married her cousin Francis Menefee White, the son of Jesse White and Mary Menefee White, original members of the Alabama Settlement. Another daughter, Frances (called Frankie), married Lucky Francis Wells, the son of Francis F. Wells, who had been Stephen Austin's doctor. Like the younger Robertson children of Elijah Sterling Clack Robertson, the four youngest Sutherland children were born during and after the Civil War: Thomas Shelton was born in 1861, William DePriest in 1865, Robert in 1867, and Lillian Belle in 1869. Their mother died when Willie was six, Robert four, and Belle two years old, so they were cared for by their father and older sister Talitha. She taught them their first grades in school, and their father's sister, Aunt Betty, took Lillian Belle and a cousin, Jennie Gayle, to live with her in Georgetown, Texas, where they could attend a better school. Later Willie was also sent to Georgetown, where he attended Southwestern University, but after a few semesters he came home to make a living.

Frankie Heard was especially taken with his cousin Belle, who was a beautiful girl, full of life and as popular as she was attractive. She met and married Hamilton Dixon, the sheriff of Wharton County and a close friend of the Heard family. Dixon's first wife had died, leaving him with a son to raise. One day he and his posse went in pursuit of a "desperado," whom they found hiding in a clump of trees. Dixon announced that it was his job to go in and arrest the outlaw and that the others should not risk their lives. He walked into the cluster of trees, was shot, and died at once. The widowed Belle would not remarry for a long time, but then she met a pharmacist named Edward Lee Faires, and they had a long married life together. Belle never lost her beauty. Even when she grew old, Frankie Heard described her as "fresh as a young woman."[6]

Both Thomas and Willie were shorter in stature than the other Sutherland boys, who were mostly six-footers like their grandfather George Sutherland. Lizzie Laura, the fifteen-year-old bride, thought that because they began raising and smoking tobacco when they were just boys, their growth was affected. Tobacco, like spirits and gambling, was certainly frowned on in their strictly Methodist family, but these were high-spirited boys. Because of their slighter build and no doubt because they were riding horses as soon as they could hold the reins, they were jockeys in the quarter-horse races held around Jackson County.

Like the other young men, Tommy and Willie also rode in ring tournaments, which were a type of riding contest. A line of poles would be set up with small iron rings hanging from each pole. As a boy rode along the line with a long, sharp lance, he would try to hook as many rings as possible. The boy who snagged the most rings won a gold crown, and the next two or three in line won wreaths. The boys in the tournament were called "knights" and dressed accordingly. Frank Rogers had a handmade uniform that was navy blue with gold strips down the pant legs and on the shirt. He wore a George

Washington hat with a large yellow feather waving in the center. For the top winner, the real reward came when he placed his crown on the head of a girl he favored, while the onlookers cheered and whistled. Lizzie Laura was crowned one year by Tommie Menefee, and in the next tournament Willie Sutherland won a wreath and presented it to a neighbor, Josie York. Emma recalls the following:

> I was about 14 at the time and I was really hoping he would call for me. Miss Josie York was a beautiful girl but when she went to Victoria to be her sister's brides-maid, she took pneumonia and was buried in the dress she was bridesmaid in.
>
> I married W. D. Sutherland four years later . . . on Dec. 8, 1889[. We were married] by Brother A. C. Biggs of the Methodist church, in the one room school house on Devers creek near Ganado, Texas. We were to be married after the ser-vices with no organ for music. We marched in unattended, whether it was time or not. They told me they were singing "Hark from the Tomb.". . . Then we drove in his new buggy with a large brown horse to my home where my mother had our Infare dinner [a reception]. Then to my husband's father's home where we lived for four years except for a few months when we stayed with my father and mother when our first child, John D. Sutherland was born on Oct. 20, 1890.[7]

On February 13, 1891, Sam Rogers died. At eighty-two, he had lived longer than most of the original settlers from Alabama, and now his three youngest daughters were married to the grandchildren of the man who led him to Texas. His death marked the end of the Alabama Settlement in Jackson County and the beginning of the next—and last—migration of their descendants as the twentieth century came into view.

CHAPTER 20

The Migration to Uvalde

T he migration of the large extended groups—grandparents, parents, aunts, uncles, children, grandchildren, and cousins—of the Sutherland, Rogers, White, Heard, and Menefee families from northern Alabama to what is now Jackson County, Texas, was a well-organized move, undertaken in successive waves that brought them all to Texas in 1830 and 1831. Careful coordination was necessary partly because they were going to a "wild" area, a place where they had to construct their lives and community completely from scratch—build houses, clear fields, and plant crops while they lived on deer meat and survived for at least year.

The next migration of the descendants of those groups to the Texas Hill Country was the last one undertaken as an extended family. Beginning in 1892 some of the offspring of the Alabama settlers moved to Uvalde over a period of several years. The relocation was undertaken by individual families who were closely related and intermarried as before, but without the overriding authority of the patriarchs and matriarchs of the last generation. This was a group of siblings who decided to make a new life in a new area where they could become ranchers. They were going to a remote, rough country, but it was not "wild," as Texas had been when the first migration took place. There were roads and railroads, and they would find towns where folks would rent them lodgings or take them in until they built their own homes. The first sibling to migrate was Rosa Rogers and her husband, Frank Witt. Then the three Rogers sisters who were married to three Sutherland brothers followed. Several cousins such as Willie White, Shelton Wells, and Mack Rogers (a brother of the four Rogers girls) also joined them.

Nueces Canyon is in the Hill Country in Uvalde County, a rocky, dry cedar brush area that barely supported cattle but was perfect for Angora goats. The settlers were drawn to the region by rumors that one could make a living by raising goats. A friend in Jackson County told them, "All you need is a Mexican goat herder for $10 a month and beans, and he takes care of the herd, defends them from theft by man or beast, and the flocks increase. You sell the mohair in the nearby town of Uvalde."[1] Like many stories of the promised land, reality did not turn out to be so easy.

Rosa and Frank Witt moved to Uvalde in 1892, then Willie and Emma came a year later, bringing with them Emma and Rosa's widowed mother, Mary, and a nephew of Willie Sutherland, Willie Lee White. In the town of Uvalde they stopped and bought two beds, a small kitchen stove, four dining chairs, and a small kitchen cabinet. After arriving at the ranch, they made a dining table out of lumber and a large box to hold the groceries and used the kitchen cabinet for their clothes. Their neighbors generously gave them a few hens so they could have eggs to eat. These hens' eggs were a major part of their diet and, of course, highly valued. One day while cooking, Emma heard a squawk and saw a large hawk trying to carry off one of her precious chickens. Without hesitation she grabbed a gun and shot the predator out of an old live oak tree in the yard. Since the bird was not dead, she knocked it in the head with a stick. That hawk was not going to take food from her children.

The Witt group bought 2,080 acres of land through which the Nueces River ran for a mile and a half. The people who sold the land to them had been their neighbors in Jackson County. Willie had ranched with his father since 1885, running horses, cattle, and mules, but in Uvalde he began breeding and raising Angora goats, Delaine sheep, and cattle.[2] Later they built a house that had two front rooms, a shed room that was used as a kitchen, and a small bedroom. From a well in the backyard they drew their water. When they first arrived, their son, John D., was two and a half years old, but the next six children were born in this house: Sam, Robert, Laura Mae, Gayle, and the twins Virgil and Viola. Gayle and Robert eventually went deaf like their grandfather Sam Rogers. In all, Willie and Emma had eleven children.

Although Uvalde was supposed to be a more healthful place to live than fever-ridden Jackson County, all kinds of diseases were still lurking. When five of the children caught whooping cough, Emma put them all in one bedroom and burned a vapo-cresolene lamp all night. Later the family expanded the structure until it was a ten-room house. During the construction, Emma cooked for two carpenters and a painter and fed them goat meat, cornbread, pinto beans, and ginger cake. They had no other food except coffee and buttermilk.

Then, in October 1895, Lizzie and Tommie decided to join their siblings in Uvalde County. Tommie went ahead, and Lizzie came by train with their four living children: Tom (age 8), George (age 4), Mary (age 3), and John (age 2). Baby Sam had died the year before. The whole family stayed with Willie and Emma. It was wrenching for Lizzie to leave her family and home in Jackson County, where she not only knew everyone but was also related to them.

The two families, Rogers and Sutherland, used kinship terms for each other, never referring to each other as in-laws. Lizzie called Mary Sutherland (her husband's mother) Mama and her husband's father Papa. Her sisters-in-law she referred to as sisters and her husband's aunt as her own aunt. This practice felt natural to her since she had grown up with her husband's sister Belle, whom she was particularly close to and who was only one year younger than she, just as she had known her husband all his life. When Lizzie got to Uvalde, she immediately wrote Belle the first letter of what was to become a long correspondence between the two women, one that presents us with a glimpse into the lives of these women through their own words:

Dear Belle,
We arrived here yesterday morning—will go up this morning to the Ranche [sic]. I write you first because I neglected to get the Bank Book that Papa [Thomas Shelton Sutherland] was so kind to get for me. It is in Sister Frank's [Frankie Sutherland Wells] top bureau drawer. I wish you would take care of it until I notify you where to send it. As soon as we get home and find out where we get our mail from I will write to Mama [Lizzie's widowed mother, Mary Evans Rogers] and Papa [Lizzie's husband's father, Thomas Shelton Sutherland]. I am very sorry I forgot the book. It may possibly be in my trunk, but I have no remembrance of taking it out of the drawer.

If I had not met Mr. Pervance's mother I don't think I would have been able to get to the train at all that night with three sleepy children, but she took Mary for me. George went along crying to go to sleep and I carried John.

We all have very bad colds. Tommie [Lizzie's husband] is very near sick. I believe he has a pretty bad case of Catarrh. I have nettle rash all over me.

Tommie saw the man yesterday that once owned the Ranche [sic]. He told Tommie he was sorry that he carried horses there, that it was too rough for horses, but a splendid hog ranche [sic]. And that they made good crops every year. They had never failed, but it is very rough, and I am afraid we have no road to Utopia. I guess we will get in there and stay until the year is out. I can tell more about it after I get there.
Your Aff. sister Lizzie [3]

It was much more difficult than she had expected to get out to the ranch they had found in Utopia, Texas. For one thing, there was no road to the house, and it was not really livable for a woman with four children: "November 12, 1895 . . . Tommie says the house at Mr. Box's really is not fit to live in, but we will have to put up with it. It is a rent house and I suppose you have some idea about rent houses out here as you saw Rosey's [Rosa Witt, her sister], although I think it is some better than that."[4]

Although Lizzie tried to be cheerful about Uvalde, she was full of doubts about living there and seemed happiest when family came to visit: "Well,

I suppose you have heard that Shelton [Shelton Wells, a cousin] has at last gotten here. I have just asked him how he liked it out here. He says 'Oh, well, I am very well satisfied, but if I had a million I would not buy land here.' So you all can have no fear of his investing out here."[5]

Shelton Wells was, according to my father, "a somewhat unusual bachelor." Unlike the men around him who wore the same work clothes to town that they used for handling livestock and doing outdoor chores, Shelton was a natty dresser. Moreover, he did not ride horses for work; rather, he raced them to bet on their speed. But while the men found him strange, Lizzie was grateful for the presence of a loyal kinsman who would hold her baby while she was busy with the household chores.[6]

Meanwhile, the main problem for the men was to round up the stock they had bought. It had rained every day since they had come to Uvalde, and Tommie had to ride his horse in the downpour to find the animals: "Tommie found 26 head of his stock and said he saw so much sign [hoofprints] he supposed the others were there. He has rheumatism a little in his wrist tonight. I suppose it is from being out in the damp weather."[7]

The men hunted as well, not only for deer to eat but also to eliminate the pumas, which liked to feed on the goats: "Tommie went hunting with Mr. Box and killed a young panther. Mr. Box has killed four panthers and three catamounts (or leopard cats I should have said) since we came."[8]

The family had to abandon the idea of renting Mr. Box's house at Utopia, partly because of its rundown condition and partly because the land was not very good for farming. After two months, they finally leased the Threadgill place, which was one mile from Willie and Emma's home in Nueces Canyon. Then another complication arose. The Threadgill widow had recently married a man named Atkins and was planning to move to the Atkins ranch and rent her own home to the Sutherlands, but her grown sons were unhappy with this arrangement:

Montell, Texas
December 3, 1895
Dear Belle:
Well, you supposed we were in our house at Mr. Box's but you were wrong. We are still at Willie's, but will move tomorrow to the Threadgill place about a mile below here. We will be cramped as there are only two small rooms, but Tommie says it is much warmer than the house at Mr. Box's. I am very anxious to get moved. "Be it ever so humble there is no place like home," even if it has to be a rented one. Some of our furniture has been setting out doors since we first came. We have had it covered with an old tent cloth of Willie's which has protected it some.

Tommie has all his horse stock on the Atkins place which is much more con-
venient for him to look after. Old Mr. Atkins left here about two months ago—
told his wife [Mrs. Threadgill] he could not live with her boys [the Threadgill
boys]. I think he had no objections to the youngest one, but the oldest cursed him
once. He wanted his wife to go with him or told her if she would come to him he
would be glad to have her and take care of her the rest of her life. It has been two
weeks since Tommie leased the place and we thought she could have moved long
ago, but she had first one excuse and then another, but yesterday the mystery was
solved by Mr. Atkins coming for his wife. This is their land we have leased and
of course he did not want to live on their place. When he was married he dressed
the boys up and told them now they had nothing to do but go to school and get
stove wood and in speaking to Ed Witt about it afterwards, he said "And do you
know, they never got a stick of wood."

Write soon to your affectionate sister, Lizzie
P.S. You can send The Progress *[newspaper] now.*[9]

The ranch life was constant hard labor for the men as well as the women.
Lizzie not only had the children to care for and food to cook, but she also
made all of the family's clothes herself. Even the sheets and pillowcases were
handmade. Sewing took place in the fall and again in the spring. Because
the project was such a huge task, a woman needed another woman to help
with the sewing. In her letters Lizzie notes that, without her mother and sister Minnie to help with the task, it was a daunting job. The women also had
to do the washing and ironing. Washing was done on a rubbing board, and
since Lizzie was pregnant with her sixth child, she could not do the rubbing.
Her husband, Tommie, helped with the rubbing while she rinsed and hung
the clothes to dry, but he was not always available to assist. The children were
small, but they all helped, too. Lizzie still called Jackson County "the old
home place":

The children are a good deal of help to me. They clean up the dishes real nice.
I am trying to get me a Mexican girl or boy, but don't know that I will succeed.
I will need one very badly after a little [referring to her pregnancy]. By the way,
did you ever send The Progress?

Tommie says tell you to draft that house again for us. He might go to the Di-
vide [an area west of Uvalde] and want to build a new house this fall. As well
as I remember, it was two rooms 20 x 20, a Hall on one side, bathroom, closets,
pantry, kitchen and gallery that extended almost around the house. You might
draw several then we can take our choice as I am satisfied Tommie will want to
build a place of his own by fall.

There is a very cheap place fifty miles from here that would be much better for his stock and more healthy, but we hate to go. It is a long ways from there to any place except two or three near neighbors. The railroad fare would be less from Kerrville than it is from Uvalde. Home, I mean.

Well, I must close. Love to all. Tommie or I one will write to Papa [Thomas Shelton Sutherland] in a few days. Write soon.

Aff your sister, Lizzie [10]

As her pregnancy advanced, Lizzie spoke to her sister-in-law about it, but only in oblique terms. The etiquette of the period did not allow for direct discussion of such a delicate topic, and there was a complete taboo on the topic of sex. In the self-sacrificing mode of the women of her time, she mentions all of her family's health concerns before referring to her own:

Dear Belle,

We are all very well. George has a bad cold and John has had sour stomach for the last two days and does not look well. I suppose it is the chills wearing off. Mary is well, with the exception of teething. Tommie looks better than ever before—weighs 140 pounds. He has gained twenty one pounds since we came here. Little Tom has also gained six pounds. He carries pecans in his pockets and you seldom see him without he is eating, if not pecans it is biscuit. I feel as well as could be expected. I believe I have suffered less than I ever did. That is, when I did my own work. I suppose I am under obligations to Mitchella Compound, a medicine I am using, which is very highly recommended for such as that.

Tommie planted me a nice patch of oats for my chickens. They are growing nicely and will soon be ready to turn the chickens on. I guess I will have a poor chance to raise chickens or turkeys this spring as the very time they will need attention I will not be able to give it to them [when the baby comes]. I have only set two hens and I don't think one of them will hatch to do any good. Tom is delighted that we have at last succeeded in getting some guineas and turkeys.

Tommie is very busy with his goats, kidding. Has only fifteen but have been coming but two or three days. From now on for a good while they will be coming every day. He has four pair of twins in the fifteen. The children are overjoyed to go to the pen when their papa goes to attend to them. John claims most of them, I think, and everything else. Miss Mai Etheridge sent me a nice pone of light bread yesterday and John claimed it right away. Several time he asked me for bread and I would start to give him a biscuit when he would hallo: "Mai's bread."

Three of the neighbors came in and spent the evening with me yesterday. Mrs. McCaughan and Dollie, Mrs. Humphrey and Mrs. Luce. It just so happened that they all came at once. They have been real good to come to see me considering that I have been able to visit very little since I came.

We received The Progress *this evening for the first time.*

Little Tom will have his hands full attending to the kids [baby goats] while his Papa is gone.

Well, I don't know what else I can write. It is time to have prayers so I must close. All send love to all. Write soon to your aff sister, Lizzie Sutherland.

Tell Sister Talitha [Sutherland White] I will write to her in a few days.[11]

Life was a series of chores that started in the morning and ran until night-fall, only to start again the next day. Tom (Thomas Shelton Sutherland III), the eldest son, was only eight years old, but he had little time for education because he was always watering the horses, working at the goat camp, bringing in wood, or washing dishes. The girls cleaned house, washed potatoes, and minded the babies. It was all Lizzie could do to cook for so many people, care for the children, and wash and iron everyone's clothes. The family saw few people and were lonely and homesick for their relatives and friends back in Jackson County. Lizzie wrote of getting "the blues" and noted that her husband, Tommie, also got the blues. With no schools and no social life, they relied completely on their relatives for any conversation.

A month later, March 15, 1896, Lizzie gave birth to a little girl, her seventh child. She now had five living children, and they were running out of names. They named the baby after Lizzie's sister Minnie and Tom's sister Belle: "We still cling to family names but have combined the last one on each side (that is, in age). Guess we will call the baby for you and Minnie—the full name Minnie Bell. Enclosed you will find a lock of your namesake's hair."[12]

In June 1896 Tom's father, Thomas Shelton Sutherland, came to visit:

Dear Belle:

Well, Papa is here. We were very glad to see him, but sorry to see him so weak. He has been in the bed ever since he came. He was taken sick on the train with bowel complaint. When he got to Uvalde he did not make any effort to get off the train. Willie went in and got him up and off. Went to Sansoms and Papa laid down on the bed to rest. We were in town when he came. We went and spoke to him but he did not seem to notice us or know who we were. Along in the evening Emma and I were in the room and he asked if we had all seen Johnnie. I told him Johnnie was not there. I suppose he thought where he was by my voice, and he asked where is Lizzie. I said, here I am. So from that on he knew everything he said. I did not know his brain was addled, but it was.

We are all well. Minnie Bell is a perfect beauty to me. You may know as I think she is very much like her Papa and you. Well, today is wash day. Tommie [her husband] does the rubbing [on a rubbing board] while I rinse.

All send love to all. Do not be uneasy about Papa. He is doing all right now. Write soon.

Your aff. Lizzie [13]

Not long after this, they received the sad news that Frankie Sutherland Wells, Tommie's sister, had died suddenly of kidney failure. Shelton Wells, Frankie's son, was boarding with Mrs. Box at the time. Lizzie wrote Belle the following news:

Mrs. Box told Emma she never saw a more gloomy, restless mortal than Shelton was the day after he heard of his mamma's death, seemed like he did not know what to do with himself. I know Mr. Wells, children and yourself all miss Sister Frank very much and I can only offer the consolation that Georgie did to myself. I had read the telegram—gave it to Tom to take to his Uncle Willie—and had sat down on the bed. Georgie said, "Mamma, what is the matter?" I said, "Georgie, Aunt Frankie is dead and we will never see her again in this world." He said, "But Mamma, we will see her in Heaven." Georgie is a strange child. I don't think he would care if he should die. Very often in having prayers in the morning I will talk to them about the Bible and the precious promises therein, and he remarked to me the other morning, "Mamma, why don't God take us to Heaven? We have been here long enough," then he said, "Whenever I am bad, you read me that Book," meaning the Bible, and he told me he loved Jesus. But they are not always glad when I have prayers. Sometimes they are playing and will say now, Mamma, don't read a long chapter, read Psalms, when they want me to finish quickly.

Love to all. Write soon. Your aff. sister, Lizzie [14]

In 1897 Tom bought a ranch near Vance, and that October Tom's brother John Wiley, who lived in Jackson County, was killed when his wagon overturned. Stunned by the death, they moved back to Jackson County for a few months to stay with Tom's father and family. According to Frankie Heard, "John was a great favorite with many of the kin-folks and just about the time he reached his majority he was accidentally killed. He was driving a span of rather spirited horses, hitched to a wagon and in some manner the horses became scared, started to run and before they could be controlled, had overturned the wagon and the fall killed John instantly. He was laid to rest in the family cemetery, on the green hill side across the swag from home, and his was the largest funeral I remember attending." [15]

When they came back to Nueces Canyon, they bought the Riverside Ranch, with its one small log cabin, with money they had borrowed from Tom's father. The children lived in tents. The oldest son, Tom III, was now ten, old enough to provide the extra labor for his father. The oldest girl, Mary, had to help her mother with the children and the housework. That year they were so poor they could not send any Christmas gifts to their relatives or get presents for their children. Lizzie wrote the following:

Emma and Willie spent Thanksgiving with us and instead of turkey and pump-kin pie we had duck and sliced potato pie. If the weather is good we will eat dinner with them Xmas and they with us New Year. Xmas is most here again— another year numbered with the past. I hope we have profited thereby and are more ready today to meet our Maker than ever before. Let us strive to live very near to Him who is always near us.

We would like to be able to make a good many presents, but are financially embarrassed, which I guess is one of our many crosses, and I hope we may be able to bear it patiently.

I had hemorrhage of kidneys, suffered a great deal. Am a great deal better, but not well at all, and my physician tells me I can never get well and drink the well water in this country. So the very first money we get will be used in an under-ground cistern. You know, I had an attack of that kind two years ago at Home. I am now taking medicine, drinking boiled water, and hope to soon get well.

I am trying to teach the children a little which, though very little, takes most of my time in the evening. Mary has learned her large letters in the last few days and is now learning the small ones. George can learn as fast as Mary and has a splendid memory, but does not apply himself as well. I find it harder to teach Tom than any because he does so many jobs such as watering horses, going to the goat camp, bringing in wood, washing dishes and various other things too numerous to mention. The others also have something to do. I asked Mary what I must tell you and she said tell her I clean the lamps. Yes, cleaning lamps, dusting bureau, table, machine, etc. is her work of morning which she does real well. George minds the baby while I am in the Kitchen in the morning and then he washes the potatoes and puts them in the stove, then brings in an armful of wood. John brings in wood which is about all he does. Tom helps clean up in morning if his Papa hasn't him otherwise engaged. And Minnie Bell—well, she makes us attend to her, is what she does. They help a great deal for little children and yet they make a great deal of work.

This is a right pretty place and as good a place as you can find in this coun-try. The house—you can't conceive how rough it is and open. We are anxious to improve it some, but like all people without money, we have to wait. It is so far from market is one great drawback.[16]

Another disadvantage was the loneliness. The ranch at Vance was so far from the nearest neighbors and Lizzie's relatives that it was difficult to socialize. Making a visit in person was the only way to communicate with others, but the never-ending labor the ranch required meant that there was little time left for calling on people. Lizzie depended almost entirely on her correspondence with Belle to give her a chance to talk with another woman. Although opportunities for social calls were extremely limited, Lizzie saw it as selfish that she did not go visiting more often:

> *Emma [her sister] and Willie came up two weeks ago and spent two nights with us—the second time they have visited us here. Rosey [her sister] has not been up at all. She has been busy moving. I returned two calls last week and went to Willie's Christmas—only three times I have been off the place since we came here. I would like to return one or two other's calls, but parties live so far over rough roads I can hardly get off I am afraid. I dislike to see people live to themselves and hate to appear selfish, but I have so many other little duties and things to take up my time that there is little time to spare in visiting. The children help a great deal, especially Tom [her eldest son]. I could not do without him. But there is so much to do; five men to cook for besides myself and children. Two of them are the Mexican herders. They clean the dishes at night. They will only be here about a month—came in to shear and kid. This is a very busy time with the men folks.*
>
> *They have just finished planting and Mexicans are coming this evening to begin shearing tomorrow. Will have young kids coming by the middle of the week. There is not much rest on a goat Ranche [sic]. Still, I don't mean to be complaining. I get along comparatively well with the work, but you know where there is breakfast to get, house to clean, baby to attend to, dishes to wash, dinner to get and I always try to find time to have prayers with the children in the morning so in the evening I can hear a few lessons from Tom that by the time all that is done the day is pretty well spent, to say nothing of numerous other things to be done.*
>
> *George and Mary say a lesson now and then when I have time to teach them. They are spelling in three letters such as net, get, boy, eyes and John almost knows his letters. I think they would all learn fast if I had the time to teach them. Hope I can soon. I don't believe in letting children get to be 10 or 12 years old before they begin with their books. Tom, now, is entirely too much interested in his Papa's business to be much interested in books. Still he studies very well when the men are away from the house.*
>
> *We are all right homesick and Tommie says we can think about going Home this summer, but I can't see where we are to get the money myself, even if we*

should go in the hack. I want to see you all very bad, but I think sometimes that I don't want to go back there until I can stay for I know if I were to go back I would hate worse than ever the separation. Of course, this country is best for our business, but it can not compare with [Jackson County] in any way except for goats and hogs and, of course, it is natural that we should rather live there. . . . Tommie is just as homesick as can be. I know he tries to keep it from me just like I do from him, but he knows it too well. He tells me I think more about it than I want to acknowledge, which I guess I do, for it does no good to let him know it. Just makes him feel bad because we could not go. As long as no one has the "blues," so to speak, but myself I can stand it, but I can't bear to see him get low spirited. I always think whenever he seems the least that way that I will try to be cheerful no matter what the circumstances are because I think Tommie hates very bad having his family out here where we have so little association. It is worse here than at Montell. It is not so much homesickness as it is tired of the sameness of things which you know anyone gets tired of and feels occasionally like seeing good old fashioned Homefolks.

Love to all, Your aff. sister, Lizzie [17]

Loneliness, hard work, a lack of money, lots of children to feed, no school nearby for the youngsters—these were difficult times, as arduous perhaps as when their forebears first came to Texas. But Lizzie and her sisters Emma, Minnie, and Rosey were strong women who relied on their family, their Methodist religion, and their sense of self to make a life. That they undertook another migration from Jackson County to Uvalde to start a new life demonstrates that they had the same grit as their ancestors.

CHAPTER 21

Getting an Education

The ranch families in Uvalde were meat eaters. Putting food on the table meant raising and butchering animals and curing the meat. Tommie and Lizzie raised cattle and goats for sale, horses for working the ranch, and hogs for food. The hogs ran loose on the range until fall, when the barrows were penned and fed corn in preparation for butchering. Their son John Lee described the process:

Usually Papa butchered eight or ten hogs for our pork supply. Butchering took place during cold weather and all members of the family took part. We ground sausage, made lard, laid outside shoulders and hams to cool out before packing in salt and then curing by smoking. We usually used the loins fresh. After the lard was rendered I had the job of making soap with the crackling and lye. Mama supervised the project. Some of the sausage was used fresh but most of it was cured along with the ham, bacon and shoulders. Papa would also butcher a fat cow in the fall and pickle the meat. During the spring and summer he and neighbors would take time about butchering calves for fresh meat. We also butchered goats. We were meat eaters.

We not only ate meat but vegetables and fruit. Papa bought corn, tomatoes by the case and dried apples, peaches prunes apricots and raisins by the 25 pound box. Sugar and dry beans by the 100 lb sack—also coffee which was green and had to be parched. We had a good garden and orchard from which we got most of our fresh vegetables and fruit.

Goats and cattle were the main source of our income though we had income from pecans that were gathered from the native trees that grow along the Nueces. We had our goats sheared twice per year. One time during shearing Marty went for the mail and brought the paper to Papa. The paper—The Semi-Weekly Express—had an account of the assassination of President McKinley. The shearing crew gathered around and listened while Papa read the account.

Christmas was a time we looked forward to, for all the relatives would gather for the day at one of the homes. We would play games and eat. What a feast we would have—turkey, ham, venison, and beef with all that goes with it (except liquor of any kind). Mama would begin preparing by baking her fruitcake by

Thanksgiving. Other cakes and pies were baked during the week before Christ-mas. Christmas was the one time of year that we had apples and oranges. Papa would go to Uvalde and buy a box each of apples oranges and dried cluster rai-sins. He also bought nuts—English walnuts, Brazil nuts and milked candy. The children usually got one toy.[1]

Now that the children had grown up so much, the biggest problem was finding schooling for them. School was not free; it cost five dollars per month per child, an amount the Sutherland family could not afford, so they hired a series of girls from Uvalde who had just completed high school to come and teach the children at home. The first years in the canyon, they attended a school with Willie and Emma's children near their home. However, this was a long way for the kids to go, and with the school term only four months long, the family decided to find a tutor to live with them just to teach their growing family. One of the teachers, Hettie Humphreys, came to instruct the children and to help sew clothes for them. The teachers lasted only one year—that was as much of the isolated life and hard work as they could take.

In 1898 the family made a long wagon trip back to Jackson County to visit their relatives. The journey was a costly one. It meant the loss of their goat kids since they had to have the goats looked after by a Mr. Arnold, and he took the kids that were born: "Well, Mr. Arnold is to let Tommie have his goats back and while we feel that Mr. Arnold has been more than well paid for taking care of the goats, we feel that we are lucky to get them back. We do not get them until after the first of October as he will not shear before then. He, Mr. Arnold, is to pay us no interest, get the increase (and Aubrey said our goats raised more kids in proportion to number than Mr. Arnold's); he gets all the spring clip of hair. We are to get half of the fall clip."[2] Living on the edge as they did, this situation put a financial burden on them, and they had to rely on the food they grew and the deer they hunted: "Tommie has walked out into the pasture to see if he can kill a deer. I hope he will as it is right hard to get something to eat. Hope we may be able to sell our crop there soon so that we can pay Papa. I do not like to be in debt. Our money has about run out. With much love from all to all, I am your aff. sister, Lizzie."[3]

When the school year began in 1899, Lizzie and the children moved to Uvalde so the children could attend classes, and the three brothers, Tom, Willie, and Bob Lee, built a house on the Riverside Ranch. Because the river water caused so many intestinal problems, they made a well by digging about thirty feet and then blowing up the rock with blasting powder. Even then, they still could not get water, so they selected a different site for the new house, this time close to water.

In the summer of 1901 they moved into the house, which was based on the design their sister Belle had sent them in 1896. It had a large kitchen and two bedrooms, one of which was at least twenty feet by twenty feet, to hold all of the children. A bathroom adjoined the kitchen, and a porch wrapped around two sides of the house. Later they added a living room, two more bedrooms, and a large hall, which also served as a bedroom with a folding bed. Across the front of this wing was another wide veranda. The house had two fireplaces, one in the living room and one in a bedroom.[4] This was their first real home.

The family joined the Methodist Church in Montell, which held services in their home until a small church was built. According to their son John Lee,

Edwards, Kinney and Uvalde Counties were sparsely settled so people took advantage of every opportunity to get together for any and every social event. We went to church in Barksdale or Montell—most of the time in Montell for the other Sutherlands, Witts, Merriweathers and later the Mack Rogers attended church there. The Sutherlands and Merriweathers were Methodist. The Witts and Rogers were Baptist. Most of the other families were Episcopalians though there were a few Presbyterians and Church of Christ people. It made no difference. All went to church for no denomination held services over once a month and it was arranged for each to have a Sunday. When it was time for the Methodist, Baptist and Church of Christ and later the Presbyterian to preach there were two services and dinner on the ground. Everyone spread the food on a long table. I marvel when I think of what our mother would do to get her family to church which was 8 or 9 miles away. She would prepare a large basket of food including at least three pies (usually pineapple custard) and get the small children dressed for church. Of course the older children helped for we were taught to take care of ourselves and help the younger. As I mentioned, most everyone went to church. Not only was it church but a social gathering for after the morning service people gathered on the grounds to visit and get all the available news. During the service Papa sat at one end of the bench and Mama at the other with the children in between. There was no talking nor squirming.[5]

The church they built is still used today in the Montell community. Sunday was an important day. The women prepared food and their clothes on Saturday, and then on Sunday morning the women and girls piled into the surrey, and, with the men and boys on horseback, they traveled to the little church to attend the morning service. There they spread out their baskets of food for the lunchtime picnic, attended the afternoon service, and then went home late in the afternoon to do their ranch chores. The Methodist pastor, A. T. White, lived with them, sleeping in the large bedroom they called the boys' room.

Other people occupied the big bedroom, including a regular boarder, Shelton Wells, his uncle Rob Wells, and Nelson Rogers, a relative of Lizzie's. People stopped in frequently and stayed for the night. Lizzie wrote the following to Belle: "Shelton says we have more company here than any place he has struck in this country, but it's mostly people who know Tommie stopping in to stay overnight. You see we live just half way between Uvalde and Rocksprings, 38 miles to each place and are known all along the road. It's also known we have a large house and it is very convenient for them to stop."[6]

John Lee commented later in life that "Our house seemed headquarters for all the preachers—Methodist and Baptist. I remember Brother Gibbons, Brother and Sister Keith, Brother Knox who had been a Confederate soldier, Brother Barr, Brother A. J. White, Brother Stovall, Kickapoo Brown or Buckalew who had been captured by the Indians and carried to Mexico. Reverend Abe Mulkey, a prominent evangelist, spent a night at our house and later sent some sheet music to Mary,

> *Last night as I lay on the prairie*
> *Looking up at the stars in the sky.*
> *I wondered if ever a cowboy*
> *Would drift to the sweet by-and-by.*[7]

It had been four years since the last visit to their relatives in Jackson County, so in the summer of 1903 Lizzie and Tom, with Willie and Emma, packed up their hoard of children in wagons and embarked on the overland trip back home. According to John Lee,

> *The older boys rode in a wagon with baggage and camp equipment and supplies. Our parents, the girls and young children rode in hacks or carriages. It was on this trip that I became acquainted with "Sweet Dreams" a concoction to ward off mosquitoes. Uncle Willie had a bottle which he used one night when we camped near Hondo Creek. The mosquitoes swarmed around us in spite of sweet dreams. A night or two later we camped near San Pedro Springs then on the outskirts of San Antonio. There were only a few Mexican jacalas [huts] scattered about. We visited the Alamo where our great uncle William DePriest Sutherland died with the other heroes on March 6, 1836. On our way back from the Alamo George was missed and was found on Houston St. looking at an automobile, the first any of us had ever seen. After leaving San Antonio we traveled through pioneer country until we reached Edna and the homes of Uncle Frank Rogers, then on to Ganado to visit the R. L. Sutherlands, the Mack Rogers, Clark Rogers and other relatives. After several days we went back to Edna and visited Aunt Talitha and Uncle Frank White. We also visited Aunt Bell and Uncle Lee Faires in Edna.*[8]

Russell Ward, a nephew of the three Rogers women, described the emotion of the parting: "All of us regretted to see them leave. It was a sight I shall never forget. The feeling of all was most intense, and all eyes were wet as we waved goodbye."[9] John Lee Sutherland described the journey home: "We went back home by way of Cuero, San Antonio and Hondo. When we got to Hondo the rains came and Papa and Uncle Willie put Mama and Aunt Emma and the younger children on the train for Uvalde. We arrived during a heavy rain and went to the Keith home and stayed until the men arrived two days later. It was still raining when we left for the canyon and home. In Benson Flats the mud was so bad that we had to walk by the wheels and poke the mud from between the spokes. It was with great relief and joy that we finally arrived home."[10]

In 1904 the family was headed for a Fourth of July picnic in Barksdale, when they suffered a terrible tragedy. The women drove ahead in buggies carrying the food, while the young boys raced each other on their horses. Thirteen-year-old George, the son who spoke of going to heaven when Aunt Frankie died, was racing his double first cousin William when his horse shied. His head hit a branch that was sticking out in the road, and he was killed instantly. For three days Lizzie sat in a rocking chair on the porch singing to herself the Methodist hymns "Rock of Ages" and "How Great Thou Art."

ROBERT AND MINNIE SUTHERLAND

Robert and Minnie's first three children, Robert Lee, Bettie, and Frank, were born in the "old home place" in Jackson County. Then they moved to Ganado, where Robert Lee worked in the livery stable business. The next three children, Rogers, Faires, and Mary, were all born in Ganado. In 1900 Robert Lee Sutherland and Minnie Rogers, as well as Frank and Herman White, Thomas Menefee, and S. M. and Nettie Rogers, were counted in the Ganado census.

It was not until 1905 that Robert Sutherland and Minnie Rogers moved to Nueces Canyon. By this time Bob's health was bad, and they felt it important to join their relatives—his brothers and her sisters—in Uvalde. They had visited several times before deciding to move there. Once they paid a visit when their son Rogers was eight or nine months old and unable to digest anything. They tried giving him goat's milk, but even that did not help. At last they fed him roasted sweet potato, and he was fine after that.

In August they shipped all of their household goods, as well as their horses, chickens, and ducks, on the train. It was one of those searingly hot Texas

Augusts when the temperature does not drop below one hundred degrees. When they arrived, they quickly let the chickens and ducks out to get water, but it was too late. The fowl flopped over in the heat, and the ground was immediately covered with dead poultry.

Robert and Minnie bought a house in Montell and sent for their own teacher, Mamie Jackson, from Ganado, who lived with them and taught the youngsters in a one-room, one-teacher school. Most of the teachers were just out of Uvalde High School and were working mostly for the experience. None of them lasted for more than a year. Emma boarded the teachers, one of whom gave music lessons to her children. Eventually a high school was organized in Montell.

The nearest church was ten miles away, but the family managed to attend once a month, traveling in a hack, taking their dinner, and spreading it on the ground to eat with neighbors. They had cold chicken, fish, goat meat, salads, cakes, pies, and coffee. Montell was very much in need of a church building. Contributions were collected, but after several years they still lacked sufficient funds for construction until T. S. Sutherland, who had been one of the main contributors, gave the last eight hundred dollars needed. They called their house of worship the Montell Methodist Church. Like the school teachers, the ministers came for only one year and then left.

Minnie had two boarders, as well as Lizzie's son Tom Sutherland III, living with her while going to school in Montell. Rob Wells, who had just finished medical school and was a nephew of Bob's, also stayed there. Minnie soon had three more children, Harrell, Flora, and Marguerite. The family moved to a ranch to raise goats but lost many of them when a hard cold rain came just after shearing. Bob died on November 16, 1911. The family then moved to Uvalde, where the oldest son, nineteen-year-old Bob Lee, became the head of the family of eight children. He did not leave his mother to get married until his brother Frank was old enough to take over.

In 1904 Lizzie and Tommie had another baby, whom they called Frank Rogers. Lizzie now had ten children, and the effort was taking a toll on her health:

Montell, Texas
March 2, 1904
Dear Bell: I have so little time from my babies as all the children go to school, with the exception of Tom who has had to stop to help with the goats, much to our regret, as Tommie is paying for two months of private school (one month of which has passed). It is bad that Tom cannot go when we are paying the hard earned cash for it.

Yes, I have help and am very thankful for it for I don't see how I could get along without it. She is a very good cook and right neat about her work, but slow is no name for her. I believe she is the slowest mortal I ever saw though you know our cooking and cleaning dishes alone are no little jobs. She does that and the ironing and washes the diapers and flannels. I send the regular washing every week to Pablo's wife.

No, I am not feeling very weak, but have such a trembling feeling in the back of my neck, head and all down my spinal column. I was not at all well before my baby came—suffered a great deal with internal trouble and also with indigestion. I retained very little that I ate or drank—even water—or anything that I ate (excepting green apples) and if I did not spit it up I was in misery with colic and I guess Baby inherited both from me as he has had colic ever since he was born and throws up all the time. He throws up more than all the rest of my babies even at his best. He does not only have colic in the evening, but all the time nearly especially if he get a little cool, and almost every time he nurses, he will cry until he throws up or belches the wind off his stomach. In spite of it all he is fattening right along. He is the first baby I ever had to have colic. I doctor him with castor oil and have given him asafetida; rub him with quinine and Vaseline for his cough which I know does him good. The oil is also fine, I give him a small dose at night which makes him sleep well until about four o'clock when he has to have a vomiting spell, after which he usually rests very well. I think maybe I have saved his life by doctoring him as there were three babies born the same week he was at Rocksprings. All of them died at about two or three weeks old with cold. They and my baby all came in that very severe spell of cold weather in January and considering everything I think we have done well.[11]

By 1908, when she was still only thirty-nine years old, Lizzie seems to have become worn out from all the birthing and toil. She could no longer work.

My dear Belle,

Thomas asked me a few days ago to write you, but there is so much of the time these days that I do not feel like writing that I have put it off until now. Tommie and all the children, from the oldest to the youngest, are celebrating the Fourth today with the rest of the people in this canyon. I am at home. A young lady we have just recently been fortunate enough to employ for help is with me. She is not the best of help, but very good and willing and I judge a girl of good principles. I expect her to get better all along. I want to try and keep her as long as we are here, which will only be till the first of September. Especially do I want her on Mary's account. As I am not able to work it has fallen very hard on her, entirely too hard after studying hard until May 26 then to be overtaxed with work. It has made her thin and pale, though Tom [Lizzie's son] always got up and prepared the breakfast. He is a very good cook. They always make good bread. Though Tom only had time to get the breakfast, or when I was able or Bro. White here, one of us would help, nearly all the rest of the cooking fell on Mary.

I have not been well for months. Besides having bladder trouble and blind piles or hemorrhoids, I suffer a great deal from spells that I believe Rob calls interlocal neuralgia [probably migraines]. I think it is caused from the run down condition my system is in. I was just simply worked down trying to do the work while the children were in school. I felt all this coming, but could not help myself and must say that I am very thankful that it is no worse.[12]

She had her fifteenth child in 1908 and named her Ara, after Ara Cook, the schoolteacher her children liked so much: "I feel as President Roosevelt that I have twice done my duty along the line of populating the world. He, you know, says that if a woman has had six children she had done her duty, and when one starts out on the second dozen, it seems it is most too many, but my consolation is that there may be some great work in this world for one that is coming and that God makes all things, without Him was nothing made that was made. We do not happen by chance. He has some purpose in making us."[13]

Ara Cook convinced the family that without some kind of schooling beyond what she could provide, the children would not get an adequate education. Tom and Lizzie thus sent their oldest son, Tom, to Cornel Institute in San Marcos, but the other children were not so fortunate. Ara Cook stayed on an extra year, but in 1908 the family decided to move to Salado in Bell County, where the Robertson family had established Salado College:

Well, our home is sold or traded and the contract signed. The deeds and abstracts have not passed yet, but will as soon as [they] can get them ready. We are not to give possession till 1st of September. Tommie traded our Ranch here of 4,866 acres for property in Bell County, a 450 acre farm valued at $50.00 per acre, a stock farm of 924 acres valued at $15.00 per acre, six houses and lots in Temple valued at $9,500 (these rent houses bring in $73.00 per month) and $4,100.00 in cash. We will live on the stock farm at Salado just one mile from Town. We go there to send the children to school. They claim to have fine folks and schools also at Salado. Our ranch with 250 head of stock cattle, 30 head of stock horses and 200 head of hogs was valued at $50,000.

I surely hate to leave here as so many of our folks are here and Mamma especially, as she is so old and feeble. Seems to me I hate to leave worse than I did Jackson the first time, though I hope and pray it is best for all concerned. This

*ranch life, the way I have had to live, is killing on me, though I dread to change
for fear we will not like it.*

*Tommie thinks he can do better there than here. Expects to feed steers through
winter for market, though when he pays his debts he will have no money. He has
at least 400 head of cattle besides those sold with the ranch, but he owes for most
of them, and will have to borrow to go into business. We only get half of the crop
on the farm this year.*[14]

Having borrowed from family to make ends meet, they were more than
anxious to settle their debts now that they had sold the ranch.

Lizzie Rogers Sutherland's life consisted of hard work, childbearing, and
undying faith. Married at sixteen, she eventually gave birth to fifteen children—seven boys and eight girls. All of the girls lived to adulthood, but only
four of the boys survived. Two boys died in infancy, and George died at thirteen. In a financial bind, unhappy with the struggles of ranching, and eager
for the girls to have educational and social opportunities, Lizzie and Tom decided to move to Salado, where there the girls could attend Salado College.
If the four youngest children had been boys and if three sons had not died,
Tom Sutherland might have stayed in the ranching business, as did the other
Sutherland brothers, who became successful ranchers. But with the girls' future to consider, a more populated area provided more opportunities. Salado
had a college, the land there was black soil, and a cotton boom was beginning, which promised a better living than goats could offer.

My grandfather, the eldest son, was twenty-one when his mother, father,
brothers, and sisters moved to Salado. He had grown up as a rancher, helping
his father since he was a small boy. Because he was needed to work the ranch,
his education was limited, though his letters show him to be intelligent, literate, and articulate about what he knew. He had done every chore there was
on the ranch, and as a grown man of twenty-one, his knowledge of ranch
work was extensive. He roped and wrangled with the greatest of ease. Riding
a horse all day with a lariat in hand in case a steer or goat shot out of the brush
was a familiar part of his life. He did not know or care about the cowboy image of Texas. He would not have recognized as anything but a sorry joke the
cowboys portrayed by John Wayne or Clint Eastwood or even the moraliz-
ing rancher Homer Bannon, portrayed by Melvin Douglas in *Hud.* None of
these characters bore any relation to his life. He was, however, without having thought about it, a Texas cowboy.

My grandfather attended Salado College for a short time, and at the
Methodist Church he met Mary Elizabeth Robertson, granddaughter of Elijah Sterling Clack Robertson. They were practically the same age—he was

Mary Elizabeth Robertson and Thomas Shelton Sutherland II (center couple sitting),
Robertson's sisters and their beaus, courting on the banks of the Salao River.

born on June 21, 1887, and she on June 9 of the same year. They courted along
the banks of the Salao, hunting for violets in the beautiful spring-fed stream
brimming with watercress and water lilies shaded by pecan trees. Even though
the water was clear, cold, and very inviting on a hot Texas summer day, the
most they did, since they were exceedingly modest, was wade in it.

Mary Elizabeth Robertson had a memory book, and the young men who
called on her were invited to write poems in it, such as this one:

> *As sure as the vine*
> *Grows round the stump*
> *You are my darling*
> *Sugar lump.*[15]

Mary Elizabeth was the oldest daughter of Maclin and Alice Robertson.
From childhood, she cared for the other children as well as her mother, just as
Mary, the oldest girl in the Sutherland family, did for her siblings and mother.
Both her husband's mother, Lizzie Rogers Sutherland, and her own mother,
Alice Robertson, were frail from so many years of childbearing. Even though
Mary Elizabeth did not go to public school until seventh grade and then went

for only part of a year to the College of Industrial Arts in Denton, Texas, she was very literate. With the help of a governess at home, she had learned to read from the great Robertson library. According to my father, "The characters and stories of the Waverly novels by Sir Walter Scott were as familiar to her as the family and the events of the day, and this influence of the universally famous romancer was characteristic of the entire south. She also knew Charles Dickens and was quite familiar with the plays of Shakespeare. The men in her family, such as her father, while mostly men of ranch life and action, knew Robert Burns, as she did, and my grandfather Maclin who never appeared to be in any way related to the written word, was capable of reciting 'A Man's a Man for All That' in case anyone needed the instruction."[16]

Before she turned twelve, Mary Elizabeth Robertson had read *Ivanhoe, The Talisman,* and *The Abbot and the Monastery* by Guy Mannering Scott. She read Sir Walter Scott's *Scottish Chiefs,* Jane Porter's *Eight Cousins, Rose in Bloom,* and *Jack and Jill,* and all of Louisa May Alcott's books. In 1900, when she was twelve, she kept a diary of the twenty-five books she read that year, along with her comments on them. As part of the Robertson library, some of these works were bought by her grandmother when she belonged to the Amasavourian literary society. Mary Elizabeth read the Grimm brothers' *Fairy Tales; Two Little Confederates* by Thomas Nelson Page ("a very interesting and delightful book. A story that when you finish it you are sorry you are through"); *The Story of an African Farm* by Olive Schreiner ("I did not like it at all"); *Alice in Wonderland* and *Through the Looking-Glass* by Lewis Carroll ("very silly"); *Swiss Family Robinson* ("contains valuable information on astronomy and science"); *Robin Hood; Hamlet* ("did not like it very much"); *The Lord of the Isles* by Sir Walter Scott; *The History of New York* by Washington Irving; *New England Girlhood* by Lucy Larcom ("a good story of a girl's life in the Puritan days in which I don't think I would have liked to live"); *Little Men* by Louisa May Alcott ("a delightful story by one of the best writers today"); *Lady Jane* by Cecilia Viets Jamison ("the story of a little girl who, although left friendless in the world, soon won many friends by her gentle manners and sweet disposition. The moral of it is: be good and you will not have as bad a time as if your were naughty and rude"); *The Story of a Bad Boy* by Thomas Bailey Aldrich ("I like it so much and imagined I would like to play as many jokes off of people as he did, particularly when they shot off the twelve cannon, for then nobody was hurt and the boys were never found out. And besides he was not bad but only mischievous."); *The Courtship of Miles Standish* by Longfellow ("I think Miles Standish was a better man than John Alden"); *My Lady, a Story of Long Ago* by Marguerite Bouvet ("I was sorry when Lucine Dancourt married Llora instead of Philippe. I had hoped

Phillippe would marry Llora for he had a better nature than Lucien"); *Remember the Alamo* by Amelia E. Barr ("I liked it very much but if Rachela and Fray Ignatius had been shot instead of Dar Grant and Jack Worth it would have been still better"); *When Knighthood Was in Flower* by Edwin Caskoden ("Two brave persons who were an example of the proverb 'where there's a will there's a way' "); and *Tom Brown's Schooldays* by Thomas Hughes ("a fine story of two brave boys, Harry East and Tom Brown, who were not afraid to stand up for the right, no matter who or how many were against them").[17]

After Tom and Mary Elizabeth agreed to marry, Tom went back to Uvalde to set up his own ranch. He wrote her letters about his difficulties with horses and cattle, the long lonely rides on horseback between ranches, and the weather, which affected every move he made since he lived mostly outdoors. Living a cowboy's life, he was more attuned to horses and cattle than to a sensitive, patrician wife. His mind hardly ever strayed from his work. Once at dinner he began a prayer that started out fine, but as he began to think about his milk cow, "Buttercup," it deteriorated somewhat. "Ho lor we hum beg mumble ings damn that old she-devil if she ever kicks the bucket over again I'm gonna jerk her hind leg off and beat 'er bloody with it. Amen." To which Mary E. added gently, "Now, Tom."[18]

My father once described his parents in the most romantic tones. The values they held were the same ones, he said, that "had guided both the Sutherlands and Robertsons since their arrival in the 17th century from the British Isles. That is to say, they possessed the all-powerful family loyalty to kin of the Scots and the moral dicta handed down from Moses and Jesus. They were basically without fear of anything on earth except the loss of their loved ones and accepted that sometimes with weeping on the part of women and sadness, as the will of God. They were strict in the observance of the ten commandments, and they loved people in the spirit of the humble master of Nazareth. They were protective of the young and responsible by long habit for the care of animals and of the changing condition of the land which produced the harvest to feed them. They were close to the land by a long history and were at home inside or outside their houses. I am perhaps the last generation to share this simple pastoral background."[19]

CHAPTER 22

Family Reunions

THE SUTHERLAND-ROGERS REUNIONS

T he three Sutherland-Rogers families and the Rogers-Witt family began having reunions so that the thirty-two double first cousins could get together. Their grandparents, Thomas Shelton Sutherland and Samuel Rogers, each had twelve children, but only sixteen of these twenty-four firstborn Texans lived to adulthood. The first gathering, held in the summer of 1930, was attended by eight of the nine living first-generation Texans who were the children of Sutherland and Rogers: Talitha Menefee White, William DePriest Sutherland, Belle Sutherland Faires, Clark Rogers, Rosa Rogers Witt, Lizzie Laura Sutherland, and Emma and Minnie Sutherland, as well as the widows of Frank and Mack Rogers. Of that group, only Mamie Sutherland Crockett was unable to come, but 110 of their descendants gathered.[1]

The reunion was so successful that a second get-together was held the next year and another one in 1934, this time on the Texas coast. In 1936 the fourth meeting was held, when only Belle Sutherland Faires was left of the first-generation Sutherlands; all of the Rogers brothers and sisters were still living, however. The men went fishing together, the women laid out on long tables the home-cooked food they had brought, the "cousins" ran off and got to know each other, and everyone talked the whole time. The last of these early gatherings took place in 1940, and then the war intervened.[2]

In 1948 more than 150 Sutherland-Rogers relatives convened, hungry for news of their kinfolk and stories about their origins. The next get-together did not occur until 1952, and at that reunion Minnie Sutherland, Clark Rogers, and Emma Sutherland, who, as the last of the first-generation Texans, embodied the living memory of the American history of Texas, suggested that there be a family meeting every year.[3] Their gentle statements became an eleventh commandment. The reunions are now an annual event. When we congregate, we pay homage to those who came before us, listen to the stories of their Texas adventures, and get to know the next generation. These assemblies have been the vital conduit of a sense of family, of Texas identity, and of the art of storytelling. We continue to pass down the tales of our fore-bears, who arrived in Texas in 1830.

By 1957 Florence Sutherland Hudson, daughter of Thomas S. Sutherland II and Lizzie Rogers Sutherland, had put together a book called *We Cousins,* which records the genealogy and history of these families. Everyone got a copy. In 1958 the reunion had grown to 237 relatives, and the family began renting the entire Garner State Park in Uvalde, named after "Cactus Jack" Garner, Uvalde's favorite son and vice president to Franklin Roosevelt. Cactus Jack was a favorite character, a blunt-speaking, colorful man who once said the vice presidency wasn't worth a bucket of warm spit. The get-togethers were held there until 1967. I remember the one in 1958 as the most fun of my whole teen-anguished thirteenth year. I could hardly wait for the reunion in 1959, where I met 231 of my aunts, uncles, and cousins. Since I grew up going to these gatherings, when I had children of my own, I brought them as often as I could, even from faraway places such as England and Minnesota, so they too could learn what family and Texas meant.

THE ROBERTSON REUNION

The Robertsons were not the child-producing machines that the Sutherland and Rogers families were. A more patrician and prickly lot, they also were not as close. They did, however, have their own single moment of reunion. In 1936, during the centennial of Texas independence from Mexico, celebrations all over the Lone Star State spurred a movement to transfer the remains of the heroes of early Texas colonization and the war of independence to the Texas State Cemetery in Austin. The cemetery is on a beautiful, peaceful hill just east of the state capitol, now in one of the poorest parts of town. There you will find the heroes of early Texas buried alongside the revered writers and intellectuals of Texas history: J. Frank Dobie and Walter Prescott Webb, as well as my father, who sneaked in, thanks to the influence of his sister Liz Carpenter, Lady Bird Johnson's former press secretary. In December 1935 Sterling C. Robertson's remains were disinterred from his burial place in Robertson County and brought to the state cemetery, where an elaborate funeral was arranged. The interment turned into a huge family reunion of Robertsons, who came from all over Texas and the rest of the United States to attend, including those still living in Salado, those who had become urbanites in Austin and Houston, and those who had moved as far away as Miami, New York, Los Angeles, and Mexico City.

The Robertsons are a proud group, comfortable with their sense of superiority but not so adept at getting along with each other. Attending the funeral were four granddaughters of the empresario and twenty-eight great-grandchildren, including my grandmother Mary Elizabeth Robertson Sutherland. The number of great-great-grandchildren was too daunting for anyone to count, but since they were among the more physically able, several of them served as pallbearers, including my father and his cousin Malcolm McLean, who, along with his wife, Margaret, published the nineteen volumes of the Robertson papers, thus ensuring the empresario a position in Texas history forever.

The pallbearers were given white gloves to wear. My father, who never much cared for the white-glove society and also possessed a mischievous streak, very slowly and carefully began to examine his gloves during the ceremony. As the eulogies wound their way slowly and monotonously on, the audience began to show signs of boredom. Tom Sutherland had inherited George Sutherland's physique—a large frame and a hefty weight. He stood out in the audience of the mostly smallish Robertsons. When he began to put the glove—meant for a dainty Robertson hand—on his large Sutherland paw, it turned out to be quite a struggle. Raising his huge hand up into the air, he tried to squeeze his fingers into the glove, with exaggerated grimacing and feigned agony. Slowly the audience began to focus on the spectacle. My father's sister Alice, with whom he had a loving, but tense, relationship ever since he had stuck a go-devil on her wet rear end, knew exactly what he was saying to the somewhat pretentious Robertsons. This was a serious occasion, and she was not going to let him get away with it. Suddenly she wheeled around and shouted for all to hear, "Tommy, if you don't stop that, I'm going to scream!" My father jerked his hand down, happy that he had nettled his sister once again, and the funeral took on a lighter air.[4]

IDENTITY AND TEXAS

In this book I have tried to answer basic questions about Texas identity: Why is it so strong, and how does it get reproduced from one generation to the next? Why do Texans, no matter where they go, keep coming back to the Lone Star State, certain that it is the best place on earth to live? And why do newcomers to Texas immediately sniff this identity in the air, like the smell of bacon sizzling in the early morning? When I watched George W. Bush, who identifies the state as his home, departing for Washington to become president of the United States and choking back tears with the words "I'll be back," I was reminded of Tanya Tucker's song "Texas When I Die," in which she sang that if she couldn't get into heaven because they had no place for cowboys, "just let me go to Texas / Texas is as close as I've been."

Much has been said about the powerful role of the images of Texas that movies, television, and books have promoted. In them, local Texas history is projected first as a story of the quintessential westward movement of American history and then as a statement of the archetypal American character— willful, individualistic, self-reliant, independent, and violent. A whole generation of Europeans, Asians, and Latin Americans saw in the soap *Dallas* the essence of not just Texas but also the United States. In the 1950s the movie *Giant* had that effect on me. Each generation of Texans can point to a media image of the state that reinforces the ethos of Texas identity. Nonetheless, I do not think that the role of the media is sufficient to explain the Texas phenomenon.

The forces I have explored in this book are the emotions about identity that were developed through my own family's history. The family identity and the Texas identity, at least in the case of my gigantic family, became intertwined through their experiences in the Lone Star State. Those experiences—migration, births and deaths, war and hunger, hard work, and financial setbacks—were turned into stories told to generations of family members. The tales they told about themselves, to themselves, are the gist of their Texas identity.

WHAT IS HOME?

When my father's sister Liz Carpenter moved back to Texas from Washington, D.C., after years of frenetic politics in the LBJ White House, she asked him, "What is home?" My father loved such questions and often answered them by leafing through the writings he loved to find the most eloquent answer. When, as a child, I asked him, "Why do we die?" he read me Cervantes and Shakespeare. When I said to him, "Why do people hate?" he would pull from our bookshelves Mark Twain and Robbie Burns. But to my aunt's question, he replied in another one of his slow, thoughtful ways. He wrote her a poem:

> *A restless sister asks me, "What is home?"*
> *A thousand years ago, from hill and heather*
> *Our people watched the thieves and murderers roam,*
> *Back to the rock we fought in cruel weather.*
> *Here in this place of sun and grass and flowers*
> *One hundred fifty years ago we stood.*

We fought a tyrant's army and his powers
To take our lives and what to us is good.
Home is a high place in the head
Held for the virtues and the better way.
Here Wisdom rules, Beauty and Truth are wed,
And Loyalty stands guard till break of day.
Evil can stalk our path, hide in his hole.
Home is the lighted sanctum of the soul.[5]

My father was in the habit of writing poetry to express his thoughts and feelings. Since a sense of family was one of the bedrock values of his life, many of his poems were about his ancestors, whom he tended to romanticize. Having been taught that it was wrong to say anything bad about one's relatives, he brought them to life and mentioned their many flaws only in a way that showed how painful it was for him to do so. His writings point to a long tradition in my family of writing poems, letters, and journals, a habit that goes back to the first Texas generation. His poems became a living part of my childhood, a constant reminder that home is a "high place in the head."

In describing his own father, who was a genuine cowboy, my father would quote the first poem he ever wrote, "Lone Cowboy," in his honor. He was eighteen when he wrote it and so flushed with the thrill of writing that he sent it to *Boy's Life,* the Boy Scout magazine that he avidly read. When the next issue of *Boy's Life* arrived in the mail, he was overwhelmed at seeing his words in print, an event that undoubtedly spurred him to write poetry the rest of his life.

Lone Cowboy

Now stop your horse beside a stream,
And stake him to a willow;
Stretch your body on the ground
And make your arm a pillow.
Tomorrow, no one cares or knows,
How far you both may travel;
Tonight you rest and listen to
The water on the gravel.[6]

Excited, he ran to his father to show him his son's first published poem. His father, hardly glancing at the words on the page, asked my father, "How much did you make?"

"Nothin,'" my father replied.

"Well, then, you'll never make a living, boy."

Crushed, he took his poem to his mother, who wrote poetry herself, and she praised his efforts, leading him to become painfully aware that, in his family, there were those who wrote and those who had no use for writing.

From our early visits to the Alamo, my sisters and I knew that we had relatives from the Alabama Settlement who had fought and died there. We asked my father about his great-great-uncle Willie who, at seventeen, rode off to the Alamo in good spirits, young and innocent, joking with his sister that he planned to be married when he returned. My father then wrote, "San Antonio Spring," which he dedicated "In Memory of William DePriest Sutherland, March 6, 1836."

San Antonio Spring

In San Antonio where the huisache is a glory
Of many yellow blossoms thick as rain,
We know it's Spring again,
And we recall a story.
There is a one-time chapel called the Alamo;
And when the huisache lifts its many limbs of yellow
To say that life is mellow,
Then do we know
This was the time of year
That men were fighting in the mission here.
They must have looked at some such glorious tree
Outside the door—
Its beauty must have helped them when they swore
They would not run.
Then the Mexican cannon increased its thunder,
Each looked at the other's eyes with wonder,
Priming his gun,
And died that Spring.
Who knows but what the blood springs in the leaves
And brightens the same flowers that bring
Our memory back to bloom, our hearts to sing,
Nor is that lost which causes us who write
To think on men who learned instead to fight,
And make us pray that we can meet our foe
After a hundred years

As well as they met theirs
At Spring, inside the Alamo.

THOMAS SHELTON SUTHERLAND IV[7]

I believe he was thinking of his father, a man of action with a complete disinterest in the written word, when he wrote "nor is that lost which causes us who write / to think on men who learned instead to fight." Perhaps that is why he instilled in me the idea that memories, written down for posterity, are a priceless gift from our ancestors.

Notes

PREFACE

1. *Texas History Movies*, 1956.

CHAPTER 1

1. Originally released in 1956, the movie *Giant* was directed by George Stevens and starred Elizabeth Taylor, Rock Hudson, James Dean, Chill Wills, and Mercedes Mc-Cambridge. For James Dean, *Giant* would be the last film of his short career.

2. George N. Green, "The Felix Longoria Affair."

3. Thomas S. Sutherland IV, "Our Forebear Was George Sutherland," in Carol Sutherland Hatfield, ed., "The Poems of Thomas S. Sutherland," 14.

CHAPTER 2

1. Florence S. Hudson, *We Cousins*, vol. 1, 19.

2. Malcolm D. McLean, *Papers concerning Robertson's Colony in Texas*, vol. 18, 106–107.

3. Thomas S. Sutherland IV, "The Texans," in "Poems by Tommy Sutherland, 1930–1950," 166.

4. Ibid., "Here on These Rolling Acres of Land," 84.

5. John Henry Brown, *History of Texas, from 1685 to 1892;* Frederick Law Olmsted, "Olmsted's Texas Journey"; Frédéric Leclerc, *Texas and Its Revolution.*

6. John Sutherland, *The Fall of the Alamo.*

7. John Sutherland Menefee, Papers and Letters, letter, June 1841.

8. John Sutherland Menefee, "Early Jackson County Settlers."

9. Ibid.

10. Ibid.

CHAPTER 3

1. Malcolm D. McLean, *Papers concerning Robertson's Colony in Texas* (hereafter cited as *PCRCT).*

2. Malcolm D. McLean, "Hot Pursuit: Collecting Material concerning Robertson's Colony, Texas."

3. William C. Harllee, *Kinfolks.*

4. McLean, "Hot Pursuit."

CHAPTER 4

1. *Texas History Movies*, 1956.

2. Ibid.

3. Ibid., 4.

4. Ibid., 36.

5. Ibid., 47.

6. Ibid., 60.

7. Ibid., 81.

8. Ibid., 83.

9. Ibid., 91.

10. Ibid., 94.

11. Ibid., 100.

12. Ibid., 107.

13. Ibid., 108.

14. Ibid., 109.

15. *Texas History Movies: A Cartoon History of the Lone Star State*, 1985.

16. Kent Biffle, "A Revival of Book on Early Texas Stirs Objections."

17. John H. Brown, *History of Texas, from 1685 to 1892.*

18. Ibid., 3–4.

19. Lawrence Honig, *John Henry Brown: Texian Journalist, 1820–1895*, 7.

20. James M. Day, "James Kerr: Frontier Texian," 24–25.

21. Honig, 30–31.

22. Ira T. Taylor, *The Cavalcade of Jackson County*, v.

23. Andrés Tijerina, *Tejanos and Texas under the Mexican Flag, 1821–1836*, 5–25.

24. Robert A. Calvert and Arnoldo De León, *The History of Texas*, 48.

25. Randolph B. Campbell, *Gone to Texas: A History of the Lone Star State*, 126; Calvert and De León, *The History of Texas*, 63.

26. Michael Geyer and Charles Bright, "World History in a Global Age."

27. John Comaroff and Jean Comaroff, *Ethnography and the Historical Imagination*, 25.

28. Ibid.

29. Peter Applebome, "Out from under the Nation's Shadow," A15.

CHAPTER 5

1. Gregg Cantrell, "A Matter of Character: Stephen F. Austin and the 'Papers concerning Robertson's Colony in Texas.'"

2. *PCRCT*, 1974–1993.

3. Ibid., vol. 1, xlii.

4. *The Handbook of Texas Online,* s.v. "Austin, Stephen Fuller."

5. Eugene C. Barker, *The Life of Stephen F. Austin, Founder of Texas, 1793–1836: A Chapter in the Westward Movement of the Anglo-American People,* 47.

6. *PCRCT*, 1986, introductory volume.

7. Ibid., 498–99.

8. *PCRCT*, vol. 2, 269–88, 296–301.

9. Ibid., 60.

10. Ibid., 60–68.

11. Ibid., 620.

12. Ibid., vol. 1, 10.

13. Ibid., vol. 4, 65.

14. Ibid., vol. 5, 42–43.

15. Ibid., 44–45.

16. Ibid., 46.

17. Ibid., 49–54.

18. Cantrell, "A Matter of Character," 234.

19. *PCRCT*, vol. 7, 24.

20. Ibid., 28–29.

21. Ibid., 3–34.

22. Ibid., 34–35.

23. Ibid., 38.

24. Ibid., 496.

25. Ibid., vol. 8, 30–35.

26. Ibid., 42–45.

27. Ibid., 46–47.

28. Ibid., 50.

29. Ibid., 51.

30. Ibid., 53–54.

31. Barker, *The Life of Stephen F. Austin,* 404.

32. *PCRCT*, vol. 7, 21.

33. Barker, *The Life of Stephen F. Austin,* 318.

34. Ibid., 320.

35. Ibid., 391, footnote.

36. Letter from Austin to ayuntamiento of San Antonio, Oct. 2, 1833, ibid., 374.

37. Ibid., 384.

38. Brown, *History of Texas, from 1685 to 1892,* 467, 466.

39. *PCRCT*, vol. 14, 35.

40. *The Handbook of Texas Online,* s.v. "Republic of Texas," 4.

41. Francis Richard Lubbock, *Six Decades in Texas; or, Memoirs of Francis Richard Lubbock, Governor of Texas in War Time, 1861–1863. A Personal Experience in Business, War, and Politics,* 108.

42. *PCRCT,* vol. ii, 89.

43. Birdie Robertson, letter, 1896.

CHAPTER 6

1. Ira T. Taylor, *The Cavalcade of Jackson County,* 36.

2. Martha D. Freeman, "The Sutherland Plantation and the Alabama Settlement: A Study in Cluster Migration."

3. Kay Sutherland, "Gone with Gypsy Time: Conversations with a Texas Poet and Storyteller," 117.

4. Florence Hudson, *"We Cousins" (Virginia to Texas): A Genealogy of Several of the Families Comprising the Alabama Settlement of Austin's Colony, 1830 and 1831, Now Texas, and including the Other Virginia Lines of the Sutherland Family.*

5. Contract between Stephen F. Austin and George Sutherland, Feb. 19, 1830, in Martha Doty Freeman, "The Sutherland Plantation and the Alabama Settlement: A Study in Cluster Migration," 21.

6. Villamae Williams, *Stephen F. Austin's Register of Families.*

7. F. L. Heard and Mrs. F. L. Heard. "Texas, Their Reward," 10–11.

8. Freeman, "The Sutherland Plantation and the Alabama Settlement," 8–13, 21; Laura Ann Sutherland Gipson, personal correspondence.

9. Freeman, "The Sutherland Plantation and the Alabama Settlement," xi.

10. Ibid., 22.

11. John Knox, *A History of Morgan County, Alabama,* 28, 67–68.

12. Freeman, "The Sutherland Plantation and the Alabama Settlement," 8–13, 21; Laura Ann Sutherland Gipson, personal correspondence.

13. Freeman, "The Sutherland Plantation and the Alabama Settlement," 24.

14. Russell Ward, letter to Florence Hudson, June 14, 1960.

15. Samuel Rogers, "Autobiography of S. C. A. Rogers," 5.

CHAPTER 7

1. Macum Phelan, *History of Early Methodism in Texas, 1817–1866;* William Warren Sweet, *The Story of Religion in America,* 316–20.

2. Sweet, *The Story of Religion in America,* 327–31.

3. Francis Ward, *An Account of Three Camp-Meetings Held by the Methodists,* 12.

4. Ibid., 5.

5. John Knox, *A History of Morgan County, Alabama,* 288.

6. Martha D. Freeman, "The Sutherland Plantation and the Alabama Settlement: A Study in Cluster Migration," 5.

7. Homer S. Thrall, *History of Methodism in Texas,* 34.

8. F. L. Heard and Mrs. F. L. Heard, "Texas, Their Reward," 45–48.

9. Ibid., 48.

10. Thrall, *History of Methodism in Texas,* 82–83.

11. Ibid.

12. Heard and Heard, "Texas, Their Reward," 51–55.

13. Ibid., 59–61.

14 Ira T. Taylor, *The Cavalcade of Jackson County,* 222–23.

15. Heard and Heard, quoting George Simons's pamphlet "Methodist Church History," 62.

16. *Texas Methodist Historical Quarterly,* July 10, 1909.

CHAPTER 8

1. Ira T. Taylor, *The Cavalcade of Jackson County,* 53.

2. Verne Huser, *Rivers of Texas.*

3. Martha D. Freeman, "The Sutherland Plantation and the Alabama Settlement: A Study in Cluster Migration," 26; John Sutherland Menefee, Papers and Letters, letter, 1833.

4. Freeman, "The Sutherland Plantation and the Alabama Settlement," 27; John Sutherland Menefee, "Early Jackson County Settlers," June 3, 1880.

5. Freeman, "The Sutherland Plantation and the Alabama Settlement," 29.

6. Ibid., 28.

7. Taylor, *The Cavalcade of Jackson County,* 98.

8. Freeman, "The Sutherland Plantation and the Alabama Settlement," 29.

9. José Enrique de la Peña, *With Santa Anna in Texas: A Personal Narrative of the Revolution,* 100–101.

10. *Ganado Tribune,* Feb. 6, 1964.

11. Brownson Malsch, "Some Highlights of 400 Years in Jackson County, 1532 to 1932," 4D.

12. John Sutherland Menefee, Papers and Letters, diary.

13. Freeman, "The Sutherland Plantation and the Alabama Settlement," 35.

14. Ibid., 39–40.

15. Ibid., 60.

16. Ibid., 61.

17. Ibid., 60.

18. Thomas Shelton Sutherland, last will and testament, Mar. 1, 1899 (Anne Sutherland Collection).

CHAPTER 9

1. William W. Newcomb, *The Indians of Texas: From Prehistoric to Modern Times,* 335–37.

2. Ira T. Taylor, *The Cavalcade of Jackson County,* 46.

3. Kelly Himmel, *The Conquest of the Karankawas and the Tonkawas, 1821–1859*, 83–84.

4. Kay Sutherland, "Gone with Gypsy Time: Conversations with a Texas Poet and Storyteller," 41.

5. John Sutherland Menefee, "Early Jackson County Settlers," June 17, 1880.

6. F. L. Heard, "I Remember."

7. Jack Weatherford, personal correspondence, 2000. Harris may also have been referring to Anglo men taking Comanche wives.

8. Rachel Plummer, *Narrative of the Capture and Subsequent Sufferings of Rachel Plummer*.

9. John H. Brown, *History of Texas, from 1685 to 1892*, vol. 2, 70.

10. *The Searchers* was directed by John Ford and released in 1956.

CHAPTER 10

1. Brownson Malsch, "Some Highlights of 400 Years in Jackson County, 1532 to 1932," 4D.

2. Ibid.

3. William C. Binkley, *The Texas Revolution*, 8–9.

4. Ibid., 14–15.

5. Ibid., 19–21.

6. *The Handbook of Texas Online*, s.v. "Lavaca-Navidad Meeting."

7. Samuel Rogers, "Autobiography of S. C. A. Rogers," 7–8.

8. John H. Brown, *History of Texas, from 1685 to 1892*, 297–98.

9. Binkley, *The Texas Revolution*, 36–45.

10. Malsch, "Some Highlights," D5.

11. Martha D. Freeman, "The Sutherland Plantation and the Alabama Settlement: A Study in Cluster Migration," 33.

CHAPTER 11

1. José Enrique de la Peña, *With Santa Anna in Texas: A Personal Narrative of the Revolution*.

2. Ira T. Taylor, *The Cavalcade of Jackson County*, 62–63.

3. John Holmes Jenkins III, ed., *The Papers of the Texas Revolution, 1835–1836*, 16.

4. Ibid., 218.

5. Ibid., 233.

6. Ibid., 251, 276.

7. Ibid., 149–50.

8. Jeff Long, *Duel of Eagles: The Mexican and U.S. Fight for the Alamo*, 376–77.

9. John Sutherland, *The Fall of the Alamo,* 15; Bill Groneman, *Alamo Defenders: A Genealogy, the People, and Their Words,* 107–108.

10. Groneman, 108–109.

11. Peña, *With Santa Anna in Texas.*

12. John Sutherland Menefee, *Texana Clarion,* Aug. 5, 1880.

13. *The Handbook of Texas Online,* s.v. "White, Francis Menefee."

14. *Ganado Tribune,* Jan. 30, 1964.

15. Ira T. Taylor, *The Cavalcade of Jackson County,* 79–83.

16. Samuel Rogers, "Autobiography of S. C. A. Rogers," 10–11.

17. Frances M. Sutherland, letter to her sister in Alabama, June 5, 1836.

18. Mary A. Maverick and George Maverick, *Memoirs of Mary Maverick,* 14–16.

CHAPTER 12

1. Arnold van Gennep, *The Rites of Passage,* 1960.

2. Victor Turner, "Betwixt and Between: The Liminal Period in *Rites de Passage.*"

3. *The Last Command* (1955) stars Sterling Hayden; *Davy Crockett, King of the Wild Frontier* (1954–1955) features Fess Parker; and *The Alamo* (1960) stars John Wayne and Richard Widmark. Lon Tinkle, *Thirteen Days to Glory;* James A. Michener, *Texas;* Randy Roberts and James Olson, *A Line in the Sand: The Alamo in Blood and Memory.*

4. José Enrique de la Peña, *With Santa Anna in Texas: A Personal Narrative of the Revolution,* 87–91.

5. Holly B. Brear, *Inherit the Alamo: Myth and Ritual at an American Shrine.*

6. T. R. Fehrenbach, *Lone Star: A History of Texas and the Texans,* 204–205.

7. Robert A. Calvert and Arnoldo De León, *The History of Texas,* 228–29.

8. Fehrenbach, *Lone Star: A History of Texas and the Texans,* 190–233; Ben Procter, *The Battle of the Alamo;* James W. Pohl, *The Battle of San Jacinto;* William C. Binkley, *The Texas Revolution.*

CHAPTER 13

1. José Enrique de la Peña, *With Santa Anna in Texas: A Personal Narrative of the Revolution,* 134–64.

2. Samuel Rogers, "Autobiography of S. C. A. Rogers," 12.

3. Brownson Malsch, "Some Highlights of 400 Years in Jackson County, 1532 to 1932"; muster roll of Capt. George Sutherland's company, June, 26, 1836.

4. Rogers, "Autobiography of S. C. A. Rogers," 12.

5. Ibid., 14.

6. Ibid., 14–15.

7. Ibid., 14.

8. Ibid., 16.

CHAPTER 14

1. Samuel Rogers, "Autobiography of S. C. A. Rogers," 6.
2. Lizzie Laura Rogers Sutherland, postscript, "Extracts from 'Reminiscences of My Father, Reverend Samuel C. A. Rogers.'"
3. Rogers, "Autobiography of S. C. A. Rogers," 18.
4. Ibid.
5. Ibid.
6. Ibid., 19.
7. Ibid., 20.
8. Tyler, 1936, 180–83.
9. Ibid., 184.
10. Ibid., 187–88.
11. Ibid., 189–90.

CHAPTER 15

1. Ira T. Taylor, *The Cavalcade of Jackson County,* 168–81.
2. J. Frank Dobie, *Tales of Old-Time Texas,* 15–33.
3. J. Frank Dobie, letter to Alice Sutherland Romberg, Jan. 15, 1955.
4. "Reminiscences of Mrs. Dilue Harris."
5. Taylor, *The Cavalcade of Jackson County,* 170.
6. Samuel Rogers, letter to Russell Ward, his great-grandson, undated.
7. Taylor, *The Cavalcade of Jackson County,* 17.
8. Ibid., 180–81.

CHAPTER 16

1. *PCRCT,* vol. 7, 497–98.
2. Elijah Sterling Clack Robertson, Letters.
3. Elijah Sterling Clack Robertson, Biography File.
4. *PCRCT,* vol. 16, 301.
5. *Telegraph and Texas Register* (Houston, Feb. 24, 1838); "Laws of Texas," *PCRCT,* vol. 2, 103–104.
6. *PCRCT,* vol. 8, 61; vol. 16, 130.
7. Ibid., vol. 17, 97.
8. Ibid., 239–40, letter to Colonel Porter, May 17, 1839.
9. Ibid., 291.
10. Ibid., vol. 18, 92, 187.
11. Ibid., 93.
12. Ibid., 374.

13. Ibid., 374–75.

14. Ibid., 378.

15. Elijah Sterling Clack Robertson, "Journal of Incidental Matters," 1845.

16. Ibid., May 21, 1845.

17. Ibid., Feb. 4, 1846.

18. Mary Ann Moore, *Rekindled Embers: The Story of the Robertson Family of Washington County, Texas,* 18–19.

19. Robertson, Letters, 1847.

20. Ibid.

21. Ibid.

22. George Tyler, *History of Bell County,* 256–57.

23. *Texas Catalog, Historic American Buildings Survey: A List of Measured Drawings, Photographs, and Written Documentation in the Survey,* 1974.

24. Mary Dickey Robertson, Letters.

25. Robertson, Biography File, charter, town of Salado.

26. Ibid., charter of Salado College.

27. Ibid.

28. Tyler, *History of Bell County,* 355.

CHAPTER 17

1. Elijah Sterling Clack Robertson, Letters.

2. George Tyler, *History of Bell County,* 196–97.

3. Robertson, Letters.

4. Tyler, *History of Bell County,* 199; William S. Riggs, personal communication.

5. Tyler, *History of Bell County,* 236–38.

6. Elijah Sterling Clack Robertson, Biography File.

7. Ibid.

8. Ibid., letter from Henry McCulloch.

9. Ibid., diary, June 19, 1865.

10. Ibid., June 22, 1865.

11. John Henry Brown, letter from to Marion Robertson, Feb. 22, 1894.

12. Robertson, Biography File, July 5, 1865.

13. Ibid., July 8, 1865.

14. Ibid., Aug. 15, 1865.

15. Ibid., Aug. 26, 1865.

16. Ibid., Aug. 27, 1865.

17. Ibid., Aug. 28, 1865.

18. Cile Robertson Ambrose, personal communication.

19. Malcolm Dallas McLean, "Elijah Sterling Clack Robertson's Participation in the Civil War."

CHAPTER 18

1. Kay Sutherland, "Gone with Gypsy Time: Conversations with a Texas Poet and Storyteller," paraphrased, 104.

2. Ibid.

3. Ibid.

4. Elijah Sterling Clack Robertson, Biography File, diaries, 1873–1875.

5. George Carmack, "Salado's House of Texas History," 1B.

6. George Tyler, *History of Bell County*, 349–59.

7. Liz Carpenter, *Getting Better All the Time*, 116–17.

8. *The Handbook of Texas Online*, s.v. "Robertson, Luella."

9. Kay Sutherland, "Gone with Gypsy Time," 97–98.

10. Cile Robertson Anderson, personal correspondence.

11. Sutherland, "Gone with Gypsy Time," 99.

12. Tyler, *History of Bell County*, 263.

13. Sutherland, "Gone with Gypsy Time," 101–103.

14. *Belton Journal*, July 13, 1876.

15. Sutherland, "Gone with Gypsy Time," 163–66.

CHAPTER 19

1. F. L. Heard, "I Remember."

2. Emma Rogers Sutherland, "My Life Story," 2.

3. Ibid., 4.

4. Ibid., 1.

5. Ibid., 2–3.

6. Heard, "I Remember."

7. Sutherland, "My Life Story," 4.

CHAPTER 20

1. Kay Sutherland, "Gone with Gypsy Time: Conversations with a Texas Poet and Storyteller," 42.

2. Ellis A. Davis and Edwin H. Grobe, *The New Encyclopedia of Texas*, 3651.

3. Lizzie Laura Rogers Sutherland, Letters, Oct. 18, 1895.

4. Ibid., Nov. 12, 1895.

5. Ibid.

6. Sutherland, "Gone with Gypsy Time," 70–71.

7. Sutherland, Letters, Nov. 12, 1895.

8. Ibid.

9. Ibid., Dec. 3, 1895.

10. Ibid., Jan. 19, 1896.

11. Ibid., Feb. 15, 1896.

12. Ibid., Mar. 22, 1896.

13. Ibid., June 19, 1896.

14. Ibid., Sept. 11, 1896.

15. F. L. Heard, "I Remember."

16. Sutherland, Letters, Dec. 6, 1896.

17. Ibid.

CHAPTER 21

1. John William Lee Sutherland, "Recollections of an Octogenarian."

2. Lizzie Laura Rogers Sutherland, Unpublished letters to Lillian Belle Dickson Faires, 1895–1908, letter, Aug. 30. 1898.

3. Ibid.

4. Florence Sutherland Hudson, "Thomas Shelton Sutherland II, Family of Nueces Canyon."

5. Sutherland, "Recollections of an Octogenarian."

6. Sutherland, Unpublished letters to Laurie Belle Dickson Faires, 1895–1908, letter from 1898.

7. Sutherland, "Recollections of an Octogenarian."

8. Ibid.

9. Russell Ward, letter to Florence Hudson, June 14, 1960.

10. Sutherland, "Recollections of an Octogenarian."

11. Sutherland, Unpublished letters to Laurie Belle Dickson Faires, 1895–1908, letter of March 2, 1904.

12. Ibid., letter, July 3, 1908.

13. Ibid.

14. Ibid.

15. Kay Sutherland, "Gone with Gypsy Time: Conversations with a Texas Poet and Storyteller," 54.

16. Ibid., 55–56.

17. Mary E. Robertson Sutherland, Diary, 1900.

18. Sutherland, "Gone with Gypsy Time," 50.

19. Ibid., 64.

CHAPTER 22

1. Florence Sutherland Hudson, "A History of the Sutherland-Rogers Reunion."

2. Ibid.

3. Ibid.

4. *PCRCT,* vol. 18, 106–107.

5. Thomas Shelton Sutherland IV, in Carol Sutherland Hatfield, ed., "The Poems of Thomas S. Sutherland," 10.

6. Ibid., 5.

7. Thomas Shelton Sutherland IV, "Poems by Tommy Sutherland, 1930–1950," 144–46.

Bibliography

Alabama: A Guide to the Deep South. Compiled by workers of the Writer's Program of the Work Projects Administration in the State of Alabama. American Guide Series. New York: R. R. Smith, 1941.

Appadurai, Arjun. *Modernity at Large: Cultural Dimensions of Globalization.* Minneapolis: University of Minnesota Press, 1996.

Applebome, Peter. "Out from under the Nation's Shadow." *New York Times,* February 20, 1999, A15, A17.

Barker, Eugene C. *The Life of Stephen F. Austin, Founder of Texas, 1793–1836: A Chapter in the Westward Movement of the Anglo-American People.* 1925. Reprint, Austin: Texas State Historical Commission, 1949.

Barr, Alwyn. *Black Texans: A History of African Americans in Texas, 1528–1995.* Norman: University of Oklahoma Press, 1996.

Biffle, Kent. "A Revival of Book on Early Texas Stirs Objections." *Dallas Morning News,* November 4, 1984, 60A.

Binkley, William C. *The Texas Revolution.* 1952. Reprint, Austin: Texas State Historical Association, 1979.

Brear, Holly B. *Inherit the Alamo: Myth and Ritual at an American Shrine.* Austin: University of Texas Press, 1995.

Brown, John Henry. *History of Texas, from 1685 to 1892,* vols. 1–2. St. Louis: L. E. Daniell, 1893.

———. *Indian Wars and Pioneers of Texas.* 1890. Reprint, Austin: State House Press, 1988.

———. Letter to Marion Robertson, February 22, 1894. In John Henry Brown Papers, 1948, Barker Texas History Center, University of Texas–Austin (also Anne Sutherland Collection).

Calvert, Robert A., and Arnoldo De León. *The History of Texas,* 2d ed. Arlington Heights, Ill.: Harlan Davidson, 1996.

Campbell, Randolph B. *Gone to Texas: A History of the Lone Star State.* New York: Oxford University Press, 2003.

Cantrell, Gregg. "A Matter of Character: Stephen F. Austin and the 'Papers concerning Robertson's Colony in Texas.'" *Southwestern Historical Quarterly* 104(2) (October 2000): 231–61.

———. *Stephen F. Austin, Empresario of Texas.* New Haven, Conn.: Yale University Press, 1999.

Carmack, George. "Salado's House of Texas History." *San Antonio Express News,* April 19, 1975, 1B.

Carpenter, Liz. *Getting Better All the Time*. New York: Simon and Schuster, 1987.

Carroll, Patrick. *Felix Longoria's Wake: Bereavement, Racism, and the Rise of Mexican American Activism*. Austin: University of Texas Press, 2003.

Comaroff, John, and Jean Comaroff. *Ethnography and the Historical Imagination*. Boulder: Westview Press, 1992.

Connor, Seymour V. *Texas: A History*. New York: Crowell, 1971.

Cooksey, Alice J. "A Woman of Her Time: Birdie Robertson Johnson." *East Texas Historical Journal* 24 (1986). Eliza S. R. Johnson, Special Collections, Texas Woman's University Library, Denton, Texas.

Curl, R. F. *Southwest Texas Methodism*. N.p.: Inter-Board Council, Southwest Texas Conference, Methodist Church, 1951.

Davis, Ellis A., and Edwin H. Grobe. *The New Encyclopedia of Texas*, s.v. "W. D. Sutherland." Dallas: Texas Development Bureau, 1931, 3651.

Day, James M. "James Kerr: Frontier Texian." *Texana* 2(1) (Spring 1964): 24–43.

De Shields, James. *Border Wars of Texas: Being an Authentic and Popular Account, in Chronological Order, of the Long and Bitter Conflict Waged between Savage Indian Tribes and the Pioneer Settlers of Texas*. Austin: Herald Company, 1912. Extract of pamphlet, "The Fall of Parker's Fort," Waco: Texian Press, 1972.

Dixon, Sam Houston. *The Men Who Made Texas Free*. Houston: Texas Historical Publishing, 1924.

Dobie, J. Frank. Letter to Alice Sutherland Romberg. January 15, 1955 (Anne Sutherland Collection).

———. *Tales of Old-Time Texas*. Boston: Little, Brown, 1955.

Dugger, Ronnie, ed. *Three Men in Texas: Bedichek, Webb, and Dobie*. Austin: University of Texas Press, 1967.

Fawcett, William B., Jr. "Archeological Investigations of Historic Sites." *The Antebellum Period in the Stephen F. Austin Colony: Historical and Archeological Research in the Palmetto Bend Reservoir Area, Jackson County, Texas*. Texas Archeological Survey. Research report 70, part 2. Austin: University of Texas, 1980.

Fehrenbach, T. R. *Lone Star: A History of Texas and the Texans*. New York: De Capo, 2000.

Fenley, Florence. *Oldtimers of Southwest Texas*, s.v. "Mrs. Minnie Sutherland, Daughter of Mexican War Veteran." Uvalde, Tex.: Hornby, 1957, 267–73.

Ferber, Edna. *Giant*. Garden City, N.Y.: Doubleday, 1952.

Flores, Richard R. "Private Visions, Public Culture: The Making of the Alamo." *Cultural Anthropology* 10(1) (1995): 99–115.

Fly, Stephen R. "Descendants of George Sutherlin III." Unpublished ms. March 14, 2000.

Freeman, Martha Doty. "The Sutherland Plantation and the Alabama Settlement: A Study in Cluster Migration." *The Antebellum Period in the Stephen F. Austin Colony: Historical and Archeological Research in the Palmetto Bend Reservoir Area, Jackson County, Texas*. Texas Archeological Survey, research report 70, part 1. Austin: University of Texas, 1980.

Friedman, Jonathan. "Myth, History, and Political Identity." *Cultural Anthropology* 7(2): 194–211.

Ganado Tribune. Yoakum, Tex., January 30, 1964; February 6, 1964.

Garcia, Hector P. *In Relentless Pursuit of Justice.* Houston: Arte Publico, 2002.

Garrison, George P. *Texas: A Contest of Civilizations.* New York: Houghton Mifflin, 1903.

Geyer, Michael, and Charles Bright. "World History in a Global Age." *American Historical Review* (October 1995): 1034–60.

Gipson, Laura Ann Sutherland. Personal correspondence. 2000.

Green, George N. "The Felix Longoria Affair." *Journal of Ethnic Studies* 19 (Fall 1991): 23–49.

Groneman, Bill. *Alamo Defenders: A Genealogy, the People, and Their Words.* Austin: Eakin, 1990.

Handbook of Texas Online, The. Texas State Historical Association and the General Libraries of the University of Texas–Austin, 1997 (updated February 15, 1999).

Hardin, Stephen L. *Texian Iliad: A Military History of the Texas Revolution, 1835–1836.* Austin: University of Texas Press, 1994.

Harllee, William Curry. *Kinfolks: A Genealogical and Bibliographical Record of Benjamin and Mary Curry, Samuel and Amelia (Russell) Kemp: Their Antecedents, Descendants, and Collateral Relatives,* vols. 1–3. New Orleans: Searcy and Pfaff, 1937.

Hatfield, Carol Sutherland, ed. "The Poems of Thomas S. Sutherland." Unpublished collection. 1990. Artwork by Gayle Sutherland DeGregori (Anne Sutherland Collection).

Heard, F. L. "I Remember." Unpublished memoirs of F. L. Heard, c. 1963 (Anne Sutherland Collection).

Heard, F. L., and Mrs. F. L. Heard. "Texas, Their Reward." Unpublished manuscript on the Heard, Menefee, Dever, Sutherland, White, Davis, McFarland, Reed, Jones, Borden, Owens, and Morton families, c. 1959 (Anne Sutherland Collection).

Himmel, Kelly. *The Conquest of the Karankawas and the Tonkawas, 1821–1859.* College Station: Texas A&M University Press, 1999.

History of Knox County. East Tennessee Historical Society. Quoted in F. L. Heard and Mrs. F. L. Heard, "Texas, Their Reward," 45–47.

Honig, Lawrence. *John Henry Brown: Texian Journalist, 1820–1895.* El Paso: Texas Western Press, 1973.

Hudson, Florence Sutherland. "A History of the Sutherland-Rogers Reunion." Unpublished manuscript, 1960 and May 1973 (Anne Sutherland Collection).

———. "Thomas Shelton Sutherland II, Family of Nueces Canyon" (n.d., Anne Sutherland Collection).

———. *"We Cousins" (Virginia to Texas): A Genealogy of Several of the Families Comprising the Alabama Settlement of Austin's Colony, 1830 and 1831, Now Texas, and including the Other Virginia Lines of the Sutherland Family.* 2 vols. San Benito, Tex., 1957–1970.

Huser, Verne. *Rivers of Texas.* College Station: Texas A&M University Press, 2000.

James, Marquis. *The Raven: A Biography of Sam Houston.* Garden City, N.Y.: Halcyon House, 1929.

Jenkins, John Holland. *Recollections of Early Texas: The Memoirs of John Holland Jenkins.* Austin: University of Texas Press, 1958.

Jenkins, John Holmes, III, ed. *The Papers of the Texas Revolution, 1835–1836,* vols. 1–2. Austin: Presidial Press, 1973.

Knox, John. *A History of Morgan County, Alabama.* Morgan County Board of Revenue and Control. Decatur, Ala.: Decatur Printing, 1967.

Lamar, Mirabeau Buonaparte, Papers, vol. 1, edited by Charles Gulick Jr. Texas State Library. Austin: A. C. Baldwin and Sons, 1920–1927.

Leclerc, Frédéric. *Texas and Its Revolution.* Translated from the original French by James L. Shepherd III. Houston: Anson Jones Press, 1950.

Long, Jeff. *Duel of Eagles: The Mexican and U.S. Fight for the Alamo.* New York: William Morrow, 1990, 376–77.

Lubbock, Francis Richard. *Six Decades in Texas; or, Memoirs of Francis Richard Lubbock, Governor of Texas in War Time, 1861–1863. A Personal Experience in Business, War, and Politics,* edited by C. W. Raines. Austin: Ben C. Jones, 1900.

Mallouf, Robert J., Daniel E. Fox, and Alton K. Briggs. "An Assessment of the Cultural Resources of Palmetto Bend Reservoir, Jackson County, Texas." Texas Archeological Survey. Research report 11. Austin: Texas Historical Commission and Texas Water Development Board, 1973.

Malsch, Brownson. "Some Highlights of 400 Years in Jackson County, 1532 to 1932." *Edna Herald,* Twin Centennial ed., Edna, Tex., 1982, D1–D34.

Maverick, Mary A., and George Maverick. *Memoirs of Mary Maverick,* edited by Rena Maverick Green. San Antonio: Alamo Printing, 1921.

McLean, Malcolm Dallas. "Elijah Sterling Clack Robertson's Participation in the Civil War." Paper read at acceptance of the Earl R. Davis Award, March 31, 1990.

———. "Hot Pursuit: Collecting Material concerning Robertson's Colony, Texas." *Quarterly Newsletter* 56(2) (Spring 1991): 31–35.

———, comp. and ed. *Papers concerning Robertson's Colony in Texas,* vols. 1–3, Fort Worth: Texas Christian University Press, 1974–1976; introductory vol. and vols. 4–18, Arlington: University of Texas–Arlington Press, 1977–1993.

———. "The Robertson Colony: Success in spite of Politics." Lecture, University of Texas–Arlington, October 11, 1990 (Anne Sutherland Collection).

Menefee, John Sutherland. "Early Jackson County Settlers." *Texana Clarion* (May 20, May 27, June 3, June 17, July 15, August 5, 1880). Texana Museum, Edna, Texas.

———. Papers and Letters. Center for American History, University of Texas–Austin.

Michener, James A. *Texas.* New York: Random House, 1985.

Montejano, David. *Anglos and Mexicans in the Making of Texas, 1836–1986.* Austin: University of Texas Press, 1987.

Moore, Mary Ann. *Rekindled Embers: The Story of the Robertson Family of Washington County, Texas.* A Sesquicentennial Project. Houston: MAM Productions, 1987.

Newcomb, William W. *The Indians of Texas: From Prehistoric to Modern Times.* Austin: University of Texas Press, 1961.

Olmsted, Frederick Law. "Olmsted's Texas Journey." 1857. Reprint, *Time-Life,* Classics of the Old West Series, 1981.

Parsons, Uncle Jeff. Interview by *Galveston News*. In Ira T. Taylor, *The Cavalcade of Jackson County*, 79–83.

Peña, José Enrique de la. *With Santa Anna in Texas: A Personal Narrative of the Revolution*, translated and edited by Carmen Perry. College Station: Texas A&M University Press, 1997.

Phelan, Macum. *History of Early Methodism in Texas, 1817–1866*. Nashville: Cokesbury Press, 1924.

Plummer, Rachel. *Narrative of the Capture and Subsequent Sufferings of Rachel Plummer*. 1839. Reprint, Waco: Texian Press, 1968.

Pohl, James W. *The Battle of San Jacinto*. Austin: Texas State Historical Association, 1989.

Procter, Ben. *The Battle of the Alamo*. Austin: Texas State Historical Association, 1986.

"Reminiscences of Mrs. Dilue Harris." *Southwestern Historical Quarterly* 4(2) (October 1900): 88–127.

Richardson, Rupert N. *Texas, the Lone Star State*, 6th ed. Englewood Cliffs, N.J.: Prentice Hall, 1993.

Roberts, Randy, and James Olson. *A Line in the Sand: The Alamo in Blood and Memory*. New York: Free Press, 2001.

Robertson, Birdie. Letter, 1896 (Anne Sutherland Collection).

Robertson, Elijah Sterling Clack. Biography File. Special Collections. University of Texas–Arlington Library.

———. "Journal of Incidental Matters, 1845–1846." Special Collections. University of Texas–Arlington Library.

———. Letters. Special Collections. University of Texas–Arlington Library.

Robertson, Eliza Hamar Robertson. Letters to husband, 1847. Special Collections. University of Texas–Arlington Library.

Robertson, Mary Dickey. Letters. Special Collections. University of Texas–Arlington Library.

Robertson, Pauline, and R. L. Robertson. *Panhandle Pilgrimage*. Amarillo: Paramount, 1978.

Rogers, Samuel. "Autobiography of S. C. A. Rogers." Compiled by his daughters, Lizzie Laura Sutherland, Emma Sutherland, and Minnie Sutherland. Unpublished manuscript, August 18, 1891 (Anne Sutherland Collection).

———. Letter to Russell Ward, his great-grandson. Undated (Anne Sutherland Collection).

Rutersville College. Second Annual Catalogue, 1841. Fayette Co., Texas. Austin: S. Whiting, 1842. Fifteen pages.

Salado College. Charter. Special Collections. University of Texas–Arlington Library.

Sánchez Lamego, Miguel A. *The Second Mexican-Texas War, 1841–1843*. Waco: Hill Junior College Press, 1972.

Shivley, JoEllen. "Cowboys and Indians: Perceptions of Western Films among American Indians and Anglos." *American Sociological Review* 57 (December 1992): 725–34.

Simons, George. *Methodist Church History*. August 23, 1934, in F. L. Heard and Mrs. F. L. Heard, "Texas, Their Reward," 59–60.

Sinks, Julia Lee. "Rutersville College." *Southwestern Historical Quarterly* 2(2) (October 1898): 124–33.

Sowell, A. J. *Rangers and Pioneers of Texas.* New York: Argosy-Antiquarian, 1964.

Sutherland, Emma Rogers. "Autobiography of Emma Maria Rogers Sutherland." Unpublished, 1959 (three pages) (Anne Sutherland Collection).

———. "Biography of William DePriest Sutherland II." Uvalde, Tex., October 30, 1959. Unpublished (one page) (Anne Sutherland Collection).

———. "My Life Story." Unpublished manuscript, no date, compiled by Barbara Sutherland Chitwood (Anne Sutherland Collection).

Sutherland, Frances Menefee. Letter to her sister in Alabama, June 5, 1836. Center for American History, University of Texas–Austin.

Sutherland, George. Company muster roll. Mustered June 26, 1836 (Anne Sutherland Collection).

Sutherland, John. *The Fall of the Alamo.* First published in the *Texana Clarion,* 1880. San Antonio: Naylor, 1936, 1–47.

Sutherland, John William Lee. "Recollections of an Octogenarian." Handwritten manuscript by Mabel Sutherland, December 7, 1987 (thirteen pages) (Anne Sutherland Collection).

Sutherland, Kay. "Gone with Gypsy Time: Conversations with a Texas Poet and Storyteller." Unpublished manuscript, 1996 (based on interviews with Thomas Shelton Sutherland IV in 1992) (Anne Sutherland Collection).

Sutherland, Lizzie Laura Rogers. Postscript to "Reminiscences of My Father, Reverend Samuel C. A. Rogers." December 10, 1929 (Anne Sutherland Collection).

———. Unpublished letters to Lillian Belle Sutherland Dickson Faires, 1895–1908 (Anne Sutherland Collection).

Sutherland, Mary Elizabeth Robertson. Diary, 1900 (Anne Sutherland Collection).

Sutherland, Minnie Rogers. "Aunt Minnie's Story." Unpublished manuscript, March 9, 1953 (twenty pages) (Anne Sutherland Collection).

Sutherland, Thomas Shelton, IV. "Here on These Rolling Acres of Land." Unpublished poem (Anne Sutherland Collection).

———. "Lone Cowboy." *Boy's Life,* 1931. Also in "The Poems of Thomas S. Sutherland," edited by Carol Hatfield, 1990, 5 (Anne Sutherland Collection).

———, Estate of. "Oh, the Things I've Sworn That I Would Do." In "Poems by Tommy Sutherland, 1930–1950," 1995, 118 (Anne Sutherland Collection).

———. "Our Forebear Was George Sutherland." In "The Poems of Thomas S. Sutherland," edited by Carol Hatfield, 1990, 14 (Anne Sutherland Collection).

———, Estate of. "Poems by Tommy Sutherland, 1930–1950," 1995 (Anne Sutherland Collection).

———, Estate of. "San Antonio Spring." In "Poems by Tommy Sutherland, 1930–1950," 1995, 144–46 (Anne Sutherland Collection).

———. "The Texans." In "The Poems of Thomas S. Sutherland," edited by Carol Hatfield, 1990, 167 (Anne Sutherland Collection).

———. "What Is Home?" In "The Poems of Thomas S. Sutherland," edited by Carol Hatfield, 1990, 10 (Anne Sutherland Collection).

Sweet, William Warren. *The Story of Religion in America.* New York: Harper and Brothers, 1939.

Taylor, Ira T. *The Cavalcade of Jackson County.* San Antonio: Naylor, 1938.

Texas Catalog, Historic American Buildings Survey: A List of Measured Drawings, Photographs, and Written Documentation in the Survey, compiled by Paul Goeldner. Office of Archeology and Historic Preservation. San Antonio: Trinity University Press, 1974.

Texas Historical Boards Survey. Inventory of the County Archives of Texas, no. 120, Jackson County, Tex., 1940.

Texas History Movies. Illustrations by Jack Patton; text by John Rosenfield Jr. 1928. Reprint, Dallas: Magnolia Petroleum, 1956.

Texas History Movies: A Cartoon History of the Lone Star State. Illustrated by Joe B. Frantz. Sesquicentennial edition. Dallas: Pepper Jones Martinez, 1985.

Texas Methodist Historical Quarterly 1(1) (July 10, 1909). Published by the Texas Methodist Historical Association, Georgetown, Tex.

Thrall, Homer S. *History of Methodism in Texas.* New York: Lange, Little, and Hillman, 1872.

Tijerina, Andrés. *Tejanos and Texas under the Mexican Flag, 1821–1836.* Texas: Texas A&M University Press, 1994.

Tinkle, Lon. *Thirteen Days to Glory.* New York: New American Library, 1958.

Tunnell, Curtis. "A Cache of Cannons: La Salle's Colony in Texas." *Southwestern Historical Quarterly* 103(1) (July 1998): 19–43.

Turner, Victor. "Betwixt and Between: The Liminal Period in *Rites de Passage.*" In *Proceedings of the American Ethnological Society,* Symposium on New Approaches to the Study of Religion. Washington, D.C.: American Anthropological Society, 1964, 4–20.

Tyler, George. *History of Bell County.* San Antonio: Naylor, 1936.

Van Gennep, Arnold. *The Rites of Passage.* Translated by Monika B. Vizedom and Gabrielle L. Caffe. 1909. Reprint, London: Routledge and Kegan Paul, 1960.

Vernon, Walter N. *The Methodist Excitement in Texas: A History.* Dallas: Texas United Methodist Historical Society, 1984.

Ward, Francis. *An Account of Three Camp-Meetings Held by the Methodists.* Brooklyn, N.Y.: Robinson and Little, 1806.

Ward, Russell. Letter to Florence Hudson, June 14, 1960 (Anne Sutherland Collection).

Webb, Walter Prescott. *The Texas Rangers: A Century of Frontier Defense.* New York: Houghton Mifflin, 1935.

Weems, John Edward. *Dream of Empire: A Human History of the Republic of Texas, 1836–1846.* New York: Simon and Schuster, 1971.

Williams, Villamae. *Stephen F. Austin's Register of Families* (from the originals in the General Land Office, Austin, Tex.). Baltimore: Genealogical Publishing, 1984.

Index

ISBN 978-1-58544-520-2

52995